THE THEORY OF DEMAND

FOR HEALTH INSURANCE

THE THEORY OF DEMAND

FOR

HEALTH INSURANCE

JOHN A. NYMAN

STANFORD ECONOMICS AND FINANCE
An Imprint of Stanford University Press

© Stanford University Press
Stanford, California

© 2003 by the Board of Trustees of the Leland Stanford Junior University. All rights reserved.

Printed in the United States of America on acid-free, archival-quality paper.

Library of Congress Cataloging-in-Publication Data

Nyman, John A.
    The theory of demand for health insurance / John A. Nyman.
      p. cm.
    Includes bibliographical references and index.
    ISBN 0-8047-4488-2
    1. Insurance, Health—United States.   2. Demand (Economic theory)   3. Medical
economics—United States.   I. Title.

  HG9396 .N96   2002
  368.38'2'001—dc21   2002026922

Typeset by Interactive Composition Corporation in 10/13.5 Minion (text and display) and
Copperplate (display)

Original Printing 2003

Last figure below indicates year of this printing:

12   11   10   09   08   07   06   05   04   03

For Pat

TABLE OF CONTENTS

PREFACE

I began thinking about why people purchase health insurance during the health reform period in the U.S., in 1994. I was especially struck by the televised town meetings, the vehicle that the Clinton administration used to personalize the issues of health insurance. Each of the town meetings that I saw presented a case of a person or family who was not able to obtain the care they needed because they were uninsured. This flew in the face of the conventional model of insurance as representing a choice either to incur the spending privately or to engage insurance to pay; clearly, the former option did not exist for many Americans. From the identification of access as a motive for purchasing health insurance, this led to a rethinking of welfare implications of moral hazard, a respecification of the decision to purchase insurance as a quid pro quo transaction, and a reevaluation of the appropriateness of the von Neumann–Morgenstern (vNM) utility function in explaining the insurance decision.

While these ideas seemed to me to have intuitive appeal, they were not immediately accepted by early reviewers and journal editors. For example, one paper was originally submitted to a journal in 1995 and rejected several times before it was eventually published—four years later. As a result of this experience, this book may be overly concerned with presenting the case in favor of the new theory, rather than simply presenting the theory, and noting the differences between it and the conventional one. Still, I have tried to be even-handed in presenting this case, pointing out issues where they exist.

Part of the problem is that in many ways the new theory stands conventional theory on its head. Conventional theory holds that consumers demand health insurance to avoid the risk of financial loss, but that the welfare loss from moral hazard makes those who purchase health insurance worse off. The new theory holds that consumers demand health insurance mostly to obtain a welfare gain from moral hazard. Consumer preferences regarding risk are largely irrelevant and, if anything, inhibit the purchase of health insurance. Under the new theory, the voluntary purchase of insurance makes consumers better off. Because the new theory is diametrically opposed to the conventional one in so many ways, it is understandable how some might have difficulty accepting it.

PURPOSE OF THIS BOOK

This book presents a unified theory of the demand for health insurance and is intended for an audience of professional health economists. Still, I have tried to make it accessible to students and interested noneconomists by writing it at a level that would be understood by those with elementary training of microeconomics or decision analysis. As a result, this book is suitable to be assigned as a supplementary text in standard health economics courses, such as the undergraduate/graduate level survey course that I teach at the University of Minnesota. Moreover, each chapter is intended to be a self-contained unit, so, while this may imply some duplication, it also makes it possible to assign a subset of the book, if assigning the entire book is deemed inappropriate.

I would like to thank Michael Chernew, Bryan Dowd, Ted Frech, Tom Getzen, Richard Hirth, and Roland Maude-Griffin for thoughtful comments on aspects of this book. I would also like to thank Jane Raasch for her excellent administrative help. I am grateful to Ken MacLeod, Judith Hibbard and Kate Wahl, my editors at Stanford University Press, as well as Kathy Ewing and Rose Rummel-Eury at Interactive Composition Corporation. Their advice, expertise and, most importantly, their graciousness made the book-writing process an absolute joy. I would also like to apologize in advance to those of you who read this book years from now for the archaic examples and low prices. I hope that you find them quaint and amusing, instead of ridiculous and distracting.

On a personal note, I am grateful to my family for instilling in me the value of the intellectual life, and I hope that my children will someday know the joy of creative expression. And finally, I would like to thank my wife, Pat, for her patience and support (not to mention her occasional copyediting), and to whom this book is dedicated.

J. A. N.
University of Minnesota
Minneapolis, 2002

1 | INTRODUCTION

CONTROVERSIES

The theory presented in this book is controversial, but it shouldn't be. It merely says that the voluntary purchase of health insurance makes the consumer better off, and then explains why this is so. The controversy stems not from the radicalness of this new theory, but from what it says about conventional theory. That is, if this new theory is right, then conventional theory must be wrong.

The new theory is controversial because it rejects Mark Pauly's (1968) model of the welfare consequences of insurance that pays off by reducing price. Since the advent of Pauly's influential article, almost all economists (Fuchs, 1996) have believed in a theory that implies that the voluntary purchase of health insurance makes the consumer worse off. Empirical calculations based on this theory have borne this out (Feldstein, 1973; Feldman and Dowd, 1991; Manning and Marquis, 1996). These studies have indicated that consumers are worse off with health insurance contracts whose coverage limitations—coinsurance rates, deductibles, and limits on out-of-pocket spending—are typical of those traditionally purchased by U.S. consumers, or even those typically purchased in the U.S. today. Although it may be argued that the ability to use pretax income to purchase health insurance through their employers has encouraged U.S. workers to purchase insurance that would otherwise not be purchased, this does not explain the demand for health insurance by self-employed workers who, until recently, were not eligible for this subsidy. Thus, the new theory is controversial because it suggests that consumers who voluntarily purchase unsubsidized health insurance are better off.

The new theory is also controversial because it rejects as unnecessary the decidedly nonintuitive approach to understanding the purchase of insurance based on the utility function developed in 1944 by John von Neumann and Oskar Morgenstern. Instead of inextricably combining preferences for income and risk in one utility function, the theory presented here uses the concept of diminishing marginal utility of certain income that was originally developed by Daniel Bernoulli in 1738 (English trans. by Sommer, 1954) as the basis for understanding the consumer's decision to purchase insurance.

Finally, the theory is controversial because it rejects the standard gamble specification that has conventionally been used to describe the insurance decision. This specification, used in a classic article by Milton Friedman and L. J. Savage (1948), implies that consumers purchase insurance because they prefer a certain loss to an uncertain loss of the same expected magnitude. This book, instead, relies on the empirical evidence underlying prospect theory (Kahneman and Tversky, 1979; Tversky and Kahneman, 1981, 1986, 1988) that finds the opposite is true: namely, that consumers actually prefer an uncertain loss to a certain loss of the same expected magnitude. The theory presented in this book reconciles the empirical evidence underlying prospect theory with conventional insurance theory by modeling the decision to purchase insurance with a different specification. This specification suggests that, while the purchase of insurance has much to do with the shape of the consumer's Bernoulli utility function for certain income, it has little or nothing to do with preferences regarding risk.

OVERVIEW OF THE NEW THEORY

The central theme of this theory is that the consumer demands health insurance in order to obtain a transfer of income from the healthy if she were to become ill. This income transfer allows the ill consumer to purchase more medical care and more consumer goods and services than she would purchase without it. Sometimes, this income transfer allows the ill consumer to purchase medical care that would otherwise be unaffordable. The access that insurance provides to this care, especially if it is lifesaving, makes health insurance very valuable to the consumer.

Health insurance that pays off by reducing price generates this income transfer. The additional health care consumed because of the income transfer when ill increases welfare, but the additional health care that is attributable to price alone reduces welfare. Nevertheless, the efficient portion of this additional care, that is, of moral hazard, so dominates the welfare implications that overall, moral hazard increases welfare.

Risk preferences are largely extraneous to the new theory. If they enter the theory at all, they would decrease the demand for health insurance. Indeed, the conventional assumption that the demand for insurance is a demand for certainty has misled analysts into ignoring the fact that additional income when ill generates additional expenditures on medical care. This is because, if medical expenditures with insurance are greater than medical expenditures without insurance, then insurance could not result in certainty. Therefore, income effects are usually excluded from conventional theory and, if an increase in medical expenditures does occur, it would appear under conventional theory to be generated by the price reduction alone.

Finally, the new theory suggests that the purchase of health insurance constitutes a quid pro quo transaction: the insurance premium when healthy is exchanged for an income transfer when ill. In contrast to conventional theory, the implication of the new theory is that the voluntary purchase of health insurance makes the consumer better off.

OVERVIEW OF THE BOOK

The remainder of this book is organized into nine chapters. In Chapter 2, the conventional theory is summarized. The history of the conventional theory is traced from its origins with Bernoulli in 1738 (English trans. by Sommer, 1954) through its three cornerstones: (1) the von Neumann–Morgenstern (vNM) (1944) utility function, (2) the conventional expected utility theory using a specification first suggested by Bernoulli and later established by Friedman and Savage (1948), and (3) Pauly's (1968) model of the moral hazard welfare loss from insurance that pays off by reducing price. Then, five anomalies to this paradigm are presented. These anomalies represent assumptions within the model that are contradicted either by logic, documented evidence, or intuition. These anomalies include the following assumptions: (1) any additional health care that is consumed because of insurance that pays off by reducing price is welfare-decreasing, (2) the income payoffs that are associated with contingent-claims insurance do not elicit additional health care expenditures, (3) consumers prefer certain losses to uncertain losses of the same expected magnitude, (4) preferences regarding risk derive from the shape of the consumer's utility function, and (5) voluntarily purchased insurance at current coverage levels makes the consumer worse off. The new theory contradicts all these assumptions.

The new theory is formally presented in Chapter 3.[1] The theory shows that what appears to be a price reduction for all those who are insured, is in fact the mechanism by which insurance transfers income from those who purchase insurance and remain healthy, to those who purchase insurance and become ill. Thus, the decision to purchase insurance is essentially a comparison of (1) the expected utility lost from paying the premium when healthy, and (2) the expected utility gained from the income transfer if ill. With this specification, the decision represents a typical quid pro quo transaction, except that both utility lost from the payment of the premium and the utility gained from the income transfer are uncertain: the premium payment only occurs when healthy and the income transfer only occurs when ill.

Chapter 4 further investigates the role of risk in the model.[2] Here, I focus on the new model of insurance that pays off by reducing price under the assumption of no moral hazard. I show how the new model of price-payoff insurance without moral hazard is equivalent to the conventional model of contingent-claims insurance (also without moral hazard per all conventional models except for de Meza's [1983] model) that has simply been respecified into a quid pro quo perspective. When respecified this way, the model is consistent with the empirical evidence from prospect theory (Kahneman and Tversky, 1979) and from the other empirical studies that have investigated what motivates the consumer's purchase of insurance. This respecification suggests, however, that the decision to purchase insurance has little, if anything, to do with preferences regarding risk.

In Chapter 5, I focus on a motivation for purchasing health insurance that has gone largely unrecognized in conventional theory: the access value of insurance.[3] That is, one of the important but overlooked motivations for purchasing insurance is the desire to gain access to those health care services that would otherwise be unaffordable. The decision to purchase insurance is modeled with this motivation, and the importance of the access motive is estimated in terms of the percentage of the typical household's health insurance premium that is devoted to coverage of expenditures that the typical household could not afford to purchase if it did not have health insurance.

In Chapter 6, I develop a new demand function to be used in evaluating the welfare loss from health insurance that pays off by reducing price.[4] This demand function derives from a new decomposition of an exogenous change in price. While the Hicksian decomposition (Hicks, 1946) isolates the pure price effect by removing sufficient income to place the consumer on her original indifference curve (at the new prices), the new decomposition removes sufficient income to place the consumer on her original budget constraint (at the new prices). Applied to health insurance, this is the same decomposition that would remove all income transfers from insurance that paid off an ill person by reducing price. Using reasonable estimates for the parameters in question, this analysis concludes that the welfare loss from health insurance is only about 31% as large as the welfare loss estimated using the observed (Marshallian) demand curve implied by Pauly's (1968) analysis.

While Chapter 6 focuses on the welfare loss from inefficient moral hazard, Chapter 7 estimates the welfare gain from efficient moral hazard.[5] Although supporters of conventional theory have used persuasive examples—designer sunglasses, cosmetic surgery, and drugs to improve sexual functioning—to make the case that moral hazard is largely discretionary and inefficient, almost all the hard evidence from the clinical literature suggests that moral hazard actually consists of standard treatments for persons with common diseases. Indeed, using a study by Franks, Clancy, and Gold (1993), I find that the value of the years of life gained from having insurance for one year is about three times the cost of all the additional health care generated by insurance. This suggests that moral hazard on net makes the consumer better off and indeed, represents a central motivation for purchasing insurance.

If health insurance is so valuable, then why are about forty million Americans uninsured? Chapter 8 investigates the reasons for remaining uninsured under the new theory. It suggests that low income and the availability of Medicaid and charity in the U.S. probably explain most of the problem. In addition, however, preferences for risk—that is, preferences that are not related to the shape of the consumer's utility function for income—may also enter the decision. In Chapter 8, I outline a theory of risk preferences and discuss its application to the demand for health insurance.

Chapter 9 addresses the policy implications of the new theory.[6] It suggests that, in dealing with cost containment in the health care sector of the U.S. economy, conventional theory has inappropriately favored policies that would reduce the quantity of care at the margin. The new theory suggests that, rather than reducing quantity, it might be preferable to reduce the price instead. The new theory suggests a new optimal design for insurance policies and it represents a strong case for insuring the uninsured.

In Chapter 10, the book concludes with a summary of the new theory and a discussion of some of the apparent weaknesses and limitations of the theory, and in the final section, I revisit the theory's intuition.

INTUITION

This book is intended to persuade on the basis of logic—verbal, diagrammatical, mathematical—and empirical evidence, but also on the basis of intuition. The demand for health insurance is not complicated. Most of us purchase insurance periodically, therefore, we all must have some idea for why we do it. As economists, we must be careful not to let our technical training cloud our intuitive under-standing. We must attempt to think like a representative consumer, without bring-ing with us the prejudices that we may have absorbed from our education. For ex-ample, if a consumer were actually confronted with the decision to purchase a fair contingent-claims health insurance contract, would she be more likely to view the decision in terms of (1) paying a premium when healthy to obtain a payoff in the event of illness, or (2) a choice between a certain loss of income and an uncertain one of the same expected magnitude? Would the consumer view the price reduc-tion associated with health insurance as (1) the vehicle by which insurance pays for health care when ill, or (2) a sale on health care? This intuition must inform our thinking, too.

1. This chapter is based on Nyman (2001b) and Nyman (1999c). In the version of Nyman (1999c) that was originally submitted to the *Journal of Health Economics*, I had explained how the income transfer effect (from purchasing insurance that paid off with a price reduction) differed from the Hicksian income effect (from an exogenous reduction in price), but the editors would only permit me to use the Hicksian decomposition in the published work. This use of the Hicksian decomposition is misleading because it appears as if I am just revisiting the standard compensated demand story, and that nothing is really different in my analysis. Nyman (1999b) and Nyman and Maude-Griffin (2001) present the correct analysis.

2. This chapter is based on Nyman (2001c).

3. This chapter is based on Nyman (1999a).

4. The new demand curve was first described in Nyman (1999b). The chapter is based on that paper and on Nyman and Maude-Griffin (2001).

5. Portions of this chapter are based on Nyman (2001a, 2001b).

6. Portions of this chapter are based on Nyman (1999c, 2001a).

2 | CONVENTIONAL THEORY AND ANOMALIES

HISTORY

The theory of the demand for insurance was first proposed by Daniel Bernoulli in 1738 (English trans. by Sommer, 1954). In his seminal paper, Bernoulli postulated that an individual derives different levels of satisfaction or *utility* from different levels of income (or wealth) and that in general, an individual's utility increases with the income, but at a decreasing rate. One of his first applications of this theory was to insurance. Given a specific concave utility function and a specific insurance problem, he derived the conditions under which the utility level achieved after paying the insurance premium exceeded the expected utility level from remaining uninsured. Thus, Bernoulli suggested that insurance was purchased because people were maximizing expected utility.

While utility has always been and continues to be a useful theoretical concept, its usefulness in practice remained in question during the subsequent two centuries because no one could find a satisfactory way to measure it. An important advance, therefore, came in 1944 when John von Neumann and Oskar Morgenstern, in their book *Theory of Games and Economic Behavior* (1944), developed a practical method for measuring utility as a function of income or wealth. With the von Neumann–Morgenstern (vNM) utility function, it became possible to measure the shape of this function for an individual and to predict how individuals with variously shaped utility functions would respond to the opportunity to purchase insurance. This advance stimulated a renewed interest in insurance theory and choice theory, in general.

Shortly thereafter, the theory of the demand for insurance was refined by Milton Friedman and L. J. Savage (1948) who, in attempting to reconcile the motivations of a consumer who both gambled and bought insurance simultaneously, laid out the theory of the demand for insurance in a clear and digestible format. Friedman and Savage modeled the insurance decision with the standard gamble specification: a small certain loss (the insurance premium) is preferred to a large, but actuarially equivalent, uncertain loss. Thus, by purchasing insurance, the authors concluded that the consumer is "choosing certainty in preference to uncertainty" (Friedman and Savage, 1948, p. 279). Although Friedman and Savage acknowledge Bernoulli as originating the concept of expected utility maximization, the conventional standard gamble specification of the insurance problem can be traced to Friedman and Savage's classic paper.

John Pratt (1964) and Kenneth Arrow (1965) separately developed a statistic that could be used to measure the curvature of the utility function. Because, according to economic theory, the sole source of preferences regarding risk derived from the shape of the consumer's utility function, this measure of the curvature of the consumer's utility function became the measure of the relative *risk averseness* of the individual consumer.

In 1963, Arrow published an important article entitled "Uncertainty and the Welfare Economics of Medical Care," which was part of the national debate that resulted in the passage of the 1965 Amendments to the Social Security Act establishing Medicare and Medicaid. It focused attention on the pervasiveness of uncertainty in health care, and argued that if consumers were (1) rational expected utility maximizers, (2) "risk averse" (that is, their utility functions manifested the conventional concave functional form), and (3) charged actuarially fair premiums, the case for health insurance was "overwhelming." That is, Arrow was arguing that conventional expected utility theory supported government intervention to expand health insurance coverage in a form such as Medicare.

In response to Arrow's article, Mark Pauly (1968) wrote a short article entitled "The Economics of Moral Hazard: Comment," that was to become, perhaps, the single most influential article in the health economics literature. In that article, Pauly argued that because health insurance lowers the price of health care to consumers but leaves its costs unchanged, the additional care consumed by insured persons—that is, the *moral hazard*—is inefficient and represents a welfare loss to society. Thus, Arrow's case for expansion of insurance must be tempered by this realization. Public policy must, therefore, be directed at reducing moral hazard in order to reduce the welfare loss and ensure that insurance has a positive overall effect on society's welfare.

The influence of Pauly's 1968 paper can hardly be overstated. It is behind most policies directed at containing health care costs in the U.S. and around the world—for example, the demand-side policies of raising coinsurance rates and deductibles, and the supply-side policies of imposing utilization review, bundled payments, and managed care, in general. With regard to access, the welfare loss has probably been behind the general lack of enthusiasm by U.S. health economists for the expansion of health insurance coverage (for example, national health insurance or expanded Medicare benefits) in the U.S.[1] It would probably be fair to say that this paper established the central paradigm by which health economists viewed most health policy issues to arise during the last third of the twentieth century. A few classic studies will serve as an illustration.

In 1973, Martin Feldstein published a study of the welfare consequences of the tax subsidy of employee health insurance premiums. In this paper, Feldstein estimated net welfare effect of the additional insurance coverage generated by the tax subsidy of employee health insurance premiums, and found that for the typical policy, the welfare loss from moral hazard exceeded the gain from risk avoidance. Accordingly, Feldstein recommended raising the coinsurance rate on health insurance—he suggested raising it to 66%—as a way of reducing the moral hazard welfare loss associated with health insurance. Using more recent data, Roger Feldman and Bryan Dowd (1991) reached similar conclusions. In still another study, Willard Manning and M. Susan Marquis (1996) suggested that, because of the importance of the moral hazard welfare loss relative to the risk avoidance gain, the optimal coinsurance rate on health insurance policies should be about 50%, with no limit on the patient's out-of-pocket spending. As a result of this literature, many, if not most, economists have taken the position that the tax subsidy should be repealed.

The theory that insurance represented a movement along the consumer's demand curve was also behind the design of the RAND Health Insurance Experiment (HIE), the most costly social experiment ever to be funded in the U.S. (Newhouse, 1974). The RAND HIE was intended to measure how the demand for medical care varies with insurance, but instead it measured how the demand for medical care varied with the various prices for health care. The effect of variation in the price on demand for health care was the focus of the RAND HIE in large part because it was thought that health insurance operated in the same way: it simply changed the price of health care (Newhouse, 1974). Thus, design of the experiment was to randomize consumers into insurance plans that differed by price, just as if the consumers were dropped at random into various markets that differed by the price of health care. This design was consistent with the idea that insurance represented a simple movement along a demand curve, which was exactly Pauly's theory.

The widespread acceptance of Pauly's theory is documented by Roger Feldman and Michael Morrisey (1990) in a paper that reported the results of a 1989 survey of 518 health economists. As part of this survey, subjects were asked whether they believed that "the level and type of health insurance held by most U.S. families generate substantial welfare loss due to over-consumption of medical care services" (Feldman and Morrisey, 1990, p. 641). Sixty-three percent of all health economists surveyed either strongly agreed or agreed with this statement, and a higher percentage among Ph.D.-trained health economists.

Similarly, Victor Fuchs (1996) reported the results of 1995 survey of forty-six health economists, forty-four economic theorists, and forty-two practicing physicians regarding their opinions on various aspects of health care reform in the U.S. The item corresponding to Pauly's model and the empirical work associated with it was, "third-party payment results in patients using services whose costs exceed their benefits, and this excess of costs over benefits amounts to at least 5% of total health care expenditures" (Fuchs, 1996, p. 8). Eighty-four percent of health economists with an opinion agreed with this statement and 93% of economic theorists with an opinion agreed with it. Of the twenty statements in the survey, this item scored the highest level of agreement among health economists and economic theorists. This level of agreement, Fuchs notes, is unprecedented in previous surveys of economists.

In the remainder of this chapter, I lay out the particulars of the conventional theory of the demand for insurance that originated with Bernoulli and was modified for the health insurance context by Pauly. While various writers have made modifications in this theory to highlight specific insights, I describe the basic theory—the one that appears in the 1948 paper by Friedman and Savage and then in all subsequent health economics textbooks (Feldstein, 1999 and all earlier editions; Folland, Goodman, and Stano, 2001 and all earlier editions; Newhouse, 1978a; Phelps, 1997 and the earlier edition; Getzen, 1997; Henderson, 1999; Santerre and Neun, 2000). This basic specification is useful because it is easily understood and easily illustrated graphically. It contains all the essential components of the conventional explanation of why consumers demand health insurance, but it avoids some of the extraneous components of more sophisticated models. For example, in more sophisticated models, the consumer may choose the optimal level of the insurance payoff or coinsurance rate, given a loss which is assumed to be a fixed amount and which is determined exogenously. In most cases, however, the consumer does not have sufficient leeway to choose the exact level of coverage he wants, so models that describe the optimal level of coverage have limited practical appeal. Before reviewing the conventional expected utility theory, however, I first discuss the methods that von Neumann and Morgenstern developed to construct the consumer's utility function.

VON NEUMANN–MORGENSTERN (vNM) UTILITY FUNCTION

The specific shape that Bernoulli proposed for the relationship between utility and income (or wealth)[2] is now widely accepted by economists. Originally, Bernoulli asserted that successive additions to income result in successively smaller gains in utility, but there was little need to convince economists of the essential truth in this concept.[3] Diminishing marginal utility implied that a wealthy person would gain less satisfaction or utility from a gift of an additional $100 than would a poor person. Few other concepts in economics are as transparently obvious from a theoretical perspective. But, the measurement of the actual utility gain that consumers derived from income turned out to be difficult.

Originally, economists thought they might be able to measure utility directly by developing some machine that could physically detect the satisfaction that a consumer derived from consuming various goods and services. For example, in the late 1800s Francis Edgeworth proposed creating a "hedonmeter" and later, in the 1920s, Frank Ramsey explored the idea of developing a "psycholgalvanometer" (Bernstein, 1996). But it was not until 1944,[4] when von Neumann and Morgenstern developed their indirect method, that a practical way to measure utility existed.[5] In addition to its practical appeal, the von Neumann–Morgenstern (vNM) expected utility theory had a number of other features that made it attractive to economists. First, it was based on a series of fundamentally appealing axioms. Second, its derivation was consistent with ordinal utility and the indifference curve theory of demand. Third, it had a wide range of mathematical applications. This utility function is the basis of the conventional theory of the demand for health insurance.

The vNM utility is actually a function of lotteries rather than certain income. If these lotteries have outcomes that are represented by money (income), they can be used to construct a vNM expected utility function of income for an individual consumer. The following steps (based on an example in Friedman and Savage, 1948) show how this utility is estimated.

Step 1. The researcher identifies a range of income or wealth for which to determine the vNM utility. For example, income from $0 to $100,000.

Step 2. The researcher arbitrarily assigns utility values to the low and high endpoint of that range, say, U($0) = 0 and U($100,000) = 50, making sure that the lower utility level corresponds to the lower income level.

Step 3. The researcher identifies some intermediate level of income or wealth, say, $75,000 and asks the participating consumer to answer the following question:

What would the probability (π) of winning \$100,000 need to be to make you indifferent between,

Choice A: \$75,000 with certainty, or

Choice B: a lottery, where you have that probability π of receiving \$100,000 and $(1 - \pi)$ of receiving \$0, the two endpoints of the arbitrary income range?

Choice B can also be expressed as the lottery:

Choice B': $\pi \times \$100,000 + (1 - \pi) \times \$0$.

The probability, π', that makes the consumer indifferent to these two choices implies that the consumer derives the same level of satisfaction or utility from either of the choices. Using U(.) to represent a general utility function, the consumer's answer in Step 3 implies that the utility from Choice A equals the utility from Choice B, or

$$U(\$75,000) = U[\pi' \times \$100,000 + (1 - \pi') \times \$0]. \qquad (2.1)$$

The Expected Utility Theorem (see, for example, the discussion in Mas-Colell, Whinston, and Green [1995], pp. 176–178) presents the mathematical case that the right-hand side of equation (2.1) can be expressed in a more convenient format

$$U(\$75,000) = \pi' \times U(\$100,000) + (1 - \pi') \times U(\$0). \qquad (2.2)$$

If so, we are then able to calculate the utility of \$75,000, or any other intermediate income level, since we know π' for this consumer, and have assigned arbitrary values to U(\$100,000) and U(\$0). Thus,

Step 4. For π' that equates Choice A and B above, say, $\pi' = 0.85$, find the utility level for \$75,000 by making the following calculation:

$$U(\$75,000) = \pi' \times U(\$100,000) + (1 - \pi') \times U(\$0)$$

$$= (0.85) \times 50 + (0.15) \times (0)$$

$$= 42.5.$$

For this consumer, the vNM utility of \$75,000, relative to \$0 and \$100,000, is 42.5 units of utility, on a utility scale from 0 to 50. You can then,

Step 5. Plot the initial arbitrary points in (income; utility)-space, as illustrated in Figure 2.1, and record the intermediate point (\$75,000; 42.5) as illustrated.

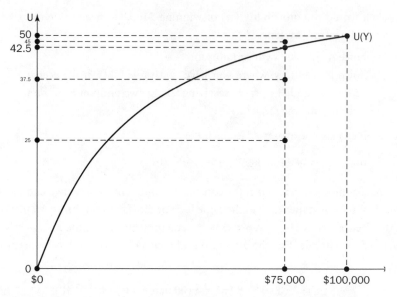

Figure 2.1 Construction of the von Neumann–Morgenstern (vNM) Utility Function.

At this point, there are three discrete points on the individual consumer's vNM utility function: ($0; 0) and ($100,000; 50) set arbitrarily, and ($75,000; 42.5) determined by the individual, given the vNM utility-eliciting procedure described. To find the complete function, repeat Steps 3, 4, and 5 for various other income levels between $0 and $100,000. Once sufficient points are determined, a complete and continuous function can be fitted to these points, and the resulting functional form can then be used to characterize the utility function of the consumer. If this function were complete and continuous, it could be represented by U in Figure 2.1.

This method can be used to derive utility for any range of income or wealth, for any arbitrary utility endpoints, and for any consumer. It is important to recognize that the answer to the question in Step 3 will likely be answered differently by different consumers, even for the same wealth level within the same range. This is because, according to the conventional interpretation of this function, different individuals have differing preferences regarding risk. For example, if a second consumer were more averse to the risk of loss than the consumer who answered that $\pi' = 0.85$ would make him indifferent to Choices A and B, this consumer might require that the probability of receiving $100,000 be set at $\pi' = 0.9$ (implying that the probability of receiving $0 is set at $[1 - \pi'] = 0.1$) in order to be indifferent between Choices A and B. If so, the vNM method would calculate that this second consumer's utility of $75,000 relative to $0 and $100,000 on a scale of 0 to 50 is 45.0, which is larger than the 42.5 of the original less risk averse consumer. Plotting the point ($75,000; 45.0) in (income; utility)-space in Figure 2.1 shows that this point would lie on a different utility function. This utility function lies to the northwest of the original one.

Conventional theory has held that the curvature of the consumer's utility function reflects the degree of risk averseness of the consumer. The more concave the utility function, the more "risk averse" the person is. Therefore, the second consumer described above is more risk averse than the original one, because her utility function is more "curved." If the consumer does not care about risk, the consumer would indicate $\pi' = 0.75$ as her answer to the question in Step 3, which would imply a different point, ($75,000; 37.5$), and a different utility function. Thus, the consumer's utility function would appear as a straight line between the two initial endpoints, in this case, ($0; 0$) and ($100,000; 50$), and the consumer would be described as "risk neutral" because her utility function exhibits this shape. If a person generates probabilities to the question in Step 3 (such as, $p' = 0.5$) that places his utility curve to the southeast of the risk-neutral person's utility curve, the person is said to be a "risk lover." The various consumers typed according to their apparent preferences regarding risk—risk averse, risk neutral, and risk lover—are illustrated in Figure 2.2. This

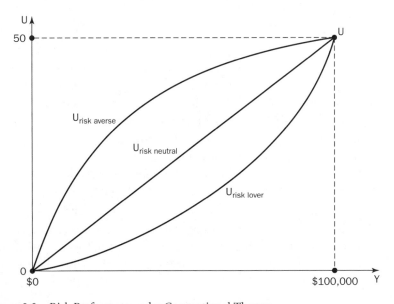

Figure 2.2 Risk Preferences under Conventional Theory.

diagram illustrates the point that the sole source of risk preferences in economic theory derives from the curvature of the consumer's vNM utility function.

Pratt (1964) and Arrow (1965) developed a measure of the curvature of this expected utility function that has been used to characterize consumer's risk preferences, and to further estimate the risk avoidance benefit gained from insurance. That measure for each level of income, Y, is $r(Y) = -U''(Y)/U'(Y)$. Again, risk preferences are derived solely from the functional relationship between expected utility and income.

Once a method for estimating a consumer's utility function existed, it could be used to explain and predict whether a consumer will purchase a given insurance contract. The conventional expected utility theory of the demand for insurance and health insurance is based on the ability to construct, or at least identify the functional form of this utility function.

CONVENTIONAL EXPECTED UTILITY THEORY

The conventional expected utility theory of the demand for insurance and health insurance assumes that the consumer's vNM utility function exhibits diminishing marginal utility of income. Diminishing marginal utility of income, however, is assumed to be equivalent to risk aversion in economic theory. Instead of specifying that marginal utility of income is diminishing, it is therefore considered equivalent simply to assume a "risk averse" utility function.

Conventional expected utility theory also assumes that there is a "loss" and that the loss is exogenously determined. For example, a consumer with Y° in income will spend M of that income on medical care if ill, leaving $Y = Y^\circ - M$ to spend on other goods and services. (Assume here that the price of medical care is normalized so that M represents the units of medical care consumed and that the price of each unit equals \$1.) Thus, M represents the "loss" in conventional health insurance demand theory, even though in reality, M represents a payment for goods and services that are valuable to the consumer.

Although in some models, the consumer's problem is to choose a lump sum payoff such that expected utility is maximized, in this simplified model, it is assumed that the consumer is presented with the more limited choice: either purchase a certain insurance policy or not. The consumer's decision depends on the expected utility with or without this insurance. Assume that the payoff, I, is equal to M, the exogenously determined loss. Further assume that the probability of becoming ill is π, and that this probability is exogenously determined. Finally, assume that the insurer has no administrative costs and therefore charges a premium, R, that is actuarially fair, $R = \pi I$. To be clear, an actuarially fair or "pure" premium is one that is equal to the expected payoff.

Thus, according to the specification first suggested by Bernoulli in 1738 (English trans. by Sommer, 1954) and later established by Friedman and Savage (1948), the consumer chooses between being uninsured, where expected utility is

$$EU_u = \pi U(Y^o - M) + (1 - \pi)U(Y^o), \qquad (2.3)$$

and being insured so that $I = M$, where expected utility is

$$EU_i = \pi U(Y^o - \pi M - M + I) + (1 - \pi)U(Y^o - \pi M) \qquad (2.4)$$

$$= \pi U(Y^o - \pi M) + (1 - \pi)U(Y^o - \pi M) \qquad (2.5)$$

$$= U(Y^o - \pi M). \qquad (2.6)$$

Under the conventional model, the consumer appears to be presented with a choice between (1) being uninsured and having an uncertain outcome with an expected utility, or (2) being insured and having a certain outcome with certain utility. If the consumer chooses to become insured, the consumer is opting for a certain level of utility over an uncertain level of utility. Thus, the demand for insurance has been interpreted as a demand for certainty or, equivalently, for avoiding risk.

Figure 2.3 illustrates this choice. Y^o represents endowed income and $(Y^o - M)$ is income after becoming ill and spending M on medical care. The consumer's utility function is such that $U(Y^o)$ represents utility if healthy and $U(Y^o - M)$ represents utility if ill. Expected income without insurance is represented by

$$Y_u = \pi(Y^o - M) + (1 - \pi)Y^o$$

$$= \pi Y^o - \pi M + Y^o - \pi Y^o \qquad (2.7)$$

$$= Y^o - \pi M$$

and expected utility without insurance is represented by

$$U_u = \pi U(Y^o - M) + (1 - \pi)U(Y^o). \qquad (2.8)$$

The point (Y_u, U_u) lies on a chord between points $[Y^o, U(Y^o)]$ and $[Y^o - M, U(Y^o - M)]$, the various other points on the chord representing other expected uninsured positions with the same loss, M, but different probabilities of illness, $0 < \pi < 1$. With insurance, income is certain at $Y_i = Y^o - \pi M$ and utility is certain at $U_i = U(Y^o - \pi M)$. Because $Y_u = Y^o - \pi M = Y_i$, expected income is the same with or without insurance, but because of the assumption of a "risk averse" utility function, $U_i > U_u$, and insurance is purchased.

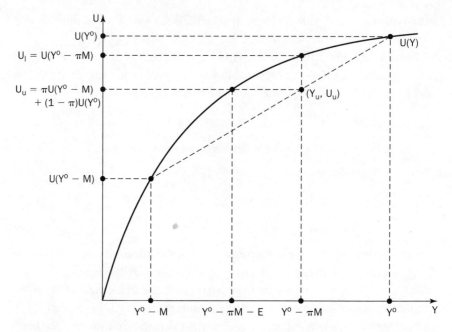

Figure 2.3 Conventional Expected Utility Theory of Demand for Insurance.

The gain in utility from purchasing insurance in Figure 2.3 is indicated by the vertical distance, $U_i - U_u > 0$. This gain in utility can be evaluated in dollar terms, representing a willingness to pay for insurance. If the consumer were to be charged the actuarially fair premium plus an additional very small amount, ϵ, the consumer would still be willing to purchase insurance because

$$U(Y^o - \pi M - \epsilon) > \pi U(Y^o - M) + (1 - \pi)U(Y^o), \qquad (2.9)$$

and thus, U_i (the left-hand side of inequality [2.9]) is still greater than U_u (the right-hand side of inequality [2.9]). If $\epsilon = E$ in Figure 2.3, the premium would be such that the utility with insurance, U_i would just equal expected utility without insurance, U_u. Thus, E is the largest amount that the consumer would be willing to pay in excess of the actuarially fair premium. This maximum additional willingness to pay represents the dollar value of insurance under the conventional model, and is called the *risk premium*.

So far, it has been assumed that the insurer charges a premium that covers only the expected spending on medical care, that is, the expected payoff. Insurers have expenses in addition to the expected payoff: claims processing, marketing, overhead, administration, and normal profits. The insurer must set a premium that covers these expenses as well in order to stay in business. As long as the insurer sets a premium that is less than the sum of the fair premium (covering the expected payoff) and the risk premium, insurance will be purchased by this consumer. Therefore, the insurer can charge a premium that covers expected payoffs, but also an additional "loading fee" that covers administrative costs and profits. Insurance is purchased, therefore, because the consumer is willing to pay an amount that not only reflects expected payoffs but an additional amount, the risk premium, caused by the curvature of the consumer's utility function. Because the consumer expects to pay an amount equivalent to the fair premium whether insured or uninsured, the loading fee is often considered the "price" of insurance in conventional theory.

Pratt (1964) and Arrow (1965) show that the risk premium depends not only on the degree of risk averseness as represented by the curvature of the utility function, but also on the statistical variance of the income distribution underlying the insurance problem in question. As noted, the degree of risk aversion is measured by the curvature of the utility function or $r = U''/U'$. The risk premium for the insurance problem is measured by $0.5\ \sigma^2 r$, where σ^2 is the variance of the income loss (in the case of health insurance, the variance in the health care expenditures) distribution associated with this problem. The greater the level of risk aversion—that is, the greater the curvature of the utility function—the greater the risk premium and the willingness to pay for insurance.

THE MORAL HAZARD WELFARE LOSS

With conventional expected utility theory in mind, Arrow (1963) argued that if consumers maximize expected utility, are risk averse, and are charged an actuarially fair premium, the case for extending insurance coverage to the uninsured is overwhelming. This is because consumers benefit from the certainty of losses of the insurance contract, and this benefit is measured by the risk premium. Pauly (1968), however, argued that this is not necessarily true because of moral hazard. *Moral hazard* can be defined as any change in behavior that is due to becoming insured. Although it may be represented by an increased probability of becoming ill—for example, an insured person may take fewer precautions to avoid becoming ill—Pauly focused on the increased consumption of medical care by an insured consumer. Implicitly, the probability of becoming ill was thought of as exogenously determined.[6]

Pauly's argument is seemingly straightforward. Rather than paying off with a lump sum dollar payment, health insurance acts to reduce the price that consumers face for health care. Consumers respond to this lower price by purchasing

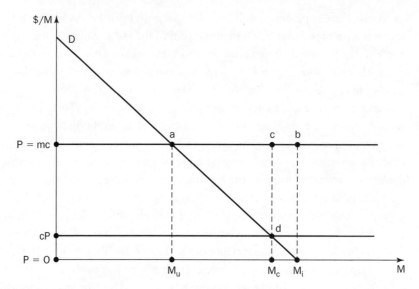

Figure 2.4 Conventional Moral Hazard Welfare Loss.

more health care. Although the price that consumers face is reduced, the cost of the resources used in producing that health care has not changed. Therefore, consumers incur a welfare loss by consuming additional health care that costs more than it is worth to the consumer.

Figure 2.4 illustrates Pauly's argument. D represents the observed demand for medical care, M. The consumer without insurance faces the market price of medical care, P, which is equal to the marginal cost (mc) of producing a unit of M, and consumes M_u medical care. If the consumer becomes insured, the price of M is reduced to 0 and the consumer consumes M_i. The moral hazard is represented by $M_i - M_u$. The cost of the moral hazard can be described as area abM_iM_u, and the value of the moral hazard is the area under the demand curve, aM_iM_u. The costs exceed the value of the moral hazard by abM_i, the moral hazard welfare loss. Imposing a positive coinsurance rate, c, raises the insured consumer's price from $P = 0$ to cP, and the movement along the demand curve reduces moral hazard from $M_i - M_u$ to $M_c - M_u$. The moral hazard welfare loss is reduced from abM_i to acd.

Thus, according to conventional theory of the demand for health insurance, there is a welfare gain from having the insurance pay for M_u (the medical care that the consumer would have purchased without insurance or the "loss") and, as a result, achieving certainty with regard to the other goods and services that can be consumed. At the same time, there is a welfare loss owing to the additional health care purchased, $M_i - M_u$, that is not worth the cost of producing it. The demand for health insurance is therefore related to this net gain from insurance.

ANOMALIES

This theory gives rise to a number of anomalies or inconsistencies. Five are described in this section.

Moral Hazard Is Welfare Decreasing

Foremost of these is the presumption that any additional health care consumed because of being insured is welfare decreasing because it implies a movement along the demand curve. That is, when economists think of moral hazard in health care, they think of those discretionary services that consumers may not wish to purchase at full price—such as cosmetic surgery, designer prescription sunglasses, or the care received by a hypochondriac—but which consumers may gladly purchase at the lower insured price. If marginal cost is reflected in the full price, there is no mechanism in the conventional model whereby the additional care purchased by consumers with insurance is anything but welfare decreasing.

Contrast this view, however, with the clinical literature describing the care and outcome consequences of being uninsured (see Brown, Bindman, and Lurie, 1998, for a comprehensive review). The clinical literature is replete with studies that show that the uninsured generally do not receive standard preventive health care, such as immunizations for children or Pap tests and mammography for women (Arnold and Schlenker, 1992; Burstin, Lipsitz, and Brennan, 1992; Freeman et al., 1987; Freeman et al., 1990; Hafner-Eaton, 1994; Himmelstein and Woolhandler, 1995; Kerr and Siu, 1993; Kirkman-Liff and Kronenfeld, 1992; Kogan et al., 1995; Monheit et al., 1985; Newacheck, 1992; Newacheck, Hughes, and Stoddard, 1996; Short and Lefkowitz, 1992). Many studies show that consumers *who are ill* do not receive standard care if uninsured (Aday et al., 1993; Blendon et al., 1992; Braveman et al., 1991; Braveman et al., 1993; Fihn and Wicher, 1988; Fleishman and Mor, 1993; Greenberg et al., 1988; Haas et al., 1994; Hafner-Eaton, 1993; Moy, Bartman, and Weir, 1995; Stoddard, St. Peter, and Newacheck, 1994; Thomas et al., 1996; Wilson and Sharma, 1995; Yergan et al., 1988; Young and Cohen, 1991; Cunningham et al., 1995; Spillman, 1992; Kuykendall, Johnson, and Geraci, 1995). For example, Overpeck and Kotch (1995) found that children with nonfatal injuries were less likely to receive medical care if uninsured, than if insured with Medicaid or private coverage. Still, other studies report that ill consumers delay or defer seeking health care if uninsured (Ayanian et al., 1993; Braveman et al., 1994; Freeman et al, 1990; Saver and Peterfreund, 1993; Weissman et al., 1991). This delaying or deferring of care often results in more expensive emergency room use and avoidable hospitalizations for the uninsured (Ahern and McCoy, 1992; Billings and Teicholz, 1990; Weissman, Gatsonis, and Epstein, 1992). Weissman and Epstein (1989) showed that uninsured also arrive at the hospital in a sicker state than the insured.

The additional care that the insured receive is far from frivolous. The insured exhibit reduced morbidity (Lurie et al, 1984; Lurie et al, 1986; Patrick et al., 1992; Short and Lair, 1995) and reduced mortality compared with the uninsured (Berg, Ross, and Latourette, 1977; Foster, Guzick, and Pulliam, 1992; Franks, Clancy, and Gold, 1993; Haas and Goldman, 1994; Hadley, Steinberg, and Feder, 1991; Shea et al., 1992; Yergan et al., 1988). For example, Young and Cohen (1991) found that uninsured patients who were hospitalized with acute myocardial infarction were less likely to receive coronary artery bypass graft or angioplasty, and also had a greater mortality rate than the insured.

Thus, the clinical literature paints a far different picture of moral hazard than economists do. In contrast to the image that economists evoke of additional care that is frivolous and discretionary (for example, designer sunglasses and cosmetic surgery), the image of moral hazard from the clinical literature is one of reasonable, effective, and often lifesaving care for people with common illnesses, care that appears to be well worth the resources spent in producing it.

Contingent-Claims Insurance Payoffs Have No Income Effects

Second, as with other insurance applications, conventional expected utility theory of the demand for health insurance specifies the loss as exogenously determined. That is, like the loss of wealth when a house burns down, the conventional theory of the demand for health insurance models health care purchases as a loss of income (or wealth) that could have been used to purchase other goods or services. The payoff represents a return of that amount of income, so that certainty of income is achieved (see equation [2.4]). For example, if a consumer who becomes ill without insurance purchases $20,000 worth of medical care, the same consumer with insurance would again purchase the same $20,000 of medical care, even though insurance has paid off with an extra $20,000 in income. In other words, the $20,000 increase in income for the consumer with insurance has generated no additional health care spending compared to the consumption of the person without insurance and with only the endowed income. Or, in still other words, the conventional model implicitly assumes that the consumer has an income elasticity of demand of 0.

This is anomalous because empirical evidence suggests that medical care is a normal good and that the income elasticity of demand is greater than 0. For example, Manning and Marquis (1996) report an income elasticity of about 0.22 using RAND HIE data. Feenberg and Skinner (1994), using tax returns of households that spent at least 3% of income on health care and might therefore be considered ill households, found a higher (0.38) income elasticity. Studies, such as Parkin, McGuire, and Yule (1987), using cross-national data typically find income elasticities exceeding unity. These studies suggest that the large additional income payment that an insured consumer would receive through the insurance payoff does not merely cancel the exogenously determined income loss, but instead generates additional consumption of medical care and, therefore, additional "loss."

Furthermore, the assumption in conventional expected utility theory that uninsured consumption is the same as insured consumption ignores the fact that many expensive procedures would be unaffordable without insurance, especially for those households with low incomes and low net worths. For example, a person with a $50,000 net worth would not be able to afford to purchase a $300,000 liver transplant procedure. The patient may be too ill or the illness may be too urgent to save the difference, and banks may be reluctant to lend money for the transplant because of the risk that the borrower will not be able to pay off the debt. For expensive, lumpy procedures like this, a consumer without insurance may receive only minimal, palliative care, even though with insurance the consumer would have access to the appropriate expensive procedure. Again, for consumers and procedures like that, the implication in the conventional model that a payoff of $300,000 does not affect the consumer's health care consumption decision is clearly wrong.

It must be noted that de Meza (1983) presents a model which shows that the availability of contingent-claims insurance results in more health care spending than if the health care were financed by borrowing or saving. This is because the cost of medical care, in terms of present consumption forgone, is lower if financed through insurance than if financed through borrowing or saving. As a result, the optimal payoff with insurance is greater than the optimal amount of income available through either borrowing or saving. If the payoff is greater and insurance is a normal good, then medical care spending is greater with contingent-claims insurance than without.

De Meza's important article is, to my knowledge, the only one to recognize that the insurance payoff generates additional medical spending. It is different from the conventional model because it compares insurance with a contingent-claims income payoff against income that is augmented by borrowing or saving. The conventional model is directed at explaining the purchase of insurance, and therefore compares insurance against no insurance, where the income without insurance is endowed income. The conventional model assumes no income effect from the insurance payoff.

Consumers Prefer Certain Losses

A third anomaly arises from comparing the standard interpretation of the expected utility model with the evidence supporting prospect theory (Kahneman and Tversky, 1979). If consumers purchase health insurance, the standard interpretation is that consumers do so because they prefer certain losses to uncertain ones of the same expected magnitude. For example, Newhouse (1978a) writes, "The purpose of any insurance policy is to convert an uncertain, but potentially large, loss into a certain, small loss. Such a conversion benefits the consumer if greater losses cause progressively larger declines in utility (that is, if there is diminishing marginal utility to wealth)" (Newhouse, 1978a, p. 19).

Thus, the demand for health insurance, like the demand for any insurance, is a demand for certainty. In sophisticated models where optimal insurance results in payoffs equal to a portion of (but not the entire) "loss," demand for insurance is interpreted as a demand for risk avoidance.[7] The demand for certainty and the demand for risk avoidance are just two sides of the same interpretation: insurance is demanded because of preferences regarding risk, and specifically, a preference for avoiding the risk of loss.

Contrast this interpretation of the demand for insurance with the empirical research underlying prospect theory. In a series of experiments, Kahneman and Tversky (1979; and Tversky and Kahneman, 1981, 1986, 1988) presented their subjects with standard gamble choices. They found that when the choice was framed as a gain—for example, a certain gain of $1,000 versus a gamble where you win $10,000 with a probability of 0.1 and $0 with a probability of 0.9—the certain choice was generally preferred to the gamble with the same expected value. However, when the choice was framed as a loss—a certain loss of $1,000 versus a gamble where you lose $10,000 with a 0.1 probability and $0 with a 0.9 probability—the risky gamble was generally preferred. These framing results have been replicated by other researchers in a series of independent studies (for example, Druckman, 2001; Bless, Betsch, and Franzen, 1998; Kühberger, 1998; Bohm and Lind, 1992; Fagley and Miller, 1990). Because fair insurance is conventionally modeled and interpreted as a choice between a small, certain loss and an actuarially equivalent larger loss, the empirical evidence on risk preferences from prospect theory suggests that consumers should not purchase health insurance, however, we know that they do. So, if consumers purchase insurance but risk preferences suggest that they should not, then the purchase of insurance must be explained by factors other than risk preferences.

Risk Preferences Derive Only from Diminishing Marginal Utility

A fourth anomaly—or perhaps, "inconsistency" is a better word—is the equating of "diminishing marginal utility of income" with "risk aversion" in economic theory.

For most consumers, the utility or satisfaction that one derives from income increases with income, but at a decreasing rate. This theoretical assumption is fundamental to economic theory. One can, however, think of an experiment where a person with an income of, say, $100,000 was asked to compare the utility of that $100,000 to the utility of, say, $50,000 and $150,000 in income, much as cost-utility analysts use visual analogue scales to determine the quality of life associated with a given health status, compared with the quality of life associated with death and perfect health (Drummond et al., 1997). For example, given an arbitrary utility scale of 0 units of utility for $50,000 and 1 unit of utility for $150,000, a person might characterize the change in utility associated with the change of income from $50,000 to $100,000 as being twice as great as the change in utility associated with a change in income from $100,000 to $150,000. As a result, the consumer would attach a comparative utility value of 0.67 to the $100,000 of income, accurately reflecting his preferences. Because the utility value is greater than 0.5, it would indicate diminishing marginal utility of income.

Now, this same consumer could be presented with the equivalent vNM procedure for eliciting the utility of income. Under the vNM procedure, the income range would be $50,000 to $150,000, and the arbitrary utility levels would be 0 to 1, respectively. An intermediate income of $100,000 would be chosen and the same consumer would be asked to identify the probability, π, that would make the consumer indifferent between the following two choices:

Choice A: $100,000 with certainty, or

Choice B: a gamble, such that, $\pi \times \$150,000 + (1 - \pi) \times \$50,000$.

The consumer in question could set this probability at 0.67, and if so,

$$U(\$100,000) = U(0.67 \times \$150,000 + 0.33 \times \$50,000)$$

$$= 0.67 \times U(\$150,000) + 0.33 \times U(\$50,000)$$

$$= 0.67 \times 1 + 0.33 \times 0$$

$$= 0.67,$$

and the utility of $100,000 would be the same under both preference elicitation procedures.

The probability, π, that makes the consumer indifferent between the vNM choices, would not necessarily yield the same utility that characterizes the utility of a certain $100,000 under the first procedure. That is, there is a fundamental difference between these two procedures for eliciting the utility of $100,000: although the standards of comparison are the same and the utility scales are the same, one procedure implicitly assumes certainty of income but the other intermingles preferences regarding income and preferences regarding risk. This difference in procedures could lead to different answers. For example, if the consumer were especially fearful of (that is, preferred to avoid) the regret from choosing the gamble and losing (that is, obtaining the $50,000 outcome), then he would set the probability that would equate Choices A and B at a level greater than 0.67, the probability that would reflect his appraisal of the relative utility of a certain $100,000 compared with the certain alternatives of $50,000 and $150,000. Mas-Colell, Whinston, and Green (1995) distinguish between these two concepts by referring to utility as a function of certain income as the *Bernoulli utility function* after the mathematician who first postulated this relationship. This book uses the same terminology.

In economic theory, the sole source of preferences regarding risk is the shape of the consumer's utility function. Thus, consumers with a diminishing marginal utility for certain income are considered to be "risk averse," because these two characteristics are deemed to be one and the same. The preceding discussion, however, suggests that the choice in the conventional model of the insurance—that is, the choice between a certain loss and an uncertain one of the same expected magnitude—depends on at least two factors instead of one: (1) the shape of the consumer's Bernoulli utility function for certain income, and (2) other preferences—perhaps, preferences that are second-order in importance—regarding risk. For example, setting the probability of loss equal to some arbitrary value and holding risk preferences constant, a consumer with a more concave Bernoulli utility function for certain income will be more likely to prefer the certain loss to an uncertain one of the same expected magnitude than the consumer with a less concave Bernoulli utility function. However, setting the probability of loss constant and holding constant the shape of the Bernoulli utility function for certain income for two consumers, the consumer who has stronger preferences for avoiding any loss at all will be more likely to prefer the uncertain loss to the certain one. Thus, "diminishing marginal utility of income" and "risk averseness" are not necessarily identical in meaning.

Insurance at Current Coverage Parameters Is Welfare Decreasing

A final anomaly derives from the economic studies that have estimated the relative benefits and costs of health insurance. As mentioned in Chapter 1, Feldstein's (1973) influential study found that the costs from moral hazard exceed the gains from "risk avoidance." He suggested that raising the coinsurance rate to 66% would improve society's welfare. Manning and Marquis (1996) use RAND HIE data to estimate that the optimal health insurance policy has a coinsurance rate of about 50% and no maximum on a patient's out-of-pocket payments. Lower coinsurance rates and reduced maximums on out-of-pocket payments would result in net losses to the purchaser. In contrast to these prescriptions, most insurance policies bought and sold in the U.S. have coinsurance rates that are much lower than 50%—perhaps, averaging 20% or less—and also include low maximums on out-of-pocket expenditures—currently, $1,000 to $5,000. That is, after, say, $4,000 of out-of-pocket expenditures, the coinsurance rate falls to 0%. The question therefore arises: Why are such insurance policies voluntarily purchased if they make the purchaser worse off?

One explanation is that health insurance is subsidized in the U.S. by the exemption from income taxes of premium payments made by employer on behalf of employees. That is, the income that is used to purchase health insurance is not taxed, and because of the absence of a tax, health insurance receives a implicit subsidy compared to other consumption, which is taxed. This subsidy of health insurance premiums may explain the prevalence of suboptimal insurance coverage in the U.S. On the other hand, the premiums actually charged by insurers must exceed the actuarially fair premium in order to cover the administrative costs and profits, and these loading fees represent a disincentive to purchase insurance. Thus, the tax subsidy is largely an offset to these loading fees, and probably cannot explain the widespread purchase of such seemingly welfare-reducing insurance policies in itself. Moreover, until recent changes in the tax law were enacted, self-employed individuals were excluded from benefitting from the tax subsidy provision, and still, many self-employed individuals found it advantageous to purchase insurance with low coinsurance rates and low stop-loss maximums, and at premiums that included a high loading fee. Thus, either this voluntary purchase of unsubsidized insurance represents an irrational act, or the conventional theory is, in some fundamental way, flawed.

SUMMARY

These anomalies represent what appear to be five theoretical or empirically supportable truths: (1) some moral hazard appears to be worth the cost of producing it, (2) if health insurance paid off the ill with lump sum income payments, those ill consumers receiving payoffs would be likely to purchase more health care than they would without insurance, (3) most consumers prefer the risk of a loss of income to an actuarially equivalent sure loss of income, (4) framing a preference elicitation question as a choice between certainty and a lottery might elicit different answers than a preference elicitation question framed completely under the assumption of certainty, and (5) voluntarily purchased health insurance, even unsubsidized and specified at currently typical coinsurance rates, makes the consumer better off. This book attempts to incorporate these diverse anomalies together into one unified theory of the demand for health insurance. The core of this theory is presented in Chapter 3.

1. In a 1995 survey by Fuchs (1996) referred to below, health economists showed no statistically significant support for national health insurance.

2. Income is a flow concept, such as dollars received per period of time, while wealth is a stock concept, such as number of dollars in the bank. The utility function can have either income or wealth as its argument. In the general insurance theory, either income or wealth can be used.

3. Diminishing marginal utility is also consistent with indifference curves that are convex to the origin, and with downward sloping demand curves.

4. Arrow (1951) points out that Ramsey (1931) developed a early version of this theory, but the theory is now linked to von Neumann and Morgenstern alone.

5. Von Neumann and Morgenstern (1944) tout the practicality of their approach when they write that, "under the conditions on which the indifference curve analysis is based little extra effort is needed to reach a numerical utility" (p. 17).

6. Ehrlich and Becker (1972) distinguish between those measures taken to reduce the size of the loss—self-insurance—and those measures taken to reduce the probability of a loss—self-protection.

7. Other authors have variously characterized the demand for insurance by "risk averse" consumers as a demand to "avoid," "eliminate," "hedge against," "kill," "manage," "shed," "protect against," or "bear" the risk of loss (for examples, see Mossin, 1968; Schlesinger and Doherty, 1985; Mayers and Smith, 1983; Cook and Graham, 1977; Arrow, 1963; Feldstein, 1973; Feldstein and Friedman, 1977; Feldman and Dowd, 1991; Manning and Marquis, 1996).

3 | NEW THEORY

OVERVIEW

The new theory of the demand for health insurance can be summarized in a few sentences. Consumers demand health insurance because they desire an income transfer from those who remain healthy in the event that they become ill. They do not purchase insurance to avoid uncertainty. Contingent-claims insurance contracts that pay off with a lump sum income transfer can accomplish this function, but contingent-claims contracts are inefficient for health insurance because of the large transactions costs. Instead, insurance contracts that pay off by reducing the price of medical care are used. Price-payoff contracts are, in essence, contingent-claims contracts where the mechanism for transferring income is a reduction in price. Price reductions can be used to transfer income because it is primarily the ill who derive benefits from medical care and the policyholder's physician is available to constrain some of the consumption choices of the healthy policyholder. Although the pure price effect in these contracts results in welfare losses, these losses are smaller than the losses that would have occurred from transaction costs under a contingent-claims contract. The welfare gains from the additional health care and other goods and services consumed because of the income transfer far outweigh these losses. The net effect of the voluntary purchase of health insurance is to increase the consumer's welfare and the welfare of society.

MODEL

The prototypical insurance contract is a voluntary quid pro quo exchange where many consumers pay a premium in exchange for a claim on the pooled premiums, contingent on becoming ill. The smaller the probability of illness, the smaller is the premium that each purchaser of insurance must pay for any given payoff if ill. For example, to establish a payoff of $10,000 when the probability of becoming ill is 1/1,000, every 1,000 consumers would need to contribute $10 each. If the probability were 1/2 instead, every two consumers would need to contribute $5,000 each. The difference between the payoff and the premium is a transfer of income from those who remain healthy to the person who becomes ill. For example, for a payoff of $10,000 and a probability of illness of 1/1,000, the amount transferred from the healthy is ($10,000 − $10 =) $9,990, but for a probability of illness of 1/2, the income transfer is ($10,000 − $5,000 =) $5,000. Health insurance is purchased to obtain this income transfer when ill.

Because of this income transfer, those who become ill purchase more health care and other goods and services than they would without insurance. For example, they may purchase an extra day in the hospital to recuperate, or they may purchase an expensive lifesaving procedure that they would not otherwise be able to afford. This additional health care is the income transfer effect of insurance. But, because of the high costs of verifying illness, monitoring for fraud, and writing complex contingent-claims contracts, the payoffs in actual private health insurance contracts occur through a reduction in the price of health care. Thus, of the additional health care purchased—that is, of the moral hazard—a portion is an opportunistic response to the reduced price, but a portion remains the original intended response to the income transfers. The following model describes the price and income transfer effects of health insurance.

Assume that all consumers have the same preferences and endowments. Without insurance, the consumer who becomes ill solves the standard problem,

$$\max U^s(M, Y)$$
$$\text{s.t. } Y^o = M + Y, \tag{3.1}$$

where U^s is utility when ill, M is medical care, Y is income spent on other goods and services, and Y^o is the endowment. The price of M is assumed to be normalized at 1, so the first order conditions are

$$U^s_M/U^s_Y = -1 \tag{3.2}$$
$$Y^o - M - Y = 0, \tag{3.3}$$

and demand for medical care without insurance is written $M^u = M(1, Y^o)$. With insurance that pays off by reducing the price of M from 1 to c, the consumer would solve the following problem if ill:

$$\max U^s (M, Y)$$

$$\text{s.t. } Y^o - R = cM + Y, \tag{3.4}$$

where R is the fair premium, taken as a given, and c is the coinsurance rate. First order conditions are

$$U^s_M/U^s_Y = -c \tag{3.5}$$

$$Y^o - R - cM - Y = 0, \tag{3.6}$$

and the demand for medical care with insurance is written $M^i = M(c, R, Y^o)$.

The premium is assumed to be actuarially fair, so that

$$R = \pi(1 - c)M^i, \tag{3.7}$$

where π is the probability of illness. For any given payoff—that is, for any given health care expenditures paid for by the insurer, $(1 - c)M^i$—the size of the premium, $\pi(1 - c)M^i$, depends on π. If the illness is rare and π is small, then the premium is small. In the limit, as π approaches 0, the premium becomes negligible and it appears as if the consumer faces the same first order conditions that would characterize an exogenous decrease in price to c:

$$U^s_M/U^s_Y = -c \text{ and} \tag{3.8}$$

$$Y^o \approx cM + Y. \tag{3.9}$$

In reality, however, the difference between the premium and the payout in expenditures is paid for by the many purchasers of insurance who remain healthy and transfer their premium through the insurer to those consumers who become ill. That is, the net payoff to each ill consumer is an income transfer from the $(1 - \pi)/\pi$ consumers who pay their premium into the pool but, because they remain healthy, have no claims on the pool. For example, a liver transplant costs about $300,000, but the probability of illness is only 1/75,000 during the contract period. The fair premium for 0% coinsurance rate coverage of a liver transplant would be ($300,000/75,000 =$) $4, so that the aggregate income transfer to the ill consumer from the 74,999 others who do not become ill during the contract period is (74,999 × $4 =$) $299,996.

If the illness is common, a larger percentage of the payoff is paid for in the premium by each consumer who becomes ill. In the limit, as π approaches 1, the first order conditions approach:

$$U_M^s/U_Y^s = -c$$

$$Y^o - (1 - c)M \approx cM + Y, \qquad (3.10)$$

or rearranging terms,

$$Y^o \approx M + Y, \qquad (3.11)$$

and the consumer pays a premium that covers the entire cost of the price reduction so that no income transfers occur. For example, if all insured consumers required one \$100 office visit to a physician during the contract year, the insurer's portion of the cost of that visit—\$100 at a 0% coinsurance rate—would be totally included in each consumer's fair premium and the income transfer would be \$0. Thus, if $\pi = 1$, even though the price is reduced from 1 to 0, the consumer is constrained to consume within his original budget, $Y^o = M + Y$.

The probability of illness, therefore, has an important effect on consumption with health insurance. If insurance were an exogenous price decrease from 1 to c, the quantity response would simply reflect the observed price elasticity of demand for medical care, and the probability of illness would not be a factor. In fact, the private purchase of insurance is not an exogenous price decrease. The price reduction must be purchased by someone in order to exist. The extent to which the ill consumer pays for this price reduction and the extent to which those who remain healthy pay for it depends on π, the probability of illness (or more realistically, the probabilities of the various diseases that the insurance contract covers). Thus, the probability of illness determines the quantity response to insurance that pays off with any given coinsurance rate c. This is analogous to the prototypical insurance contract for a given lump sum payoff, where smaller probabilities of illness are associated with larger income transfers, and larger income transfers result in commensurately larger quantity responses. Similarly, in a price-payoff contract for a given expenditure payoff $(1 - c)M^i$, smaller probabilities of illness are associated with larger portions of the payoff that are paid for by income transfers, and larger income transfers result in larger quantity responses.

The insurer conducts an actuarial study to determine insured demand, $M^i|_{c,R,Y^o}$. Once M^i is determined, income transfers become apparent by rewriting equation (3.6), the ill consumer's budget constraint after insurance, as

$$Y^o - \pi(1 - c)M^i = cM^i + Y^i, \qquad (3.12)$$

adding $(1 - c)M^i$ to both sides of the equation, and simplifying yields

$$Y^o + (1 - \pi)(1 - c)M^i = M^i + Y^i. \tag{3.13}$$

So, compared to the ill consumer's budget constraint without insurance,

$$Y^o = M^u + Y^u, \tag{3.14}$$

spending with insurance, $(M^i + Y^i)$, is larger than spending without, $(M^u + Y^u)$, by $(1 - \pi)(1 - c)M^i$, the income transfers. That is, $(1 - \pi)(1 - c)M^i$ is the additional income that is provided by those who remain healthy and that is transferred to those who become ill, who in turn, spend this income transfer on additional medical care and other goods and services.

Empirically, the effect of this income transfer on medical care spending—that is, the income transfer effect—can be estimated by:

$$\%\Delta M = \epsilon(\%\Delta Y), \tag{3.15}$$

where $\%\Delta M$ is the percentage increase in medical spending due to income transfers, ϵ is the appropriate income elasticity of demand for health care, and $\%\Delta Y$ is the percentage increase in income due to income transfers. From equation (3.13),

$$\%\Delta Y = (M^i + Y^i - Y^o)/Y^o = (1 - \pi)(1 - c)M^i/Y^o. \tag{3.16}$$

The price effect can then be estimated as a residual if the total change in consumption is known.

GRAPHICAL MODEL

Figure 3.1 shows health care spending of the ill consumer both without insurance and with insurance that pays off by reducing the price of care from 1 to c, with a probability of illness, π, that lies between 0 and 1. Without insurance, optimal consumption by the ill consumer is (M^u, Y^u), and with insurance, optimal consumption is (M^i, Y^i). Suppose the ill consumer instead purchased a contingent-claims insurance contract where the lump sum payoffs are exactly the same as the various expenditures by the insurer—the $(1 - c)M^i$'s—under the price-payoff contract. If the contract were perfectly designed, a fair premium for this contract would reflect the same expected total expenditures as under the price-payoff contract, and the difference between the aggregated payoffs and the fair premium to the ill consumer would constitute the same income transfers.[1] After these income transfers, the corresponding budget constraint would contain point (M^i, Y^i), but

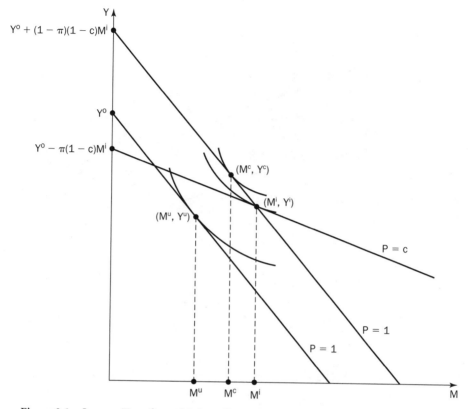

Figure 3.1 Income Transfer and Price Effects of Insurance That Pays Off by Reducing Price.

reflect the original price of medical care, $P = 1$. Optimal consumption under this contingent-claims contract would occur at (M^c, Y^c) in Figure 3.1. Thus, the pure price effect of insurance would be the increase in medical care consumption caused by using a price reduction rather than lump sum income payments as the payoff mechanism, or $(M^i - M^c)$. The income transfer effect of the price-payoff insurance would be the increase in medical care consumption caused by the contingent-claims (lump sum-payoff) insurance compared with consumption with no insurance, or $(M^c - M^u)$.

The foregoing discussion represents an "equivalent variation" type approach, where the income transfer effect is shown as the result of an increase in income transfers, evaluated at the uninsured price. Alternatively, a "compensating varia-tion" approach would isolate the price effect of insurance by eliminating the

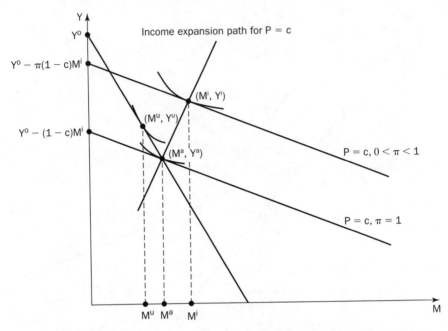

Figure 3.2 Income Transfer and Price Effects: Compensating Variation Approach.

income transfer effect after the price decrease has occurred. Figure 3.2 shows the income transfer and price effects using this approach. Again, optimal consumption is (M^u, Y^u) without insurance and (M^i, Y^i) with insurance that pays off by reducing the price from 1 to c with a probability of π, where $0 < \pi < 1$. Because the probability of illness is less than 1, income transfers have occurred, and as a result, some portion of this increased consumption of medical care $(M^i - M^u)$ is an income transfer effect. In order to eliminate the income transfer effect, it is necessary to eliminate income transfers, which would only be eliminated if π were 1. Therefore, the optimal consumption bundle without income transfers is the bundle that maximizes utility when the consumer is compelled to purchase a contract for a reduction of price from 1 to c *when already ill.* That is, the consumer faces insured prices but cannot consume beyond his budget constraint, reflecting equations (3.10) and (3.11). Such a bundle would occur at (M^a, Y^a), the intersection of the original budget constraint and the income expansion path for the insured price c. Thus, the pure price effect is $(M^a - M^u)$ and the income transfer effect is $(M^i - M^a)$.

DECISION TO PURCHASE INSURANCE

The decision to purchase insurance depends to a certain extent on which of these effects tends to dominate. If U^h describes utility in the healthy state where M is 0, the consumer's ex ante decision to purchase insurance therefore compares expected utility without insurance,

$$EU_u = \pi U^s(M^u, Y^u) + (1 - \pi)U^h(0, Y^o) \tag{3.17}$$

$$= \pi U^s(M^u, Y^o - M^u) + (1 - \pi)U^h(0, Y^o), \tag{3.18}$$

to expected utility with fair insurance,

$$EU_i = \pi U^s(M^i, Y^i) + (1 - \pi)U^h[0, Y^o - \pi(1 - c)M^i] \tag{3.19}$$

$$= \pi U^s[M^i, Y^o + (1 - \pi)(1 - c)M^i - M^i]$$
$$+ (1 - \pi)U^h[0, Y^o - \pi(1 - c)M^i] \tag{3.20}$$

$$= \pi U^s[M^i, Y^o - \pi(1 - c)M^i + (1 - c)M^i - M^i]$$
$$+ (1 - \pi)U^h[0, Y^o - \pi(1 - c)M^i]. \tag{3.21}$$

In equation (3.21), income spent on other goods and services if ill is equal to the original income endowment (Y^o), minus the premium $[\pi(1 - c)M^i]$, plus the payoff $[(1 - c)M^i]$, minus the income spent on medical care (M^i). The payoff minus the premium is, of course, the income transfers, or $[(1 - \pi)(1 - c)M^i]$ in equation (3.20). Such insurance is voluntarily purchased if $EU_i - EU_u > 0$.

The response to the income transfer and the price reduction will vary with the different illnesses, with different consumers and consumers' agents, and even at different points in time for the same consumer and same illness. Therefore, to understand the demand for insurance, it is necessary to consider the various possible responses to becoming insured. In this chapter, the case where $Y^o > M^i > M^u$ is considered. That is, insurance results in an increase in consumption of medical care caused by either a price or income transfer effect, or both, but that without insurance, the ill consumer would still be able to afford to purchase same amount of the medical care as is purchased under insurance. In other words, M^i is feasible given the consumer's original endowment, Y^o. In Chapter 4, the case where $M^u = M^i$ will be discussed, and in Chapter 5, the case where $M^i > Y^o$ (implying that the consumer requires medical care whose costs exceed her income) will be considered.

In the case where $Y^o > M^i > M^u$, the voluntary purchase of insurance implies that

$$
\begin{aligned}
EU_i - EU_u &= \pi U^s[M^i, Y^o + (1 - \pi)(1 - c)M^i - M^i] \\
&\quad + (1 - \pi)U^h[0, Y^o - \pi(1 - c)M^i] \\
&\quad - \pi U^s[M^u, Y^o - M^u) - (1 - \pi)U^h(0, Y^o) \\
&= \pi\{U^s[M^i, Y^o + (1 - \pi)(1 - c)M^i - M^i] - U^s[M^u, Y^o - M^u)\} \\
&\quad + (1 - \pi)\{U^h[0, Y^o - \pi(1 - c)M^i] - U^h(0, Y^o)\} \qquad (3.22) \\
&= \pi\{U^s(M^i, Y^i) - U^s(M^u, Y^u)\} \\
&\quad + (1 - \pi)\{U^h[0, Y^o - \pi(1 - c)M^i] - U^h(0, Y^o)\} > 0.
\end{aligned}
$$

In general, both an income transfer and a price effect are assumed to be present. If such an insurance contract is voluntarily purchased, equation (3.22) suggests that the expected net gain in utility if ill—the gain in utility from the income transfer net of the loss of utility from the pure price effect—is greater than the expected utility loss from paying the premium and remaining healthy. This case was described in Figure 3.1.

EXTREME CASES AND EXAMPLES

Consider now the case where the entire increase in consumption ($M^i - M^u$) is due to income transfers, with no pure price effect. For example, the treatment protocol for a chronic disease such as AIDS might be so standardized that there is a negligible level of substitutability between the medical care required to treat this illness on a continuing basis and other goods and services required to support life. The income transfer from insurance simply permits more of these fixed-input days to occur. This case is shown in Figure 3.3. The voluntary purchase of insurance coverage for this case would imply that the income transfers are welfare increasing because the additional medical care and other goods and services that the consumer is able to purchase are a result of the income transfer alone. That is, the expected benefits from the income transfer if ill are positive and exceed the expected costs of paying the insurance premium if healthy.

At the other extreme, the entire increase in consumption could be caused by an opportunistic price effect, with no income transfer effect. This extreme case represents the assumptions (but not the analysis) of the conventional health insurance model. The benefit derives from the effect of the income transfer on discretionary income (that is, purchases of other goods and services) alone, and the entire increase

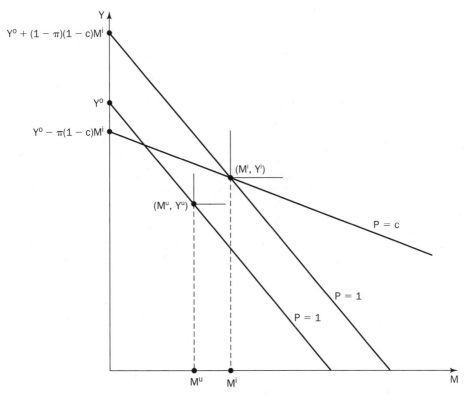

Figure 3.3 Income Transfer Effects with No Substitutability.

in consumption of medical care is the price effect. For example, some cosmetic or aesthetic surgical procedures may fall into this category. This case is illustrated in Figure 3.4. If such insurance were purchased voluntarily, it would indicate that the expected net gain in utility if ill is still greater than the expected loss in utility from paying the premium and remaining healthy. However, insurance for such illness/ treatment pairs is less likely to be purchased than insurance for illness/treatment pairs where the income effect dominates.

The same procedure could represent a price effect for some consumers or an income transfer effect for others. For example, consider a consumer without insurance who is diagnosed with breast cancer and decides, after consulting with her oncologist and surgeon, to purchase a radical bilateral mastectomy. Assume that the procedure, chemotherapy, and follow-up visits cost her $20,000. A bilateral mastectomy, however, is a disfiguring procedure, and the consumer considers purchasing a breast reconstruction. A reconstruction and implants often require two

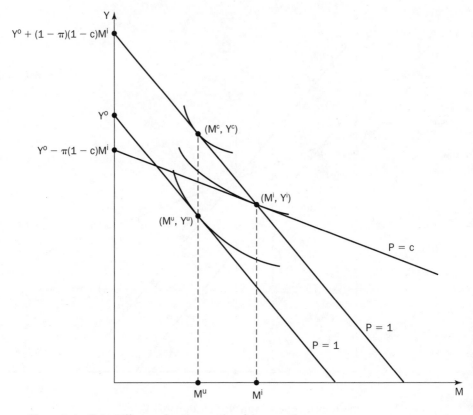

Figure 3.4 Price Effect under Conventional Assumptions.

additional operations by a plastic surgeon, plus follow-up visits, for an estimated additional cost of $20,000. Because of the competing claims on her resources, this consumer is only willing to pay $5,000 for the breast reconstruction. So, without insurance, she proceeds to purchase the mastectomy, but not the breast reconstruction.

Insurance is available to this consumer that reduces the price of medical care to zero for a premium of $3,000. If the consumer had purchased health insurance instead, she would undergo both procedures, for a total expenditure of ($20,000 + $20,000 =) $40,000, instead of just the initial bilateral mastectomy. Thus, the moral hazard would be represented by the breast reconstruction and follow-up visits, and the income transfer from insurance would be represented by $37,000, the difference between the insurance spending, $40,000, and the premium, $3,000.

The central issue is whether this moral hazard represents a welfare gain or a welfare loss. To determine this, a straightforward test is available that I will call the *consumer's income payoff test.* The test is: Would the consumer make the (same) decision to purchase an additional $20,000 reconstruction if she were given a lump sum income transfer of $37,000 in income that she could have spent on anything else? If she would purchase the $20,000 reconstruction with her original income plus the transfer of $37,000, then the $20,000 reconstruction is worth at least $20,000 to the consumer and no welfare loss exists. Indeed, a welfare gain would exist to the extent that she would be willing to pay more than $20,000 for the reconstruction, that is, to the extent that a consumer surplus existed after the income transfer.

On the other hand, if she would not have purchased the $20,000 reconstruction despite the $37,000 transfer, then the moral hazard is primarily a price effect and represents a welfare loss. Still, the income transfer would likely have increased the consumer's willingness to pay for the reconstruction above the original $5,000, but because the consumer did not purchase the $20,000 reconstruction with the additional income, we would know that her willingness to pay is still less than $20,000. Thus, by increasing the consumer's willingness to pay, the income transfer from insurance reduces the welfare loss from the price effect.

Under conventional theory, this procedure could only have been considered a welfare loss. Under the new theory, this procedure could still be considered a loss, but it could also be considered a welfare gain. The important distinction is that in conventional theory, willingness to pay is determined before the income transfer, but in the new theory it is determined after the income transfer. If insurance is purchased to provide an income transfer from those who remain healthy to those who become ill, then the willingness to pay of the ill consumer after the income transfer is the appropriate metric with which to evaluate the moral hazard.

CONTINGENT-CLAIMS VERSUS PRICE-PAYOFF INSURANCE CONTRACTS

As Figure 3.1 indicates, if a price effect is present, a price-payoff insurance contract results in a reduction of utility compared with a contingent-claims contract that pays off with the same income transfers as does the price-payoff contract. If contingent-claims contracts yield higher utility, why do price-payoff contracts dominate the health insurance market?

The result shown in Figure 3.1 is based on the assumption that the premiums are actuarially fair with both types of policies. That is, the premium equals only the expected payoff for medical care expenditures in the price-payoff contract, or only the expected lump sum payments in the contingent-claims contract. If the expected lump sum payments are equal to the expected medical care expenditures paid by the insurer, then the fair premiums of the two types of policies will also be equal. In practice, however, a premium would need to exceed the expected pay-offs by an amount that covers the administrative and other costs of insurance. Under the price-payoff contract, these costs would include the costs of claims processing, marketing, underwriting, overhead, and normal profits. Under a contingent-claims contract, the administrative costs would include all of the above, plus additional costs for verifying illnesses, policing against fraud, and writing complex contingency contracts. Thus, it is likely that the administrative costs of the contingent-claims contract would exceed those of the price-payoff contract.

The administrative costs are lower with price-payoff contracts in part because the insurer is able to use the policyholder's physician to avoid some of the costs. For example, under a contingent-claims contract, the insurer would need to employ physicians to verify that the policyholder has the disease that he claims to have. Under a price-payoff contract, the physician implicitly verifies that the policyholder has the disease by actually performing the treatment for the claimed disease on the policyholder before the payoff is made. Also, under a contingent-claims contract, the policyholder alone might fraudulently claim that he has a disease that warrants a large payoff, but under a price-payoff contract, this policyholder would need to enlist the cooperation of the physician as a co-conspirator in the fraud, a more difficult task. Under contingent-claims insurance, the contract would not only need to specify a schedule of payoffs for each disease but also the payoffs for all the possible levels of severity, complications, sequellae, and courses that each disease might take. Under a price-payoff contract, the physician (and other providers) would be paid for those services that the physician (as the policyholder's disease treatment manager and agent) deems medically necessary for treating each idiosyncratic patient/disease combination.

While using a price-payoff mechanism saves some administrative costs compared to using a contingent-claims payoff mechanism, it increases others. Foremost of these is the welfare cost from the additional medical care that the consumer demands because he is responding opportunistically to the reduced price, that is, the pure price effect. Thus, the welfare costs associated with the price effect in a price-payoff contract can be viewed as an offset to the additional administrative costs that would have been incurred under a contingent-claims contract (this issue is discussed further in Chapter 8). It may be further inferred that because price-payoff contracts dominate the market, the price effect costs are less welfare-decreasing than the additional administrative costs of the contingent-claims contract would be.

THE PHYSICIAN AND SUBSTITUTABILITY OF MEDICAL CARE FOR OTHER GOODS AND SERVICES

Not only does paying off the consumer by paying the physician eliminate some transactions costs, but the involvement of the consumer's physician also constrains the consumer's choice set and as a result, eliminates some of the consumer's welfare-decreasing responses to the price reduction. In effect, the physician is able to impose a lower degree of substitutability between health care and other commodities than actually exists for the insured consumer.

Consider, for example, a hospital stay. Hospitals provide health care, but they also provide food and housing services. Thus, for a consumer who is traveling, there is a degree of substitutability between a stay in a hotel and a stay in a hospital. If the decision were left entirely to the consumer, insurance may reduce the relative price of a hospital stay sufficiently so that the consumer may desire to substitute a stay in the hospital for a stay in a hotel. This does not occur, however, because a hospital stay must be ordered by a physician, and physicians (at least in theory) only order hospital stays for those who are ill. Therefore, one of the important roles of the physician is to reduce the degree of substitutability between health care and nonhealth care-related uses for health care. This role is also manifested in consumers not being able to obtain some prescription drugs (for example, narcotics, barbiturates, steroids, and so on) or some medical care (for example, surgical interventions for those who are not obese but want to weigh less, counseling for those who lack a mental health diagnosis, and so on) without the physician's consent.

Diagrammatically, it is as if the physician imposes preferences like those in Figure 3.3 on a consumer who has preferences like those in Figure 3.4 or Figure 3.1. It is, perhaps, no wonder that physicians have been accused by economists of having a fixed-input view of medical technology, that is, a view that tolerates little substitutability among treatments, and by extension, little substitutability between the treatment of choice and other goods or services.

Paying off the insurance contract by reducing the price of medical care also solves the problem of societal responsibility for caring for the ill. A lump sum income payment to the ill person can be spent on anything. It is possible, therefore, that a consumer who is severely ill may receive a large payoff and spend the income on goods and services (entertainment, gifts, and so on) other than health care. Society, however, may not want to permit such spending because of ethical or altruistic reasons. Constraining the consumption choice by using health care price reductions to pay off the contract avoids this problem.

Finally, it should be noted that paying off the insurance contract by reducing the price of medical care may result in inefficient consumption decisions if true substitutability exists and the illness can be treated by nonhealth care inputs. For example, paying off by reducing the price for certain formal health care services may result in an inefficient reduced use of lower cost informal care.

PAYOFFS, TREATMENT COSTS, AND FULL COVERAGE

In price-payoff contracts, the payoffs and income transfers are automatically correlated with the cost of treating the various diseases. Likewise, a contingent-claims contract with payoffs, premiums, and income transfers corresponding to the payoffs, premiums, and income transfers of a specific price-payoff contract, will also have payoffs and income transfers that are correlated with medical care expenditures for the various diseases. Under an actual contingent-claims contract, however, any schedule of payments would need to be developed explicitly and any correlation between payoffs and treatment costs for the various diseases would need to be intentional. A perfect correlation between the cost of treating the disease and the payoff may not necessarily be desirable. For example, if it is difficult to verify the presence of certain diseases, it may be in the interest of the consumer to have payoffs for some diseases set at or near zero to avoid the costs of monitoring for fraud, even though the disease has positive treatment costs. Or, as mentioned above, consumers may want payoffs set well above treatment costs for diseases with long convalescent periods and extended periods without income to cover some of the indirect costs of the disease.

Under the conventional model, the degree to which the contract provides "full coverage" is determined by the coinsurance rate alone: a coinsurance rate of 0% would indicate full coverage and any lesser rate would be less than full coverage. Under the new model, "full coverage" would be determined by both the chosen coinsurance rate and the largely exogenous probability of illness. That is, the treatment of a disease is only fully covered by the healthy if both c and π are (approach) zero, a different definition. If c were 0% but π were 1, there would be no "coverage" at all since the entire cost of the care would be borne by the consumer up front in the premium.

ADVERSE SELECTION AND MORAL HAZARD

An implication of this model is that the behavior that has conventionally been identified as moral hazard may actually be adverse selection instead. That is, moral hazard has conventionally been conceptualized as an opportunistic price effect that occurs after becoming insured. If an exogenous price change were the only mechanism for increasing consumption when insured, then a person with a chronic disease who becomes insured would purchase more care only because of the price effect. For example, suppose a consumer with myopia does not purchase designer prescription sunglasses—regarded by some as a quintessential example of a frivolous moral hazard purchase—when uninsured, but purchases them when insured at a 0% coinsurance rate. For the consumer who purchases insurance with the preexisting condition of myopia, this consumption effect is conventionally attributed to an opportunistic price effect and moral hazard under the conventional model, not adverse selection.

Under the new model, when purchasing insurance, the consumer compares the premium if healthy to the income transfers if ill. Therefore, it is clear that part of additional consumption of those who are ill and become insured is an adverse selection demand effect that is due to this comparison. Without insurance, again the consumer does not purchase designer sunglasses, but in considering whether to purchase insurance, the consumer recognizes that not all policyholders will have the condition of myopia during the contract period. If the coinsurance rate were 0% and only about 10% of the population have myopia (all of whom are assumed to purchase designer sunglasses if insured), then the consumer could purchase insurance for a fair premium representing only 10% of the cost of designer sunglasses; the remaining 90% would be paid for by income transfers from those without myopia. Thus, the consumer with myopia purchases insurance in part because of this income transfer and the resulting additional medical care consumption that he would purchase with insurance. In contrast, if the coinsurance rate were again 0% but 100% of those in the insurance pool had myopia and purchased designer sunglasses, then 100% of the cost of designer sunglasses would be included in the myopic consumer's premium and the consumer would no longer have a selection effect reason to purchase insurance, even though the price at the point of purchase is $0.

Thus, part of the increased consumption by those with insurance (compared to those without) is due to the fact that those who know in advance that they will benefit from the income transfers within insurance are more likely to both purchase insurance and have more medical care purchases, which is an adverse selection story. That is, even though without insurance no designer sunglasses would be purchased, the consumer with myopia self-selects to purchase insurance, in part because of the income transfers and the designer sunglasses he intends to purchase if insured. This effect is due to the convention that insurers sell contracts that cover some preexisting conditions, not to moral hazard.

WELFARE CONSEQUENCES AT THE MARGIN

Another implication of this model is that a change in the coinsurance rate, holding π constant, will change the size of both the price effect on medical care and the income transfers, which will affect purchases of both medical care and other goods and services. (This point is expanded upon in Chapter 9.) Unless all the utility gains from the income transfers can be evaluated, it will be difficult to determine the welfare implications of any coinsurance rate change or to find an optimal coinsurance rate.

In the case of an income transfer that pays for otherwise unaffordable but life-preserving care (discussed further in Chapter 5), any price effect would probably be negligible, and only a gain from income transfers would occur: the otherwise unaffordable medical procedure. As a result, the utility gain is related to the willingness to pay for the procedure, but information on the willingness to pay for expensive procedures may not be available. In lieu of the willingness to pay for the procedure, a measure of the willingness to pay for the outcome of the procedure can be used. For example, if the medical procedure for a certain illness results in an average increase of seven additional quality adjusted life years (QALYs) and if the willingness to pay for a QALY is $100,000, then the willingness to pay for the procedure can be measured at approximately (7 $\times$ $100,000 =) $700,000. Finally, to distinguish affordable care from unaffordable care, the distribution of wealth would need to be accounted for. For example, fewer procedures would be unaffordable to a rich consumer than a poor one.

The utility gained from an income transfer that is used to purchase additional *affordable* medical care in the ill state would be more difficult to ascertain. For those affordable medical procedures for which there is a positive consumer surplus, insurance coverage that resulted in their purchase would be welfare-increasing. Willingness to pay for these procedures could be estimated from demand analyses, if demand after the income transfer could be ascertained (as in the consumer's income payoff test referred to earlier). These income-related gains would then need to be netted against the welfare losses from the price effect in order to determine the net marginal gain.

It would be difficult to determine a functional relationship between utility and spending on medical care. Every disease is different, each requires different technologies and different expenditures, and the procedures are generally lumpy rather than continuous. Because information about the form of the utility function for spending on medical care is not available, and because the costs of an illness include more than just the cost of medical care, it would be difficult to determine an optimal coinsurance rate for medical care. For this reason, the model of the demand for health insurance proposed in this chapter specifies the conditions under which consumers would choose to purchase insurance if given a choice between (1) an insurance policy with a given coinsurance rate, c, and (2) no insurance. To do more would require structure for which information is just not available.

SUMMARY

This chapter has presented the basic model of the demand for health insurance. It argued that the demand for health insurance is a demand for an income transfer in the ill state. The price payoff in health insurance acts as the mechanism by which this income transfer occurs. In subsequent chapters, I focus on various aspects of this model. In Chapter 4, I consider the case where the medical expenditures that occur with insurance are the same as those that would occur without insurance. This is the same assumption that underlies the conventional expected utility theory of the demand for health insurance.

1. That is, if the payoff is $(1 - c)M^i$ in a lump sum income payment and the premium is $-\pi(1 - c)M^i$, then income transfers are $(1 - \pi)(1 - c)M^i$.

4 | EXPECTED UTILITY THEORY FROM A QUID PRO QUO PERSPECTIVE

OVERVIEW

This chapter examines the demand for health insurance under the assumption that medical care expenditures with insurance are exactly the same as medical care expenditures without insurance. That is, it is assumed that medical care expenditures do not exhibit either an income transfer or a pure price effect. This assumption underlies the early models of the demand for insurance—those that concluded that insurance is demanded because consumers prefer a small certain loss (that is, a premium payment) to an actuarially equivalent, but larger uncertain loss (that is, a naturally occurring event that generates an exogenously determined financial loss). As discussed in Chapter 2, however, this conventional interpretation of expected utility theory is diametrically opposed to the empirical findings that show that consumers prefer large uncertain losses to smaller certain ones of the same expected magnitude.

In this chapter, an alternative specification of the conventional expected utility theory is presented that is consistent with the demand for health insurance as a demand for an income transfer in the ill state. Then, arguments are presented that this specification is more consistent with the way that consumers actually regard the decision to purchase insurance than the conventional specification.

EXPECTED UTILITY THEORY RESPECIFIED

The assumption that no additional health care is consumed as a result of becoming insured can be specified as the case where $M^i = M^u = M^*$. For example, the illness may be so predictable in its course and the procedure for curing it so standardized

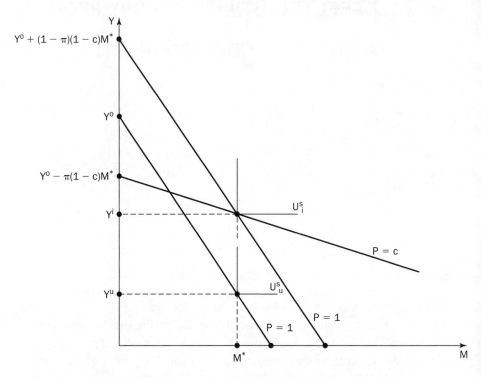

Figure 4.1 The Gain from Insurance with No Moral Hazard.

that there is no difference between the treatment with insurance and without. This case is illustrated in Figure 4.1. This figure indicates that the ill consumer does not respond to income and, because there is no substitutability between medical care and other goods and services, does not respond to price as well.

In the case where $M^i = M^u = M^*$, equation (3.18) can be rewritten as

$$EU_u = \pi U^s(M^*, Y^o - M^*) + (1 - \pi)U^h(0, Y^o), \qquad (4.1)$$

and equation (3.20) becomes

$$EU_i = \pi U^s[M^*, Y^o + (1 - \pi)(1 - c)M^* - M^*]$$
$$+ (1 - \pi)U^h[0, Y^o - \pi(1 - c)M^*]. \qquad (4.2)$$

The expected utility gain from being insured is

$$EU_i - EU_u = \pi U^s[M^*, Y^o + (1 - \pi)(1 - c)M^* - M^*]$$
$$+ (1 - \pi)U^h[0, Y^o - \pi(1 - c)M^*]$$
$$- \pi U^s(M^*, Y^o - M^*) - (1 - \pi)U^h(0, Y^o)$$

$$= \pi\{U^s[M^*, Y^o + (1 - \pi)(1 - c)M^* - M^\star] - U^s(M^*, Y^o - M^\star)\}$$
$$+ (1 - \pi)\{U^h[0, Y^o - \pi(1 - c)M^\star] - U^h(0, Y^o)\}. \qquad (4.3)$$

Thus, whether insurance is purchased or not depends entirely on the income consequences—that is, the consequences of the income transfer on consumption of other goods and services—of this insurance. This is the conventional "risk avoidance" benefit from insurance, only in this specification, the benefit is expressed as a gain from the income transfer in the ill state net of the cost of the premium in the healthy state. Under this quid pro quo specification, the consumer weighs the payment of a premium that moves him from $U^h(0, Y^o)$ "down" the utility function to $U^h[0, Y^o - \pi(1 - c)M^\star]$ if healthy, against an income transfer that moves him from $U^s(M^*, Y^o - M^\star)$ "up" the utility function to $U^s[M^*, Y^o + (1 - \pi)(1 - c)M^* - M^\star]$ if ill. If the person voluntarily purchases this insurance, it can be assumed that the expected utility gain from the income transfer if ill exceeds the expected utility loss from paying the premium if healthy.

If it is assumed that the consumer faces the same utility function for Y when healthy or when ill, then inequality (4.3) can be rewritten as follows:

$$EU_i - EU_u = \pi\{U[Y^o + (1 - \pi)(1 - c)M^* - M^\star] - U(Y^o - M^\star)\}$$
$$+ (1 - \pi)\{U[Y^o - \pi(1 - c)M^\star] - U(Y^o)\} > 0. \quad (4.4)$$

Inequality (4.4) also suppresses medical care in the utility function because the same medical care occurs if ill, with or without insurance. If the utility function in inequality (4.4) exhibits the so-called "risk averse" functional form over income, such that $U_Y > 0$ and $U_{YY} < 0$, then insurance would be purchased.

Figure 4.2 illustrates this result. The consumer is originally at Y^o income and without insurance, would remain at Y^o if healthy. If he becomes ill without insurance, the consumer would spend M^* on medical care and have $(Y^o - M^*)$ left over to spend on other goods and services.

If the consumer purchases insurance and remains healthy, he loses income by paying the actuarially fair insurance premium, $-\pi(1 - c)M^*$, so that he experiences a loss of income from Y^o to $(Y^o - \pi(1 - c)M^*)$, with a probability of $(1 - \pi)$, or an expected income loss of $-(1 - \pi)[\pi(1 - c)M^*]$, from income level Y^o. The corresponding expected utility loss from purchasing insurance and remaining healthy is $(1 - \pi)[U(Y^o) - U(Y^o - \pi(1 - c)M^*)]|_{U(Y^o)}$ or an expected loss of utility from U_0 to U_1 in Figure 4.2.

However, if the consumer purchases insurance and becomes ill, he gains income equal to the income transfers, $(1 - \pi)(1 - c)M^*$, and the expected gain in income is $\pi[(1 - \pi)(1 - c)M^*]$, from income level $(Y^o - M^*)$, the uninsured

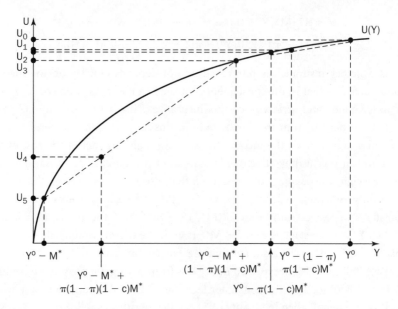

Figure 4.2 Expected Utility Theory from a Quid Pro Quo Perspective.

income level when ill. Thus, the expected dollar gain from income transfers, $\pi[(1 - \pi)(1 - c)M^*]$, equals the expected dollar loss from the fair premium, $-(1 - \pi)[\pi(1 - c)M^*]$. Because the gain is evaluated on a steeper portion of the "risk averse" utility function than is the loss, the expected utility gained will exceed the expected utility lost and insurance would be purchased.

If ill then, the consumer's expected utility gain from purchasing insurance is $\pi\{U[Y^o - M^* + (1 - \pi)(1 - c)M^*] - U(Y^o - M^*)\}|_{U(Y^o - M^*)}$ or from U_5 to U_4 in Figure 4.2. Because the expected gain in utility from the income transfer, $U_4 - U_5$, exceeds the expected loss in utility from the payment of the premium, $U_0 - U_1$, insurance is purchased.

With this specification of the expected utility model, it is simply necessary that the income transfer gain be evaluated on a steeper portion of the utility function than the premium loss, for insurance to be purchased. In Figure 4.2, the sections of the utility function representing the income transfer and the premium payment do not overlap. Indeed, if $c > 0$, these sections are separated by the portion of expenditures paid for out-of-pocket by the consumer. This implies that while a utility function with a "risk averse" functional form would satisfy the condition for purchasing insurance, a number of other functional forms would also result in insurance being purchased.

DERIVATION OF THE QUID PRO QUO SPECIFICATION

The conventional standard gamble specification was represented by equations (2.3)–(2.6) in Chapter 2. Summarizing these equations and assuming that $M^i = M^u = M^*$, insurance is purchased if $EU_i - EU_u > 0$, or equivalently if

$$EU_i - EU_u = U(Y^o - \pi M^* + I - M^*) - \pi U(Y^o - M^*)$$
$$- (1 - \pi)U(Y^o) > 0, \qquad (4.5)$$

where I, the payoff, is assumed to be equal to M^*, the medical care spending, and πM^* is the fair premium. Thus, inequality (4.5) can also be written

$$U(Y^o - \pi M^* + M^* - M^*) > \pi U(Y^o - M^*) + (1 - \pi)U(Y^o), \quad (4.6)$$

or

$$U[Y^o + (1 - \pi)M^* - M^*] > \pi U(Y^o - M^*) + (1 - \pi)U(Y^o). \quad (4.7)$$

Subtracting $(1 - \pi)U[Y^o + (1 - \pi)M^* - M^*]$ from both sides of inequality (4.7) yields

$$\pi U[Y^o + (1 - \pi)M^* - M^*] > \pi U(Y^o - M^*) + (1 - \pi)U(Y^o)$$
$$- (1 - \pi)U[Y^o + (1 - \pi)M^* - M^*]. \quad (4.8)$$

Now, subtracting $\pi U(Y^o - M^*)$ from both sides results in

$$\pi U[Y^o + (1 - \pi)M^* - M^*] - \pi U(Y^o - M^*)$$
$$> - (1 - \pi)U(Y^o - \pi M^*) + (1 - \pi)U(Y^o), \qquad (4.9)$$

or

$$EU_i - EU_u = \pi\{U[Y^o + (1 - \pi)M^* - M^*] - U(Y^o - M^*)\}$$
$$+ (1 - \pi)\{U(Y^o - \pi M^*) - U(Y^o)\} > 0. \qquad (4.10)$$

Inequality (4.10) is the same as inequality (4.5), only expressed as a net gain. Inequalities (4.10) and (4.4) are essentially identical, except that inequality (4.10) represents the conditions for purchasing a contingent-claims contract, while inequality (4.4) represents the conditions for purchasing a price-payoff contract. In both inequalities (4.10) and (4.4), the decision to purchase insurance is expressed in terms of a quid pro quo exchange: insurance is purchased when the utility gain from the income transfer received when ill is greater than the utility loss from paying the premium when healthy.

The conventional understanding of why insurance is purchased differs considerably from this interpretation. Conventional theory, based on the standard gamble specification of the expected utility model, teaches that insurance is purchased because consumers prefer certain losses to uncertain ones of the same expected magnitude. In contrast, the specification from a quid pro quo perspective described here teaches that the demand for insurance has nothing to do with the demand for certainty because uncertainty exists with or without insurance. If the consumer has insurance, the uncertainty is whether the consumer will remain healthy and incur the loss of the premium, or become ill and receive an income transfer. If the consumer does not have insurance, the uncertainty is whether the consumer will remain healthy and consume other goods and services at the level of his endowment, or become ill and consume at a level diminished by his medical care spending. Thus, under a quid pro quo specification of the insurance problem, uncertainty exists with or without insurance, and insurance is demanded not because of a preference for certainty, but because the gain from the income transfer if ill exceeds the cost of the insurance policy if the consumer remains healthy.

PROSPECT THEORY

Prospect theory is a theory of choice developed from empirical studies that show that consumers prefer certain gains to uncertain ones of the same expected magnitude, but that they also prefer uncertain losses to certain ones of the same expected magnitude (Kahneman and Tversky, 1979; Tversky and Kahneman, 1981, 1986, 1988). Prospect theory holds that decisions are made from reference points representing differing income or wealth levels. The choices that matter are with regard to changes in income—gains or losses—made relative to these reference income levels, rather than the levels themselves. Gains from a given reference point are hypothesized to diminish in value as the gain increases, and losses from a reference point diminish in (negative) value as the loss increases. Moreover, the marginal gain in value from any given gain in income is less than the (absolute) marginal loss in value for a loss of income of the same size. This theory is illustrated by the S-shaped value curve in Figure 4.3. This curve shows the value of gains and losses in income or wealth from a given reference point, as indicated by the origin.

The decision to purchase insurance in a prospect theory context is illustrated in Figure 4.3. Assume that the origin in Figure 4.3 represents endowed income of Y^o. For the decision to purchase insurance under the conventional standard gamble

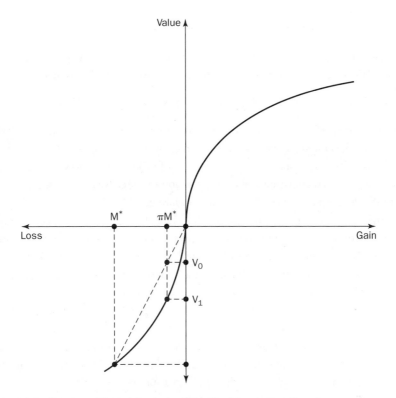

Figure 4.3 Prospect Theory Analysis of the Decision to Purchase Insurance.

specification, the consumer would compare a sure loss of the premium, πM^*, resulting in a certain loss in value of $V_1 = V(\pi M^*)$, versus an expected loss of M^* with a probability of π, resulting in an expected loss in value of $V_0 = \pi V(M^*) + (1 - \pi)V(0)$. Because $V_0 > V_1$, insurance should not be purchased according to this specification. But, we know that insurance is purchased, and for a wide variety of risks.

Prospect theory is important for two reasons. First, because the empirical evidence underlying prospect theory finds that consumers prefer uncertain losses to actuarially equivalent certain losses, it shows that the conventional interpretation of expected utility theory—a demand for certain financial losses—is incorrect as an explanation for why consumers demand insurance and health insurance. Second, prospect theory is important because it suggests that it is more useful to compare changes in utility from a reference point than to compare utility levels, when explaining the consumer behavior.

FOCUSING ON THE INSURANCE CONTRACT

The decision to purchase insurance is represented conventionally by inequality (4.5.) This inequality is often simplified, under the assumption that $I = M^*$, as:

$$EU_i - EU_u = U(Y^o - \pi M^*) - \pi U(Y^o - M^*) - (1 - \pi)U(Y^o) > 0. \quad (4.11)$$

That is, if inequality (4.11) is positive, insurance would be purchased. This is the conventional standard gamble specification of the expected utility theory and expresses the decision as a choice between levels of utility. Again, however, empirical work suggests that consumers view the decision to purchase insurance differently from the decision as represented by the standard gamble.

Slovic, Fischhoff, and Lichtenstein (1988) report on a study where 208 subjects were confronted with one of two situations: (A) a choice between a 0.001 chance of losing $5,000 and a certain loss of $5, and (B) a choice between a 0.25 chance of losing $200 and a certain loss of $50. These situations were sometimes framed as insurance and sometimes as a simple standard gamble exercise in preferences. The proportion choosing a certain loss (that is, the purchase of insurance) in the insurance context was 66 and 65%, for the 0.001 and 0.25 probabilities of loss questions, respectively. However, for standard gamble context, the proportion choosing certain loss dropped to 39 and 20%, respectively. This implies that consumers view insurance as being different than a standard gamble.

Slovic, Fischhoff, and Lichtenstein (1988) suggest that insurance may imply a different reference point, and in this way differ from a standard gamble. In the standard gamble context, the consumer's reference point is assumed to be the status quo and consumers might, therefore, prefer the gamble of a 0.25 chance of losing $200 to a certain loss of $50. But in the insurance context, the consumer's reference point might be already having purchased insurance. Therefore, the choice would be either (A) to keep insurance or (B) to forgo insurance and accept the level of expected utility associated with the following gamble: a 75% chance of a $50 gain from not paying the premium when healthy or a 25% chance of a $150 net loss because of losing $200 but getting to keep $50 that you would have paid in premiums. The authors reason that because consumers are more sensitive to losses than gains and because smaller probabilities tend to have greater weights, the person might prefer to remain insured.

While this interpretation may be consistent with prospect theory and is perhaps closer to a quid pro quo perspective than the conventional specification, it is still a choice between certainty (insurance) and uncertainty (remaining uninsured). Moreover, it does not provide an intuitively satisfying explanation for the purchase of insurance: Do consumers really assume that they have already purchased insurance when the insurance salesman comes to call?

The crucial distinction between insurance and the standard gamble is revealed by another empirical study that contrasts the standard gamble choice to the insurance choice, but also with three other choices as well. Connor (1996) presented his subjects with the following five Choice Scenarios:[1]

1. A: You will lose $40 on your next trip.
   B: You have a 2% chance of losing $2,000 on your next trip.

2. A: You will lose $40 on your next trip. In addition, you will have a 2% chance of losing $2,000 on your next trip AND getting an unexpected $2,000 gift the same day from a distant relative.
   B: You have a 2% chance of losing $2,000 on your next trip.

3. A: You will lose $40 on your next trip. In addition, you will have a 2% chance of losing $2,000 on your next trip AND recovering $2,000 the same day by searching.
   B: You have a 2% chance of losing $2,000 on your next trip.

4. A: You have a 2% chance of losing $2,000 on your next trip. You buy $2,000 in travel checks for $2,000 plus a $40 fee which will let you recover the $2,000 loss the same day if it occurs.
   B: You have a 2% chance of losing $2,000 on your next trip. You do not buy travel checks.

5. A: You have a 2% chance of losing $2,000 on your next trip. You buy travel insurance for $40 which will reimburse you for this $2,000 loss the same day if it occurs.
   B: You have a 2% chance of losing $2,000 on your next trip. You do not buy travel insurance.

When confronted with the standard gamble (Scenario 1), his subjects were almost equally divided between alternatives A and B, but when the same choice was placed in an insurance context (Scenario 5), the purchase of insurance (A) was preferred with statistical significance.

The results from the three intermediate choices are revealing. For Scenarios 2 and 3, there was no significant trend in preference (although respondents tended to prefer uncertain alternative B, consistent with prospect theory), but for Choice 4, the "certain" Choice A was preferred with statistical significance. These results suggest that it is only when the $40 payment represents a payment for an expected payoff and when the *uncertain loss is uncoupled from this uncertain payoff* (as it is with Choice 4 and the insurance context, Choice 5), that the "certain" Choice A becomes preferred. But at that point, the "certain" Choice A becomes uncertain, because the payoff gain only occurs some (2%) of the time.

These results reinforce the conclusion that the context in which insurance is purchased is not the same as the standard gamble context that is conventionally used to model the theory of the demand for insurance. They suggest that the context in which insurance is purchased is one where consumers regard the loss as separate from the insurance contract, that is, part of the environment. Thus, these results are consistent with an interpretation of the demand for insurance as being derived from the demand for something that the insurance contract can actually deliver: an income transfer to the ill from those who remain healthy.

Although inequality (4.10) is a specification derived from the conventional theory (inequalities [4.5] or [4.11]), it represents an entirely different interpretation of why consumers purchase insurance, but one that is consistent with these empirical results. In inequality (4.10), the decision is specified so that the loss is implied in a change of reference point, rather than explicitly included as part of the choice, as it is in inequalities (4.5) and (4.11). In the conventional specification (represented by inequalities [4.5] and [4.11]), the payoff is represented as merely canceling the loss, so that the consumer opts for a certain level of utility rather than an expected one. When the loss is acknowledged only as a change in reference point, such as in inequality (4.10), the specification better reflects how consumers actually regard the insurance contract: the payment of the premium when healthy in exchange for an income transfer when ill. It focuses the theory on the quid pro quo nature of the insurance contract itself and converts the decision from a choice between certain and uncertain losses of the same expected magnitude into the same sort of economic transaction that consumers make every day.

ADDITIONAL CONSIDERATIONS

The appropriateness this alternative specification of the insurance decision (represented by inequality [4.10]) is reinforced by a number of other considerations. First, the conventional specification, inequality (4.5), makes it seem as if the loss were part of the insurance contract itself. Indeed, if it were intended that the loss should be represented as part of the insurance contract, the consumer's choice would be specified exactly as in inequality (4.5). Under the quid pro quo specification, the loss remains separate from the insurance contract. The consumer purchases a contract for a payoff of income in the event that the loss occurs. The loss triggers the execution of the contract, but it is not part of the contract itself.

Second, the demand for insurance as a demand for an income transfer is consistent with the work by Rabin (2000) and Rabin and Thaler (2001). These authors question the connection between risk preferences and the shape of the consumer's utility function over defined wealth or income levels. That is, the sole source of preferences regarding risk in economic theory is the concavity (or convexity) of the consumer's utility function. These authors, however, point out that the concavity of the consumer's utility function implies intuitively implausible preferences regarding risk. For example, a person with a concave utility function of income would be expected to turn down a fair wager, such as paying $10 for a 0.5 chance of a $20 payoff. If the utility function were such that the same consumer also turned down a wager of $10 for a 0.5 chance of a $21 payoff, Rabin and Thaler (2001) show that the consumer would then be expected to turn down a wager of $100 for a 0.5 chance of an infinitely large payoff (!) in order for the utility function to be consistent with the previous decision. Because the former is plausible, while the latter is intuitively implausible, there is the suggestion that risk preferences might derive from something other than the shape of the consumer's utility function. If risk preferences are derived separately, then the shape of the consumer's utility function may be used to explain the demand for insurance (see Figure 4.2), and at the same time the role of risk preferences on the decision to purchase insurance may be largely irrelevant. This distinction is further explored in Chapter 8.

Third, because the quid pro quo specification is equivalent to the conventional specification mathematically, it preserves not only the ordinality of the insurance choice, but also its cardinality. That is, the net gain in utility from insurance under expected utility theory from a quid pro quo perspective is exactly the same as the net gain under conventional standard gamble specification. For example, Table 4.1 shows the computations of the utility gain from insurance for two commonly used utility functions: $U = \ln Y$ and $U = Y^{1/2}$. Substituting in values of $100,000 for endowed income (corresponding to Y_0), medical care spending of $50,000 with a probability of 0.2, and a fair premium of $10,000, the gains under either conventional expected utility or expected utility from a quid pro quo perspective are the same. This implies that the measures used to determine the net gain in utility under the conventional expected utility model—to the extent that they accurately measure the variance in expenditures on *other goods and services* with insurance compared with such expenditures without insurance—may be used to measure the gain in utility under a quid pro quo specification.

Table 4.1

Calculations of the gain in expected utility under conventional expected utility theory and expected utility from a quid pro quo perspective, using common functional forms for the utility function

	$U = \ln Y$	$U = Y^{1/2}$
Conventional Expected Utility Theory (inequality [4.11])	U($90K) − 0.8U($100K) − 0.2U($50K) = 11.4076 − 9.2103 − 2.1640 = 0.0333	U($90K) − 0.8U($100K) − 0.2U($50K) = 300 − 0.8(316.23) − 0.2(223.61) = 300 − 252.98 − 44.72 = 2.3
Expected Utility Theory from a Quid Pro Quo Perspective (inequality [4.10])	0.2[U($90K) − U$50K)] + 0.8[U($90K) − U($100K)] = 0.2(11.4076 − 10.8198) + 0.8(11.4076 − 11.5129) = 0.1176 − 0.0842 = 0.0333	0.2[U($90K) − U$50K)] + 0.8[U($90K) − U($100K)] = 0.2(300 − 223.61) + 0.8(300 − 316.23) = 15.28 − 12.98 = 2.3

Fourth, with regard to health insurance specifically, there is actually no "loss" of wealth if the bad (ill) state of the world occurs, in contrast to other forms of insurance, such as, automobile accident, liability, and fire insurance, where a loss of wealth would occur. (Of course, a consumer may lose income from being away from work, but that is not traditionally included as part of the loss in health insurance.) In health insurance, becoming ill is typically modeled as a change in preferences: consumers prefer to purchase other goods and services if healthy, but if ill, the same consumers prefer to purchase medical care in addition to other goods and services. A contingent-claims health insurance contract would represent a direct increase in income if ill, and that income could be spent on medical care or anything else. Likewise, price-payoff insurance also does not require that a loss of wealth occur, only that the medical care that is consumed when ill be paid for by transfers from those who remain healthy. Therefore, it would be especially inappropriate to specify the equation representing the demand for health insurance as a demand for certain versus uncertain losses, because no financial losses actually occur.

IMPORTANCE AND IMPLICATIONS

Conventional expected utility theory has traditionally been specified from a loss perspective. Because of this specification, generations of economics students have been taught that consumers demand insurance because they prefer the certain loss of paying the fair premium to the uncertain loss of a medical expenditure. If the empirical findings from the prospect theory literature are to be believed, *nothing could be further from the truth*. Replicated experiments have documented that individuals tend to prefer uncertain losses to actuarially equivalent certain losses. Therefore, if consumers buy insurance, it must be for reasons other than that they prefer certain financial losses.

The specification and interpretation described in this chapter suggest that a consumer's demand for insurance has nothing to do with a preference for certainty. Instead, the demand for insurance derives from the demand for an income transfer that occurs in the ill state, which is purchased with a premium payment that occurs in the healthy state. When these changes are made, uncertainty occurs both with and without insurance.

The key difference between these two interpretations lies in whether people integrate the "loss" into the insurance contract, or regard it as a separate characteristic —part of the environment. This may appear to be a subtle distinction, but it is at the crux of understanding why consumers purchase health insurance. It shows how the conventional specification of the expected utility model converts insurance from a quid pro quo contract, which it is in reality, into what appears to be a choice between certain and uncertain losses of the same expected magnitude. This standard gamble specification, however, so fundamentally alters the choices that these alternatives no longer reflect the way that consumers view insurance, leading analysts to make the wrong behavioral inferences about what motivates consumers to purchase insurance.

That is, there is nothing mathematically wrong with expressing the decision to purchase insurance as a choice between utility levels (that is, inequalities [4.5] or [4.11]). Such an analysis produces exactly the same empirical calculation of the net benefit as the analysis expressed as a net utility gain (inequality [4.10]). The problem with using the utility-level analysis, however, is that it appears as if consumers demand insurance for the certainty it provides. If it were recognized that this is simply an artifact of the mathematical specification chosen, and that the loss is, in fact, separate from the insurance contract and is only included to show how the reference point changes when ill, then the true quid pro quo nature of the transaction would be clear. As it is, the conventional specification has led analysts to conclude erroneously that the demand for insurance is a demand for a certainty.

This mis-specification has been far from benign. The demand-for-certainty interpretation of expected utility theory has misled analysts into specifying the insurance model so that a person could receive, say, a $30,000 income payoff in the event of illness without this additional $30,000 generating any additional health care expenditures (e.g., Newhouse, 1978a). That is, the expenditures (representing the "loss") were conventionally specified as being fixed, in order for the payoff to result in certainty. For many health economists, the implication of this specification was that the increase in health care consumption that was systematically observed in the insured could only be due (by process of elimination) to a price effect, but a price effect would reduce welfare (Pauly, 1968). It was generally not recognized that an income payoff could generate additional spending compared with no payoff (the exception being de Meza's [1983] model, but he compared the insurance payoff with saving or borrowing to obtain more income, rather than with no income payoff at all). Nor was it recognized that the price reduction in health insurance was the mechanism by which an income transfer occurs and that a portion of the additional consumption of health care was due to this income transfer. Thus, the conventional specification has indirectly led to a fundamental misunderstanding of the welfare consequences of health insurance and to the promotion of policies designed to solve problems that largely did not exist (see Chapter 9).

Under a quid pro quo specification of expected utility theory, the demand for insurance has nothing to do with the demand for certainty or for risk avoidance. This claim may seem controversial in part because the supply-side theory of insurance is about nothing other than reducing the uncertainty of payoffs (the variance) through applying the law of large numbers. It should be recognized that the demand side is much simpler and devolves into a straightforward market transaction: paying a premium when healthy in exchange for an income transfer that occurs when ill.

It may also seem controversial because of the durability of the loss perspective in insurance theory. Daniel Bernoulli (English trans. by Sommer, 1954) first postulated the concept of utility and diminishing marginal utility of income in 1738, and used an insurance example from a loss perspective to illustrate the principle that consumers maximized their expected utility by purchasing insurance. Later, Friedman and Savage (1948) summarized the insurance decision as being a choice between certain and uncertain losses that were actuarially equivalent. Although at the time, there was no empirical work to indicate that consumers actually viewed insurance from a loss perspective, or that consumers preferred certain losses to actuarially equivalent uncertain ones, these works established the demand-for-insurance-as-demand-for-certainty paradigm. This chapter presents the case that this paradigm is inappropriate, and especially so for health insurance, since no losses actually occur. For insurance theory to be consistent with empirical evidence, it is simply necessary to change the perspective of the insurance decision. A change of expected utility theory from a standard gamble specification to a quid pro quo specification may be all that is necessary to truly understand why people buy insurance.

THE GAIN SPECIFICATION

A variation of the quid pro quo specification embodied by inequalities (4.9) and (4.10) is also consistent with prospect theory. This specification takes the perspective that the consumer's insurance decision is made at the point where he is deciding whether to spend his last dollars of endowed income on (1) more consumer goods and services by remaining uninsured and having this additional income in either the healthy or ill state, or (2) an insurance premium, that would result in an income transfer if ill.

This gain specification can be derived from the previous ones by first subtracting $[\pi U(Y^o - \pi M^* - M^*) - \pi U(Y^o - M^*)]$ from both sides of inequality (4.9). The decision to purchase insurance now becomes whether

$$
\begin{aligned}
\pi U[Y^o &+ (1 - \pi)M^* - M^*] - \pi U(Y^o - M^*) \\
&- [\pi U(Y^o - \pi M^* - M^*) - \pi U(Y^o - M^*)] \\
&> - (1 - \pi)U(Y^o - \pi M^*) + (1 - \pi)U(Y^o) \\
&- [\pi U(Y^o - \pi M^* - M^*) - \pi U(Y^o - M^*)].
\end{aligned}
\tag{4.12}
$$

Simplifying,

$$
\begin{aligned}
\pi U[Y^o + (1 - \pi)M^* - M^*] &- \pi U(Y^o - \pi M^* - M^*) \\
&> - (1 - \pi)U(Y^o - \pi M^*) + (1 - \pi)U(Y^o) \\
&- \pi U(Y^o - \pi M^* - M^*) + \pi U(Y^o - M^*),
\end{aligned}
\tag{4.13}
$$

and collecting terms yields:

$$
\begin{aligned}
\pi\{U[Y^o + (1 - \pi)M^* - M^*] &- U(Y^o - \pi M^* - M^*)\} \\
&> - (1 - \pi)\{U(Y^o - \pi M^*) + U(Y^o)\} \\
&- \pi\{U(Y^o - \pi M^* - M^*) + U(Y^o - M^*)\}.
\end{aligned}
\tag{4.14}
$$

Thus, the consumer can regard the decision to purchase insurance from the perspective of whether to spend his last πM^* dollars of income on an insurance premium, or on other goods and services. If he spends it on insurance, he gains M^* in income if ill and having spent M^* on medical care, and gains nothing if healthy. If he spends it on other goods and services, he gains πM^* if healthy, or gains πM^* if ill and having spent M^* on medical care. Therefore, from a reference point of having $Y^o - \pi M^*$ of income, the consumer could gain from $(Y^o - \pi M^*)$ to Y^o, if healthy, or from $(Y^o - \pi M^* - M^*)$ to $(Y^o - M^*)$ if ill, if he decided not to purchase insurance.

This decision rule can be shown on an alternative representation of the prospect theory diagram. Figure 4.4 shows the prospect theory diagram representing only gains, and gains from two different reference points. V^s represents the value function from a reference point of $(Y^o - \pi M^* - M^*)$ worth of income, while V^h represents the value function from a reference point of $(Y^o - \pi M^*)$. V^h represents

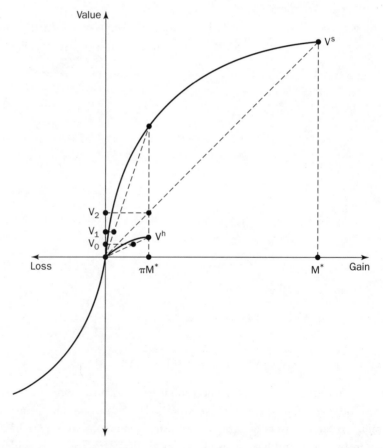

Figure 4.4 Net Gain from Insurance Using Gain Specification and Prospect Theory.

a smaller marginal gain in value for every gain in income than V^s, reflecting the assumption that gains from higher income levels are less valuable than gains from lower income levels.

The decision to purchase insurance compares two gains. First, without insurance and if healthy, the gain is πM^* income with a $(1 - \pi)$ probability, or an expected gain in value of $V_0 = (1 - \pi)V^h(\pi M^*)$ in Figure 4.4. Also, without insurance and if ill, the gain is πM^* income with a π probability, or an expected gain in value of $V_1 = \pi V^s(\pi M^*)$. The total expected gain is $V_0 + V_1$. Second, the expected gain with insurance and if ill is a gain of M^* with a π probability, or an expected gain in value of $V_2 = \pi V^s(M^*)$. With insurance and if healthy, there is no gain. Thus, insurance would be purchased because $V_2 > V_0 + V_1$.

This alternative specification is shown to make the point that of the various possible specifications of the expected utility model of the demand for insurance, only the conventional one makes it appear as if the choice to purchase insurance or remain uninsured is the same as a choice between certainty and uncertainty. Others make it clear that uncertainty is part of both options. Like the quid pro quo perspective, the gain perspective presented in this appendix is another where uncertainty occurs with or without insurance. The conventional insurance theory happened to use the one specification that led economists to draw the wrong conclusions about what motivates the purchase of insurance. We know the specification is wrong because the empirical studies referred to above show that consumers would not purchase insurance if it were presented to them as a choice between a certain loss and an uncertain one of the same expected magnitude.

1. Connor (1996) used three different contexts for his Choice Scenarios. The one described here is the trip context.

5 | ACCESS VALUE OF HEALTH INSURANCE

INTRODUCTION

In Chapter 3, an expected utility theory of the demand for insurance was presented for the case where medical care expenditures if insured, M^i, exceed medical care expenditures if uninsured, M^u, but were still less than endowed income, Y^o, that is, where $Y^o > M^i > M^u$. In Chapter 4, the case was considered where medical care expenditures if insured were the same as those if uninsured, or $M^i = M^u$. This chapter considers the case where the medical expenditures exceed endowed income, or where $M^i > Y^o$.

This case represents medical care that would be unaffordable without health insurance, and therefore, care that is likely to be inaccessible as well. That is, conventional expected utility theory assumes that for the person who is considering the purchase of insurance, the choice is between (1) insurance paying for the ill consumer's care, or (2) the ill consumer paying for the same care privately. There are, however, consumers who become ill and require procedures so expensive that their income (or wealth) is not sufficient to cover the purchase privately. In that case, purchasing an insurance contract is often the only mechanism available for gaining access to such a procedure. It may not be possible to save for the procedure because of the urgency of the illness. It also may not be possible to borrow because of the risk to the lender that the loan will not be paid off. Thus, this case represents a choice between (1) insurance paying for the care, or (2) the ill consumer not receiving the desired care.

Insurance is able to perform this access function because not everyone becomes ill at the same time, and therefore for those consumers who remain healthy, each transfers his premium through the insurer to the person who becomes ill. For example, consider again the liver transplant example used in Chapter 3. The cost of a liver transplant is about $300,000. For a person with only $50,000 in net assets, such a procedure would be unaffordable, and therefore privately inaccessible. The ill consumer would probably not be able to save the additional $250,000 needed to purchase it privately, because of limited income and the urgency of the need for care. Also, this person would probably not be able to secure an uncollateralized loan for $250,000 because of limited income earning potential of the ill consumer, and because of the possibility that the patient would die of graft versus host disease or some other complication before paying off the loan. With insurance, however, the consumer can take advantage of the fact that only about 1 person in 75,000 receives a liver transplant in a given year, and can purchase insurance coverage for an actuarially fair premium of ($300,000/75,000 =) $4. With the payment of this affordable $4 premium, the consumer with insurance has a claim on a pool of $300,000 if he were to become ill enough to require a liver transplant. This $300,000 represents the ill consumer's $4 premium plus $299,996 in accumulated premiums of the other 74,999 consumers who purchase insurance and remain healthy. Thus, each healthy consumer transfers his $4 premium through the insurer to the consumer who becomes ill. It is only because of this income transfer that the ill consumer has access to a $300,000 procedure.

In this chapter, the model developed in Chapter 3 is modified to represent insurance for expenditures that are not otherwise affordable. This case is important because unaffordable expenditures represent a large portion of what the typical consumer's health insurance premium pays for. It also has important policy implications because most of the uninsured have lower incomes, and lower-income households would benefit disproportionately from insurance that covered otherwise unaffordable medical expenditures.

MODEL

The consumer is considering the purchase of insurance covering medical expenditures that would exceed endowed income, that is, for $M^i > Y^o$. Assume that the medical care spending, M^i, can only occur with the income transfers from insurance, because borrowing or saving $(M^i - Y^o)$ dollars is not feasible. Further, assume that there are no safety net alternatives such as charity or Medicaid, and that the procedure is sufficiently lumpy so that without insurance, $M^u = 0$. Insurance coverage for such care would be purchased if

$$
\begin{aligned}
EU_i - EU_u &= \pi U^s[M^i, Y^o + (1 - \pi)(1 - c)M^i - M^i] + (1 - \pi) \\
&\quad \times U^h[0, Y^o - \pi(1 - c)M^i] - \pi U^s(0, Y^o) - (1 - \pi)U^h(0, Y^o) \\
&= \pi\{U^s[M^i, Y^o + (1 - \pi)(1 - c)M^i - M^i] - U^s(0, Y^o)\} \\
&\quad + (1 - \pi)\{U^h[0, Y^o - \pi(1 - c)M^i] - U^h(0, Y^o)\} \\
&= \pi\{U^s[M^i, Y^o - \pi(1 - c)M^i] - U^s(0, Y^o)\} \\
&\quad + (1 - \pi)\{U^h[0, Y^o - \pi(1 - c)M^i] - U^h(0, Y^o)\} > 0.
\end{aligned}
\tag{5.1}
$$

If $c = 0$, equation (5.1) implies that the value of insurance for these services is the expected consumer surplus of the medical procedure itself. Substituting $c = 0$ into inequality (5.1),

$$
\begin{aligned}
EU_i - EU_u &= \pi\{U^s[M^i, Y^o - \pi M^i] - U^s(0, Y^o)\} \\
&\quad + (1 - \pi)\{U^h[0, Y^o - \pi M^i] - U^h(0, Y^o)\} > 0.
\end{aligned}
\tag{5.2}
$$

Thus, the consumer pays πM^i, the expected cost procedure M^i, for the health benefits derived from M^i, which are expected benefits since they only occur if ill. That is, the demand for health insurance for otherwise unaffordable care is a demand for an income transfer to purchase a specific expensive medical procedure in the event of a specific illness. Thus, the demand for health insurance coverage of this type of health care is derived from the demand for medical care itself, and is perhaps most like a normal quid pro quo economic transaction.

If $c > 0$, a portion of the cost of M^i would be paid for at the time that the person becomes ill and receives the treatment. Thus, with insurance, the consumer would spend cM^i out-of-pocket with a π probability, or an expected amount, πcM^i. (Without insurance, the consumer would spend \$0 out-of-pocket if ill because he could not afford to purchase the entire procedure, and a portion of a procedure is assumed to have less value than no procedure at all.) In addition, the consumer with insurance would pay a fair premium of $\pi(1 - c)M^i$, which is the expected payout by the insurer. So, even if $c > 0$, the consumer with insurance pays $\pi(1 - c)M^i + \pi cM^i = \pi M^i$, which is still the expected cost of medical care, in exchange for the medical benefits of M^i if ill, that is, the expected medical benefits.

Because of the presumed lumpiness of the medical procedure, it is unlikely that there would be any substitutability between the procedure and other goods and services at the expenditure margin. For example, the expenditure option might be either $300,000 for the liver transplant and a possible cure, or a nominal expenditure for palliative and hospice care for the short period before death. Because of the lack of substitutability at the expenditure margin, the additional procedure that is consumed with insurance (but that would not be consumed without insurance) is entirely the result of an income transfer. Because the procedure is an income transfer effect and does not have a price-related welfare loss associated with it, its purchase is only welfare-increasing.

Substitutability at the 0,1 procedure margin could be measured empirically by the proportion of ill persons who purchase a procedure if paid off with a lump sum. In the liver transplant example, substitutability would be measured by paying off those who were sufficiently ill to warrant a liver transplant with a check for $300,000 and observing the percentage who then obtain the procedure. This percentage is assumed to be very high, reflecting a low level of substitutability, although it has never been determined empirically.

PREVALENCE OF THE ACCESS MOTIVE

A rough estimate of the prevalence of the access motive can be derived from comparing the net worth of the typical household in the U.S. with the distribution of health care expenditures. The Federal Reserve Board's Survey of Consumer Finances (Kennickell and Shack-Marquez, 1992) estimates that the median net worth of households in 1989 was $47,200. The National Medical Expenditure Survey (NMES) in 1987 estimates that the top-spending 1% of the population accounted for 30% of the total spending. The average annual individual expenditure for this 30% of total spending was $47,331 (Berk and Monheit, 1992). Comparing this figure with the median net worth suggests that, for the consumer at the median of the wealth distribution, about 30% of her health insurance premium is devoted to covering expenditures that would exceed her net worth and that she would not be able to afford privately. For consumers from wealthier households, the percentage would be lower, but for consumers from poorer households, the percentage would be higher.

This 30% figure is only a first approximation. Many adjustments would need to be made to obtain a refined estimate. For example, the elderly on Medicare would need to be excluded in order to obtain an estimate of this percentage for private insurance. Although the elderly make up a disproportionate share of the top spenders, they also have higher-than-average net worths. Therefore, it is unclear what the net effect would be of excluding the elderly. Another refinement would need to account for those who are able to obtain some level of treatment with existing resources, but not, perhaps, the preferred treatment.

The 30% estimate, however, may be conservative for a number of reasons. First, the net worth figures represent a stock, while expenditures measure a flow. To the extent that some people with annual expenditures less than $47,331 are chronically ill with diseases that draw down resources year after year, the 30% figure (as the portion of an annual insurance premium devoted to financing unaffordable health care expenditures) would be too low.

Second, in the event of illness, a portion of the existing net worth would need to be reserved to purchase other equally life-supportive commodities: food, clothing, and housing services for the ill person. To the extent that some of the net worth would be unavailable for health care purchases because of these competing claims, the 30% figure would again be too low.

Third, the net worth figures are for households, whereas the expenditure data are for individuals. Again, to the extent that the net worth would need to be used to pay for the food, shelter, clothing, and health care purchases for other members of the household, the portion of net worth available to pay for any one household member's care is less, and the 30% figure would be too low.

Last, most actual health insurance policies include cost-sharing provisions such as deductibles. To the extent that an annual deductible would cover a larger portion of a smaller annual expenditure than a larger annual expenditure, a larger percentage of the actual premiums would be devoted to coverage of the larger health care purchases, and the larger health care purchases are those that are likely to be unaffordable. Thus, a disproportionate share of any premium is devoted to coverage of large expenditures, and because large expenditures are the type of expenditures that are likely to be unaffordable, a percentage larger than 30% would likely be devoted to otherwise unaffordable expenditures.[1]

Taken together, these factors suggest that it would probably be conservative to conclude that 30% of the typical consumer's insurance premium is devoted to purchases that exceed net worth. Even so, if health care expenditures currently represent about 15% of GDP and if about 30% of these expenditures are unaffordable, this analysis suggests that health insurance would represent the mechanism for gaining access to services valued at over 4% of GDP.

ACCESS VALUATION OF A GIVEN PROCEDURE

The access value of insurance is related to the value of the otherwise unaffordable medical care to the consumer who has purchased insurance and becomes ill. Consistent with the general model presented in this book, this value can be measured by the willingness to pay of the consumer who becomes ill and receives an income transfer equal to the cost of the procedure, minus the ill person's premium contribution. It is important to recognize that the value of, say, a liver transplant would vary significantly depending on whether the consumer is ill or not. Clearly, the willingness to pay for a liver transplant, as well as most medical treatments of serious diseases, is greater for those who have the disease. It is also important to recognize that the value of the procedure depends on whether the consumer has an income transfer from insurance or not. Willingness to pay is also greater with the income transfer. Health insurance is intended to correlate the income transfer with the presence of disease.

Estimating Willingness to Pay

There are a number of potential approaches for estimating the insured consumer's willingness to pay for expensive medical procedures, such as the $300,000 liver transplant. One possibility is to identify those who are uninsured, but who are wealthy enough to purchase a $300,000 procedure privately. Perhaps, a representative group would include those consumers whose assets exceed the average net assets in the U.S. by at least $300,000. This would reflect the fact that those who are insured and become ill receive an income transfer of about $300,000 from those who remain healthy. Demand for liver transplants could then be estimated by observing behavior of those who are ill enough to need the procedure, assuming that sufficient variation in price existed.

Such market studies, however, are difficult because of the small number of qualified consumers available for observation. Only a fraction of the population has a net worth in excess of $300,000, and even fewer would have a net worth that is $300,000 greater than the average net worth. Moreover, only a tiny fraction of the wealthy are uninsured (Lefkowitz and Monheit, 1991) and of these, only a small number would become ill enough to warrant a liver transplant. Thus, a demand analysis based on a market study of the uninsured is probably not feasible.

An alternative approach is to conduct a hypothetical or contingent valuation study. Because of the high cost of many of these procedures, it would not do to simply identify a sample of consumers and ask them what they would be willing to pay for a given expensive procedure. To root the answers in real income constraints, it would be necessary to ask the question in an insurance frame: what would the respondent be willing to pay for an annual insurance policy covering the standard protocol treatment of disease X, given that there is only a 1/Y chance that the respondent would need that treatment in the coming year? Although this is a reasonable approach, hypothetical questions such as this are known to elicit strategic answering. Thus, an approach that relied on actual market behavior would be preferred.

A third approach is to estimate the value of a medical procedure based on its clinical outcome, where the value of the clinical outcome is derived from market studies. For example, a number of studies have estimated the value of a human life. For medical care that saves lives, the value of insurance that makes such medical care possible is the value of a statistical life or the value of the life years saved. Such an approach is used in cost-benefit analysis.

Valuing Outcomes

Market studies that determine the value of a statistical life are based on the same probability logic as would underlie a contingent valuation study in an insurance context. That is, the value of a life is calculated by finding the wage premium required for a worker to accept a risky job and then determining the value of life using the probability of death and wage differentials. For example, if it is observed that workers require $500 more income a year to take a job that increases the annual risk of employment-based death by 1/10,000, it implies that 1/10,000 of a life is worth $500. If so, an entire life would be worth ($500 × 10,000 =) $5,000,000. Viscusi (1993) reviewed the value of life literature and concluded that an estimate in the $3 million to $7 million range (in 1990 dollars) is most defensible.

Hirth et al. (2000) used this literature to derive values for a statistical life year. To do this, the authors converted all the values of a life from the literature to 1997 U.S. dollars, determined the life expectancy for the workers followed in each study (when not specified, the life expectancy was assumed to be that of an average forty-year-old U.S. worker, or 38.1 years), and divided the value of life by the life expectancy, discounted at 3%. Because none of the studies adjusted the remaining years for declining quality of life, Hirth et al. (2000) also did not adjust for quality of life. The authors found a large range in values. For the thirty-seven studies considered, the median value of a year of life was $265,345 in 1997 dollars.

This value exceeds the "rule of thumb" values—ranging from $20,000 to $100,000 (Tolley, Kenkel, and Fabian, 1994; Johannesson and Meltzer, 1998)— currently used in the cost-benefit analysis literature. Discounting life years, however, is controversial (see Parsonage and Neuburger, 1992; Cairns, 1992; Van Hout, 1998; Gravelle and Smith, 2001). Therefore, a more widely acceptable estimate may be found by reducing the value of a life year by 40%, the average increase in value attributable to discounting at the 3% rate (Hirth et al., 2000). Reducing $265,345 by 40% would yield a median value of just under $160,000, which is still above the "rule of thumb" values. Therefore, using $100,000 to represent the value of a life year would probably be conservative.

Specific Disease Example

This value of a year of life can be applied to clinical outcome studies to find the access value of insurance. Consider again the liver transplant example. For liver transplants performed between 1982 and 1991, 69.2% of recipients lived at least five years (Kilpe, Krakauer, and Wren, 1993), and the survival rates have been increasing over time (Busuttil et al., 1994). Also increasing over time has been the proportion of liver transplant recipients classified in the United Network for Organ Sharing (UNOS) criteria as "status 4": patients who have less than one week to live or are already on life support when a transplant is performed. This type of patient represented only 11% of a sample of patients in 1982, but 37% in 1991 (Busuttil et al., 1994). The large and growing proportion of patients in this category supports the assumption that the life expectancy of patients with liver failure who do not receive a transplant would be negligible, and that any years of life lived after a transplant represent a net gain.

About 30% of liver transplant recipients live less than five years, but 70% live more than five years, with no information on the upper bound life expectancy. If it is assumed that most of the mortality risk from the transplant occurs from possible organ rejection in the initial years, it would be reasonable to assume that expected number of survival years after a transplant is at least seven. At a value of $100,000 per year of life saved, an informed consumer's evaluation of the procedure would then be approximately (7 $\times$ $100,000 =) $700,000. Thus, with an annual rate of 1 for every 75,000 people, the expected value of the procedure is about ($700,000/75,000 =) $9.33.

To find the expected consumer surplus, the expected cost of the procedure (the fair premium) could be found by dividing the $300,000 cost of the procedure by 75,000, the annual probability of occurrence. Thus, the expected cost of the procedure is ($300,000/75,000 =) $4, and the expected consumer surplus is ($9.33 − $4 =) $5.33. Thus, $5.33 represents the access value of insurance coverage that reduces the price to $0 for a liver transplant procedure. The total access value of (zero coinsurance rate) health insurance could be found by identifying all those procedures that a certain consumer would be unable to afford to purchase privately, and by estimating the expected consumer surplus for each. The access value of insurance for that consumer is the summed expected consumer surpluses for all those procedures.

For insurance with a coinsurance rate greater than zero—for example, a coinsurance rate of 0.2 with no stop-loss on out-of-pocket expenditures—the expected value of the procedure would continue to be $9.33, but the fair premium would fall to $3.20 because an expected copayment of $0.80 would be subtracted from the total expected cost of $4.00. Thus, the access value of insurance would remain the same ($5.33) expected consumer surplus from the procedure: the expected value of the procedure is $9.33 and the expected cost is still ($3.20 + $0.80 =) $4.00. Were it not for insurance, the consumer would not have access to the entire procedure, so the entire consumer surplus is still attributed to the insurance.

ACCESS VALUE FROM COST-UTILITY LEAGUE TABLES

While the theory suggests that the expected consumer surplus represents the net welfare gain from fair insurance that covers otherwise unaffordable procedures, a more comprehensive approach would attempt to identify all the benefits and costs attributable to performing a procedure that would not otherwise be performed. Thus, a true measure of the welfare change attributable to a procedure that insurance makes possible is the net benefit from a full-fledged cost-benefit analysis from the societal perspective.

In health care, however, many procedures and health interventions have been evaluated based on the cost per quality adjusted life year (QALY). QALYs are useful because they aggregate into one measure both the mortality and morbidity effects of the treatment on the patient. The findings of such cost-utility analyses are often listed in league tables, which show the results of a series of cost-utility analyses performed on various procedures or interventions. League tables are useful because they facilitate comparison. They are particularly useful in this case because, if the value of a QALY were known, the relative net benefit per QALY gained from the various interventions can be calculated.

For example, in a league table presented in Drummond, et al. (1997, p. 269, attributed to Maynard, 1991), the cost per QALY derived from a kidney transplant is £4,710, or in U.S. dollars at the mid-year 1990 exchange rate, $5,652 (Organisation for Economic Co-operation and Development [OECD], 2001). That is, for a kidney transplant, the cost of an additional QALY worth $100,000 is $5,652, or a net benefit of ($100,000 − $5,652 =) $94,348 per QALY. Table 5.1 shows these values for a number of other expensive procedures. Most procedures would show a positive net benefit per QALY if QALYs are valued at $100,000 each. Only the "neurological intervention for malignant intracranial tumours" shows a negative value. To the extent that insurance provides access to procedures that result in a positive net benefit to society, this moral hazard results in a welfare gain.

It should be noted that the league tables only indicate the cost per QALY. They do not indicate the average number of QALYs gained from the procedure in question. Using the example of the kidney transplant, the net benefit for a kidney

Table 5.1

League table of the net benefit per QALY saved from each procedure listed, when the QALY is valued as $100,000

Procedure	Cost/QALY (£ 1990)	Cost/QALY ($ 1990)	Net Benefit/QALY ($ 1990, at $100,000 per QALY)
Valve replacement for aortic stenosis	1,140	1,368	98,632
CABG (left main vessel disease, severe angina)	2,090	2,508	97,492
Kidney transplant	4,710	5,652	94,348
Heart transplant	7,840	9,408	90,592
Home hemodialysis	17,260	20,712	79,288
CABG (1 vessel disease, moderate angina)	18,830	22,596	77,404
Hospital hemodialysis	21,970	26,364	73,636
Neurosurgical intervention for malignant intracranial tumours	107,780	129,336	−29,336

transplant that resulted in a gain of one additional QALY is $94,348, but if the kidney transplant resulted in an average gain of ten additional QALYs, the average moral hazard welfare net gain would be $943,480. Although league tables have their problems (see Drummond, et al., 1997, for a discussion of these), the procedures listed here show that a number of the expensive procedures and treatments have benefits that far outweigh their costs.

It should also be noted that the cost-utility studies are based on a comparison of the treatment in question to an alternative treatment. This alternative may be variously specified as no care, usual care, or some specific next best alternative, depending on the study. This alternative may also be unaffordable or it could be affordable, but in either case, the incremental cost-utility ratio could be used to calculate the marginal welfare gain to society (per QALY) of gaining access to the treatment in question. That is, even though the alternative is affordable, if the preferred treatment is unaffordable, a cost-utility ratio that is less than the value of a QALY would indicate a welfare gain from insurance coverage of the preferred treatment.

League tables from the cost-utility literature also provide an insight into the information that would be required to determine optimal insurance coverage. Optimal insurance for otherwise unaffordable care would be determined by identifying an individual, determining his wealth, and then specifying those otherwise unaffordable procedures that would yield a positive net benefit. Thus, the analyst would need to have information on both the costs of treating the various diseases and the distribution of income or net worth, to determine the set of otherwise unaffordable diseases for each person. Finally, the analyst would need to consult the cost-effectiveness literature to determine that subset of unaffordable procedures for which society receives a net benefit. These information requirements would make it difficult to determine the characteristics of optimal insurance.

ACCESS VALUE USING THE NMES

Still another approach to understanding the importance of the access value of health insurance is based on data from the 1987 National Medical Expenditure Survey (NMES) as cited in Berk and Monheit (1992). As noted above, NMES data showed that the top spending 1% of the population in 1987 (hence, the top-spenders) accounted for about 30% of all expenditures. The U.S. population in 1987 was about 240 million, so 1% of the population represented about 2.4 million people. If it is assumed that about half of the top-spenders would qualify under Medicaid or Medicare, those top-spenders with private insurance represented about 1.2 million Americans (Berk and Monheit, 1992).

Also as mentioned above, the Federal Reserve Board's Survey of Consumer Finances (Kennickell and Shack-Marquez, 1992) estimated that the median net worth of U.S. households in 1989 was $47,200. In comparison, the top-spenders averaged $47,331 in spending (Berk and Monheit, 1992), about the same amount. If health spending is assumed to be distributed uniformly, about half of the top-spenders (those in the lower half of the wealth distribution) would not be able to afford to purchase their expensive care privately. Therefore, for about 600,000 of the 1,200,000 top-spenders, their purchases would have been unaffordable save for private insurance.

If each of these 600,000 poorer top-spenders received medical care that reduced morbidity and mortality so as to gain, on average, 1 QALY, the access value of the care would be $60 billion, at $100,000 per QALY. In comparison, the total personal consumption expenditures on medical care in 1987 were $381 billion (Economic Report of the President, 1998). Therefore, for the access value of health insurance to completely cover the total medical care expenditures would require that each of these 600,000 top-spenders gain ($381 billion/$60 billion =) 6.35 additional QALYs, on average. If the additional expenditures due to becoming insured (that is, the moral hazard expenditures) were half of total expenditures, or about $191 billion, the benefit derived from the access value of insurance for these 600,000 top-spenders would completely cover moral hazard expenditures if the procedures saved just ($191 billion/$60 billion =) 3.18 QALYs per poorer top-spender.

The assumption that only the poorer half of the top-spenders had unaffordable procedures understates the access value. Among the richer half of top-spenders (those with net worths above $47,200), some of their procedures might also have been unaffordable without insurance. For example, a person from a household with a $100,000 net worth would probably not be able to afford to purchase a $300,000 procedure without insurance. These cases are not counted because it is not clear how many they represent.

Similarly, among nontop-spenders (those 99 percent of patients with expenditures less than $47,331, or about 237.6 million patients in all), the poorer half of the income distribution ($118.8 million patients) would have net worths less than $47,200. Some of these consumers could have received otherwise unaffordable care as well. For example, a consumer with $30,000 in net worth may not have been able to purchase a $40,000 procedure without insurance. These cases are not counted either. Therefore, the focus on only the 600,000 who represent the poorer half of the top-spending 1% of the U.S. population understates the number of ill consumers who would gain access through insurance and understates the access value of insurance.

CHARITY CARE

In the conventional model, the demand for insurance is modeled as a choice to either (1) be insured, or (2) purchase the care privately. If private purchase is not possible because the procedure is unaffordable and regular financing options are not feasible, then access requires insurance. In reality, however, other vehicles are available for gaining access to care. One such vehicle is charity (the effect of charity on the demand for insurance is developed further in Chapter 8). Although charity is common in our economy, especially for those commodities like food, clothing, and shelter that are considered necessities (in the nontechnical sense of the word), it is rarely considered as an alternative in demand analyses. In health care, however, charity has historically played such an important role that it cannot be ignored, especially in describing the counterfactual to insurance for otherwise unaffordable care.

If charity care is considered, the value of insurance again has an access value, but the access value is net of the value of the medical care that could be obtained through charity and the likelihood of receiving it. Studies have shown that important differences exist between the characteristics and outcomes of the care received by the uninsured and insured (for example, Franks, Clancy, and Gold, 1993; Young and Cohen, 1991; Currie and Gruber, 1996a), and that charity care is sometimes not available to the uninsured (for example, Himmelstein and Woolhandler, 1995; Donelan et al., 1996). Moreover, it is widely believed that for some consumers, charity has a social stigma associated with it. This stigma may reduce further the value of charity-financed care. Indeed, in some cases, the aversion to charity may be so intense that charity-financed care is not recognized as a viable alternative to insurance-financed care. This response to charity would increase the access value of insurance.

While it would be reasonable to view charity as an alternative for the exceptional individual, it would be unreasonable to view charity as an alternative for all those consumers who are not able to afford the care they need, save for insurance. This care must be paid for in some way, and it is likely that charitable contributions would be exhausted quickly if they were required to cover all the unaffordable care that insurance purchases. This implies that, from a societal perspective, there is a fallacy of composition argument that favors ignoring charity in estimating the access value of insurance. Similar arguments could be made for other mechanisms for gaining access to unaffordable care, such as through bad debts, public delivery systems, and even public insurance such as Medicaid.

IMPORTANCE OF THE ACCESS MOTIVE

The access motive for purchasing health insurance is not new. Sheer affordability of health care was recognized as the prime reason for needing or desiring health insurance as early as 1927 with the creation of the Committee on the Costs of Medical Care (Falk, Klem, and Sinai, 1933; Falk, 1936; Rorem, 1982). It was widely written about in the 1950s and 1960s (Anderson, 1956; Somers and Somers, 1961) and in the 1970s by public figures (for example, Kennedy, 1972). In the U.S. health care reform debate of 1994, the central issue was personified by individuals who were unable to obtain needed health care because they were uninsured. That economists have overlooked access in determining the value of health insurance is a puzzle.

To appreciate the importance of the access value, it must be remembered that conventionally, the value of insurance stemmed solely from the value of the other goods and services available with insurance, and that any additional consumption of medical care—moral hazard—could only be regarded as the source of a welfare loss, because it was the result of a movement along a demand curve. In the new model, a large portion of the welfare gain from insurance derives precisely from moral hazard in the form of the additional medical care that insurance makes accessible. This care is valuable largely because of the high value that we place on our lives and health. Yet even in the new model, some moral hazard is associated with a welfare loss. In the next chapter, a new demand curve is developed for the purpose of estimating this welfare loss.

NOTE

1. The 30% figure is also subject to change. Real net worth of the median household and the average real medical expenditures of the top 1% spenders may be changing. For example, managed care might result in production efficiency gains or the reduction in monopoly rents so that, over time, fewer procedures are beyond the resources of consumers.

6 WELFARE LOSS FROM MORAL HAZARD

Moral hazard is the change in behavior that occurs as a result of becoming insured. The term was originally used by insurers to describe the behavior of individuals who, when they became insured, took less care or incurred greater losses than if they had remained uninsured. This change in behavior resulted in insurers incurring greater payoffs than were expected, expectations being determined by behavior when uninsured. The hazard was, therefore, to the insurer who, when setting the premium, based it on the presumption that the insured consumers had a moral obligation to not change their behavior.

The concept of moral hazard entered the economic literature with articles by Arrow (1963) and Drèze (1961). In analyzing insurance, Ehrlich and Becker (1972) distinguished between self-protection, a reduction in the probability that a "loss" will occur, and self-insurance, a reduction in the size of the loss. Out of this distinction, moral hazard was categorized into ex ante moral hazard, which increased the probability of the "loss" occurring, and ex post moral hazard, which increased the size of the loss once the loss had occurred. For example, an insured person may not take as many precautions against illness as an uninsured one, increasing the probability that he will become ill (ex ante moral hazard), while an insured person who has become ill may incur more medical care expenditures than a person who is uninsured (ex post moral hazard).

Pauly (1968) focused on ex post moral hazard in his analysis of the welfare loss from health insurance. Accordingly, the analysis in this chapter also focuses on ex post moral hazard. As a result, it is assumed that the probability of the event that triggers the insurance payoff is given exogenously (that is, there is no ex ante moral hazard) and that the behavioral response to becoming insured is solely an increase in medical care consumption.

PAULY'S MORAL HAZARD WELFARE LOSS

Pauly (1968) characterizes moral hazard as the same change in consumption that would occur if there were an exogenous reduction in price. He measures the welfare loss for that change in consumption as the difference between (1) the Marshallian consumer surplus from the increased consumption, and (2) the cost of that increased consumption, evaluated at the pre-insurance price, which is assumed to reflect the marginal cost of producing the care (see Figure 2.3). Pauly is able to use a Marshallian demand function to describe the willingness to pay for additional units of medical care because he assumes that consumption of medical care does not increase with income. Pauly (1968) writes, "[s]uppose there are no significant income effects on the individual's demand for medical care resulting from his payment of a lump-sum premium for insurance" (p. 534). In other words, the loss of disposable income generated by the premium payment is assumed to have a negligible effect on health care spending. By eliminating income effects due to insurance premiums, Pauly implicitly eliminates the need to account for *any* income effects in the welfare analysis.

There are three income-related problems with Pauly's analysis. First, substantial income effects are present with medical care, as empirical studies have made clear. Second, the premium payment does, therefore, result in an income effect that must be taken into account when determining the welfare loss from moral hazard. Third, the price decrease is really not a market-wide price decrease, but instead is primarily a price decrease directed at the ill. As such, it represents the mechanism by which income is transferred from those who remain healthy to those who become ill. Thus, what appears to be solely a price effect is in reality an effect generated primarily by income transfers.

Still, a portion of moral hazard consumption is a pure response to price and would, therefore, represent a welfare loss. The consumer's income payoff test, discussed in Chapter 3, for determining this price effect would compare (1) medical care spending of consumers with insurance that pays off by reducing price, with (2) medical spending of consumers with insurance that pays off with an income transfer of the same amount. Modifying the example from Chapter 3, suppose that the same consumer (who became ill with breast cancer) had purchased an insurance policy that reduced the price of medical care to $0 for a $3,000 premium.

Suppose further that if that consumer had become ill without insurance, she would have purchased $20,000 worth of medical care. With the 0% coinsurance policy, however, she incurs $40,000 in spending, paid for entirely by insurance. The additional $20,000 is therefore moral hazard and would conventionally be attributed only to the price reduction.

To determine the true portion of moral hazard that is due to price, it would be necessary to pay off the consumer with the same income transfer payment that occurred in the 0% coinsurance, that is, a cash payment of ($40,000 − $3,000 =) $37,000. If the consumer purchases an additional $15,000 of medical care (for a total of $35,000) with her endowed income plus an additional $37,000 in income transfers, then the income transfer effect would be $15,000, and $15,000 of the $20,000 in moral hazard is efficient moral hazard. The remainder, $5,000 of the $20,000, is the price effect and represents inefficient moral hazard. If, however, the consumer purchased an additional $20,000 (for a total of $40,000 in medical care), the entire moral hazard would be an income transfer effect and no welfare loss would exist. Conducting an experiment of this type to determine efficient and inefficient moral hazard, however, is probably not feasible, so alternative approaches are necessary.

One alternative method, also discussed in Chapter 3, is to estimate efficient moral hazard using a measure of the income elasticity of demand of ill consumers (discussed further in Chapter 10), as described in equation (3.15):

$$\%\Delta M = \epsilon(\%\Delta Y). \tag{3.15}$$

According to this equation, the additional medical care spending that is due to income transfers, $\%\Delta M$, is determined by the product of the income elasticity of demand for the ill consumer, ϵ, and the percentage increase in income due to income transfers. For example, if it were known that on average an ill consumer spent about 1% more on medical care for every 1% increase in income due to income transfers, then the income elasticity of demand would be about 1. If the consumer in the above scenario had an endowed income of $50,000, then the $37,000 in income transfers would represent a 74% increase in income, using the endowed income as the base. With an income elasticity of 1, this would generate a 74% increase in health care spending. Thus, if spending without insurance were $20,000, a 74% increase in medical care spending would represent an increase of $14,800. One could then conclude that of the $20,000 of moral hazard, $14,800 is efficient and due to income transfers, and the remainder, $5,200, is inefficient and due to price.

OVERVIEW OF THE REST OF THE CHAPTER

This chapter presents still another method for determining the portion of moral hazard that is due to price. This method uses information from the Marshallian demand curve, that is, from the observed relationship between medical care and price. Essentially, it performs the decomposition represented by Figure 3.2 in Chapter 3. That is, it removes sufficient income to place the consumer at the intersection of his original budget constraint and the income expansion path for the coinsurance price. Thus, the portion of moral hazard that is due to price is equal to the same increase in consumption that would occur if the ill consumer were compelled to purchase the lower coinsurance price, but without any income transfers.

This method isolates the price effect by accounting for both the income transfer effect and the effect of paying the insurance premium on the purchase of medical care. To do this, it uses information on the Marshallian price and income elasticities of demand for medical care, and the share of income devoted to medical care after the insurance income transfer. This method is like the Hicksian decomposition in that it results in an income and substitution (pure price) effect. It is different, however, because the price reduction from insurance is purchased rather than exogenous. Thus, the effect of income on medical care consumption works through both the payment of the premium and the transfer of income from the healthy to the ill, rather than through an increase in real income, as is the case of an exogenous price decrease. Like the Hicksian decomposition, this new decomposition also defines a new demand curve that can be used in evaluating the portion of moral hazard due to price, and in determining the price-related welfare loss.

The chapter continues by first reviewing the different decompositions of an exogenous price reduction represented in the literature, and presenting a new decomposition of an exogenous price reduction that can also be used to decompose moral hazard into a price and income transfer effect. The welfare loss from the price effect is then described diagrammatically and mathematically. Finally, estimates of the relative price effect and welfare loss from health insurance are calculated with parameters taken from the literature.

TAXONOMY OF PRICE CHANGE DECOMPOSITIONS

It has long been recognized that an *exogenous* price decrease causes an increase in quantity demanded that is in part due to a pure price effect and in part due to an increase in real income. In order to isolate the pure price effect of an exogenous price decrease, it is necessary to hold real income constant. The existing literature offers two alternatives for accomplishing this.

Hicksian Decomposition Holding Utility Constant

The Hicksian decomposition holds constant the income that is necessary to obtain the original indifference curve. Consider a consumer who consumes two goods, X and Y, so as to maximize a quasi-concave utility function, $U = U(X, Y)$, subject to a standard budget constraint. Again, assume Y is the numeraire good. (The notation has changed to emphasize the more general level of analysis.) The consumer is originally at equilibrium consuming bundle O in Panel A of Figure 6.1. The price of good X falls from P_0 to P_1 as the result of some exogenous change in the

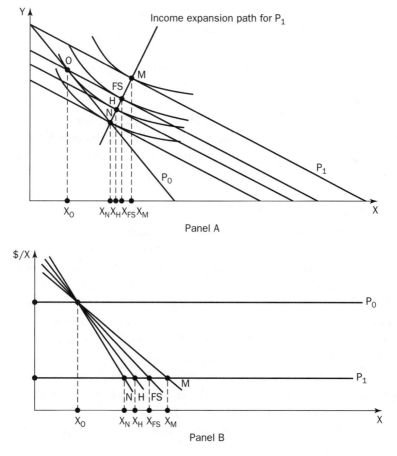

Figure 6.1 Derivation of the New Demand Curve.

market, the price of Y held constant. The consumer purchases bundle M (for Marshallian) in equilibrium, following that price decrease.

The familiar Hicksian decomposition isolates the pure price effect of a price decrease by removing sufficient income at the new prices to place the consumer on his original indifference curve. Panel A of Figure 6.1 shows this decomposition at point H. Thus, of the total change in quantity X_O to X_M, a portion, X_O to X_H, is due to the pure price effect, and another portion, X_H to X_M, is due to the increase in real income.

The welfare intuition of the Hicksian demand curve derives from the willingness to pay for good X in terms of good Y, represented by the slope of the indifference curve that contains point O in panel A of Figure 6.1 (Mishan, 1981). At point O, the consumer is willing to pay exactly the old (higher) price for a unit of X, so the Hicksian and Marshallian demands coincide at point O. As more X is purchased, the willingness to pay decreases, until at point H, the consumer's willingness to pay exactly equals the new lower price, P_1.

Hicksian demand is represented by curve H in Panel B of Figure 6.1. The area under the Hicksian demand curve is the integral of the willingnesses to pay for the various units between X_O and X_H. For example, in discrete terms, to purchase unit X_{O+1} of good X in Panel A of Figure 6.1, the consumer is willing to pay ΔY_{O+1} of good Y and still be on the original indifference curve. Because the consumer is charged the new lower price for this and all the additional units of X purchased, the difference between the willingness to pay at each successive unit and the new price is a measure of the Hicksian consumer surplus.

Friedman/Slutsky Decomposition Holding Real Income Constant

An alternative approach to removing income is identified by Friedman (1962), who attributed the decomposition to Slutsky (1915). This decomposition isolates the pure price effect by removing income sufficient to allow the consumer to purchase the original bundle of goods, point O, at the new prices, P_1. Friedman refers to this concept as holding "apparent real income" constant. Thus, if the consumer is obliged to maintain an income level sufficient to purchase original bundle O at the new prices, he would purchase good X until the willingness to pay equals the new prices, that is, until point FS in Panel A of Figure 6.1.

The welfare intuition of the Friedman/Slutsky demand is readily understood by comparing it to the more familiar Hicksian demand. The Friedman/Slutsky demand curve at price P_0 would be represented by the willingness to pay at point O, as determined by the slope of the original indifference curve. This point coincides with the Hicksian and Marshallian demand curves. As noted above, if the price were to fall to P_1, the willingness to pay for the X_{O+1} unit under Hicks is approximated in discrete terms by ΔY_{O+1}, a movement along the original indifference curve. In contrast, the willingness to pay for unit X_{O+1} under Friedman/Slutsky's decomposition is determined by the indifference curve that intersects budget line FS at X_{O+1}. That is, in order to hold constant the income necessary to purchase the bundle O at the new prices P_1, the willingness to pay at X_{O+1} would need to be evaluated at a level of Y greater than the level under the Hicksian constraint. If indifference curves are strictly convex to the origin, a greater level of Y would imply that the consumer would be willing to trade more Y for a unit of X, and the willingness to pay for the X_{O+1} unit of X would be greater than the willingness to pay under the Hicks decomposition. Similarly, the willingness to pay for all units of X purchased between X_O and X_{FS} under the Friedman/Slutsky constraint would exceed the willingness to pay under Hicks. The last unit that the consumer would be willing to purchase is X_{FS}. At X_{FS}, the willingness to pay for that unit of X equals the new price.

Demand derived from the Friedman/Slutsky decomposition is labeled FS in Panel B of Figure 6.1. The Friedman/Slutsky demand lies everywhere above the Hicksian demand for price decreases from point O, and any consumer surplus is greater than the Hicksian consumer surplus.

New Decomposition Holding Nominal Income Constant

Still another decomposition would isolate the pure price effect by removing sufficient income to allow the consumer to purchase the original bundle of goods, point O, at the old prices, P_0. That is, nominal income is held constant by constraining the consumer to his original feasibility set. Thus, the consumer is maximizing utility by responding to the new prices, but is obliged to purchase only consumption bundles within the original budget constraint. This new demand curve was originally described in Nyman (1999b).

If the price were P_0, the consumer at X_O would be willing to trade Y for X at the same rate as with the above two decompositions, so the new demand curve coincides with the Marshallian, Hicksian, and Friedman/Slutsky demands at point O. The price again falls exogenously to P_1. At X_{O+1}, the consumer would need to reduce Y in order to stay on the original budget constraint, but at that point, the consumer's willingness to pay is reflected by an indifference curve that is below the original one. At X_{O+1}, the willingness to pay for X exceeds the new price, P_1, he must pay. This would be true of those bundles along the original budget constraint from X_O until X_N, the point where the consumer is still on his original budget constraint but is willing to pay exactly the new price for that last bundle. Additional consumption of X would cease at N, the point on the original budget constraint where the willingness to pay for X equals the price P_1. X_N represents the quantity corresponding to P_1 on the new demand curve.

In comparison to the Hicks constraints, the new demand curve would be everywhere below the Hicksian demand for price decreases. To gain an additional unit of X and stay on the original budget constraint would require that the willingness to pay for X at X_{O+1} be evaluated at a lower level of Y than the level of Y required to remain on the original indifference curve. Thus, because Y is scarcer and dearer, and because preferences are again assumed to be strictly convex, willingness to pay Y for that additional unit of X at X_{O+1} would be smaller than the Hicksian willingness to pay. For any level of X between X_O and X_N, the willingness to pay for X under the new decomposition is less than the willingness to pay under the Hicksian constraints. Thus, the demand curve derived from this new decomposition is everywhere below the Hicksian demand except for at the original bundle O. The corresponding demand curve in Panel B of Figure 6.1 is labeled N.

In this analysis, the decomposition occurs by removing income (or adding income in the case of a price increase) to place the consumer at his original situation (variously defined) but at new prices. An alternative approach would decompose by adding income (or removing it in the case of a price increase) to place the consumer at the new situation, but at the old prices. This would be analogous to the compensating variation and equivalent variation versions of Hick's decomposition, respectively.

The new demand curve shows the willingness to pay for an additional unit of the good as the price falls exogenously, assuming that sufficient income is subtracted to stay on the original feasibility constraint. This is equivalent to the consumer's purchasing a contract for a reduced price where the consumer is charged an amount equal to the difference between what the consumer pays at the lower price and the total cost of the consumption. Therefore, the area under this new demand curve can be used to evaluate the additional consumption caused by the moral hazard price effect.

WELFARE LOSS FROM INSURANCE

The Hicksian demand is used in describing the welfare implications of an exogenous change in price. The new demand can be used in evaluating the welfare effects of purchasing an insurance contract that pays off with a reduction in price.

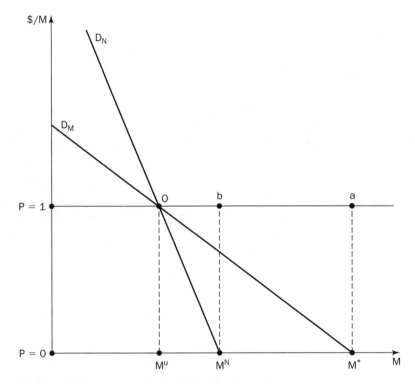

Figure 6.2 Welfare Loss from Moral Hazard.

The graphical analysis of the welfare loss from the price effect of moral hazard is shown in Figure 6.2. (Because the focus is now the welfare analysis of health insurance, we return to the original notation begun in Chapter 3.) Without insurance, the consumer purchases M^u at price $P = 1$. If insurance represented an exogenous reduction of the price to $P = 0$, M^* would be consumed consistent with the analysis in Pauly (1968). Using the Marshallian demand curve, D_M, to evaluate this increase would result in a gain of area OM^*M^u. Because the price of M has not actually changed, each unit of the additional $(M^* - M^u)$ of consumption still costs $P = 1$ to produce, thus the welfare loss under conventional analysis is characterized as area OaM^*.

Conventional analysis would lead to an appropriate measure of the welfare loss only when income is unrelated to consumption of medical care. When this is so, the Marshallian demand happens to coincide with the new demand. However, if M increases with income, then using the Marshallian demand to determine moral hazard leads to an overestimate of the welfare loss. The price effect is only isolated when income transfers are eliminated and that is only true for the new demand curve.

The price effect of moral hazard is represented by the change in quantity using the new demand curve, D_N. This is because, absent any exogenous decreases in price, a price decrease would need to be purchased in order to exist. Each successively lower price level would require a larger premium payment, thus the value of the corresponding medical care would need to reflect this reduction in income. At $P = 0$, the pure price effect of insurance results in an increase in the quantity demanded represented by M^N. Therefore, becoming insured would result in added consumption of M equal to $(M^N - M^u)$, and this moral hazard price effect is worth the area under the new demand curve, area $OM^N M^u$. The cost of acquiring this additional M under insurance is $ObM^N M^u$. Thus, the moral hazard welfare loss equals area ObM^N. This moral hazard welfare loss is smaller than the loss determined by the Marshallian demand.

MATHEMATICAL EXPRESSION OF THE WELFARE LOSS[1]

The individual's response to becoming insured is conventionally described by his Marshallian demand function for medical care $D(P, Y^o)$, where P is the price of medical care and Y^o is the consumer's income. It is assumed that only the effects of variation in the price that the consumer pays for medical care matter, thus the prices of other goods in the Marshallian demand are suppressed. Let $e(P, U)$ be the minimal expenditure necessary to reach utility level U at price P and let the consumer's Hicksian or compensated demand function be $D(P, e(P, U))$. Measuring M in units such that P, the market price of each unit, equals 1, three measures of additional consumption due to moral hazard can be defined, based on comparisons between the following four demand quantities, which are all derived from the Marshallian demand:

1. $M^u = D(1, Y^o) =$ the consumer's optimal medical care consumption when ill and facing a price of 1. This is equivalent to observed uninsured demand.

2. $M^* = D(c, Y^o) =$ the consumer's optimal medical care consumption when ill and facing a price of $c < 1$. This is equivalent to observed Marshallian demand.

3. $M^H = D(c, e(1, U^o)) =$ the consumer's optimal medical consumption when ill and insured, with utility constrained to equal U^o, the level attainable without insurance. This is equivalent to Hicksian demand derived from the observed Marshallian demand.

4. $M^N = D(c, Y^o - (1 - c)M^N) =$ the consumer's optimal medical consumption when ill and insured, where the market value of total consumption is constrained to equal income. This is equivalent to the new demand derived from the observed Marshallian demand.

The moral hazard price effects can be expressed as proportions or shares of M^u, the observed consumption of medical care without insurance. Thus, the three measures of the moral hazard are: Pauly's (1968) Marshallian measure, $(M^* - M^u)/M^u$; a Hicksian measure, $(M^H - M^u)/M^u$; and the new measure, $(M^N - M^u)/M^u$. Multiplying these measures by 100 yields the moral hazard increase in medical care consumption as a percentage of the uninsured quantity. These percentages also indicate the relative moral hazard welfare losses because, under the assumption of linear demands, the welfare losses are proportional to the change in consumption itself.

Marshallian Demand Curve Price Effect

The Marshallian price effect can be found if it is assumed that demand curves are linear and that the point estimates of the relevant elasticities approximate the values around the uninsured optima. If so, then

$$(M^* - M^u) = [\partial D(1, Y^o)/\partial P](c - 1) = (\partial M/\partial P)(c - 1)$$
$$\approx \eta M^u(c - 1), \tag{6.1}$$

and

$$(M^* - M^u)/M^u \approx \eta(c - 1), \tag{6.2}$$

which is the price elasticity of demand, η, multiplied by the decrease in effective price with a movement from no insurance to insurance, $(c - 1)$.

Hicksian Demand Curve Price Effect

The Hicksian effect measure can be estimated similarly:

$$(M^H - M^u) = [\partial D(c, e(1, U^o))/\partial P](c - 1) = (\partial M^H/\partial P)(c - 1)$$
$$= (\partial D/\partial P)(c - 1) + M^u(\partial D/\partial Y)(c - 1) \tag{6.3}$$
$$\approx [\eta M^u + \Theta \epsilon M^u](c - 1),$$

where Θ is the share of expenditures devoted to M, and ϵ is the income elasticity of demand for the ill consumer. Therefore,

$$(M^H - M^u)/M^u \approx (\eta + \Theta\epsilon)(c - 1). \tag{6.4}$$

New Demand Curve Price Effect

The new price effect can be found as follows. At the uninsured optima,

$$M^N = D(c, Y^o - (1 - c)M^N)\big|_{c=1} = M^u. \tag{6.5}$$

Therefore,

$$\begin{aligned}
dM^N &= (\partial D/\partial P)dP + (\partial D/\partial Y)(\partial Y/\partial P)dP \\
&\quad + (\partial D/\partial Y)(\partial Y/\partial M^N)dM^N \\
&= (\partial D/\partial P)dP + (\partial D/\partial Y)M^u\, dP + (\partial D/\partial Y)(c - 1)dM^N.
\end{aligned} \tag{6.6}$$

Note that at the uninsured optima, $Y^o = e(1, U^o)$, so that $(\partial Y/\partial P) = (\partial e/\partial P)\big|_{1,U^o} = M^u$, by the properties of the minimum expenditure function (Varian, 1984). Therefore,

$$dM^N/dP\big|_{(c=1)} = [(\partial D/\partial P) + M^u(\partial D/\partial Y)]/[1 - (\partial D/\partial Y)(c - 1)]. \tag{6.7}$$

So, if

$$\begin{aligned}
(M^N - M^u) &= [(dD/dP)\big|_{(c=1)}](c - 1) \\
&= [(\partial D/\partial P) + M^u(\partial D/\partial Y)](c - 1)/[1 + (1 - c)(\partial D/\partial Y)] \\
&\approx [\eta M^u + \Theta\epsilon M^u](c - 1)/[1 + (1 - c)\Theta\epsilon],
\end{aligned} \tag{6.8}$$

then

$$(M^N - M^u)/M^u \approx [\eta + \Theta\epsilon](c - 1)/[1 + (1 - c)\Theta\epsilon]. \tag{6.9}$$

Since the numerator is the same as equation (6.4) and the denominator is positive and greater than 1, equation (6.9) implies a smaller increase in consumption than under the Hicksian analysis.

ESTIMATING THE WELFARE LOSS FROM THE PRICE EFFECT

As explained in Chapter 3, it is theoretically possible to observe the new demand curve under experimental conditions—the consumer's income payoff test—but this has not been done. As an alternative, the welfare loss can be estimated as the deviation from the observed Marshallian demand curve. As equation (6.9) suggests, this deviation depends on four parameters: (1) the coinsurance rate (c), (2) the Marshallian price elasticity of demand for medical care (η), (3) the share of spending devoted to medical care in the typical ill household (Θ), and (4) the income elasticity of demand for medical care of the ill household (ϵ). What are the appropriate estimates for each?

Coinsurance Rate

The choice of a coinsurance rate to represent the price reduction associated with insurance is arbitrary. The average coinsurance rate from the plan in the RAND Health Insurance Experiment (HIE) that had a 95% coinsurance rate and $1,000 deductible is used, because it has been used in a previous study (Feldman and Dowd, 1991).[2] Therefore, the insurance payoff is assumed to embody a reduction in the price of medical care from 1 to 0.31, triggered by becoming ill.

Marshallian Price Elasticity of Demand

The new theory suggests that with insurance, it is primarily ill persons who face a reduced price of medical care. Those who are healthy do not respond to the lowered price because they would not benefit from the medical care, regardless of price. It should be kept in mind, however, that the ill consumer's choice is influenced by the physician, who as the consumer's agent, exercises a certain level of control over this choice and may even act in her own interest. For example, under certain circumstances, the physician may induce demand to obtain additional income. Or under other circumstances, the physician may constrain the medical care spending desired by the patient, as would be the case when the physician prohibits the insured consumer from using hospitals for room and board services when traveling.

The behavior ideally captured by the observed (Marshallian) demand would therefore be the medical care expenditure response of an ill person to insurance that reduces the price of medical care. In the RAND HIE, the behavior of an ill person is best approximated by the analysis of episodes of care, because by focusing on certain types of episodes, it could reasonably be assumed that the consumer was ill. The episodes of care were classified according to whether the episode involved a hospitalization or not, and according to whether the outpatient care was acute, chronic, well care, or dental care. Of these episodes, those with hospitalizations or acute care episodes seemed to best approximate the behavior of one who becomes ill.

The hospital episode, however, is problematic. Although the RAND HIE assigned participants into different RAND health plans at random, participants also remained enrolled in their previous health insurance plan. Thus, if a participant were assigned into a cost-sharing plan instead of the free fee-for-service plan and were confronted with the prospect of an expensive hospital stay that could cost the participant as much as $1,000 out-of-pocket, the participant could simply opt out of the Experiment and return without penalty to his previous insurance coverage (Newhouse and The Insurance Experiment Group [IEG], 1993). Accordingly, 0.4% of those assigned to the free plan voluntarily left the Experiment, but 6.7% of those assigned to any of the cost-sharing plans withdrew voluntarily, a statistically significant difference that represents a sixteen-fold increase in the attrition rate (Newhouse and the IEG, 1993). This implies that the reductions in hospitalizations observed in the cost-sharing plans may largely represent those participants who became ill, withdrew to their previous plan, and were still hospitalized, although without it ever being recorded as such in the RAND data. This attrition would spuriously inflate the effect of price on the likelihood of a hospitalization and on the total amount of medical expenditures.

The acute care episodes were less likely to generate large out-of-pocket spending, and as a result, less likely to represent an incentive to drop out of the RAND Experiment. To generalize from the acute care price elasticity, however, assumes that the price effect for the modest expenditures of an acute care episode (the median cost of an episode with hospitalization was $3,030, while the median cost of an acute episode without hospitalization was $59, both in 1991 dollars) are representative of expenditures on all types of medical care. The 25%–95% arc elasticity for acute care episodes (that is, the arc elasticity from the difference in acute episode spending between the 25% coinsurance plan and the 95% coinsurance plan) was nevertheless used in the calculation of the welfare loss. This elasticity was estimated to be -0.32 (Newhouse and the IEG, 1993).

It should be noted that this estimate simulated expenditures above the stop-loss (Newhouse and the IEG, 1993). That is, the $1,000 stop-loss in the 95% plan meant that as soon as $1,000 in out-of-pocket spending was generated by a participant, care became free. Thus, those in the 95% plan and those in the free plan faced the same coinsurance rate (0%) for large expenditures. To correct for this problem in the 95% plan, Newhouse and the IEG simulated a response in the spending range above the stop-loss based on behavior of those in the 95% plan whose spending was below the stop-loss. Thus, they claim that "the pure 95% rate approximates the effect of being uninsured" (p. 120).

If actually uninsured, however, the estimation would need to capture the fact that certain procedures may be unaffordable to those participants who had insured spending in the range above the stop-loss. This behavior would not be captured by observed behavior below the stop-loss. Specifically, the response from reducing the coinsurance rate from 95% to 25% for spending above the stop-loss would likely be greater than the response from the same reduction for spending below the stop-loss because of the procedures that would be unaffordable at the 95% coinsurance rate but affordable at a 25% rate. This would mean that the change from being truly uninsured (a 100% coinsurance rate for all care) to insurance with a 25% coinsurance rate would probably result in a larger consumption increase than the response that was simulated by Newhouse and the IEG (1993). Thus, although the simulation is an improvement, it probably did not capture totally the effect of becoming insured.

It is further important to remember that RAND HIE essentially measures the impact of exogenous price changes on the quantity demanded of medical care, consistent with conventional theory. A study of the effect of health insurance on the demand for medical care would, in contrast, focus on measuring the effect of the various income transfers on quantity demanded. The fact that these income transfers are generated by a price reduction and that this price reduction causes some transactions costs is secondary. In this portion of the analysis, I focus on these secondary transactions costs and base my analysis on the observed relationship between price and the quantity of medical care demanded, but the behavioral relationship that is most central to understanding the impact of insurance on behavior is the relationship between income and the quantity of medical care demanded.

Medical Care Spending Share

The appropriate measure of the medical care spending share (that is, medical care expenditures as a percentage of all household expenditures) is the share for the ill consumer. The ill consumer spends disproportionately more on medical care compared with the average consumer. From national income accounts, medical care expenditures as a proportion of all personal consumption expenditures were 0.16 in 1997 (Economic Report of the President, 1998). However, this represents the share of the average consumer, not the ill consumer. According to the NMES of 1987, about 85% of respondents had some medical care spending in that year (Lefkowitz and Monheit, 1991). Therefore, provided that consumption expenditures were similar across households with and without medical spending, the medical care spending share of an average ill person is about $(0.16/0.85 =)\ 0.19$.

This estimate does not capture the representative spending share of an ill person because the distribution of the expenditures is so skewed. As discussed in Chapter 5, the 1987 NMES found that the top-spending 1% of the population accounted for 30% of total health care spending. This survey also found that the top-spending 10% accounted for 72%, and the top-spending 50% accounted for 98% of all spending (Berk and Monheit, 1992). An approximation that is perhaps more representative of the ill person's spending share would be to use the medical expenditure share for the 10% of households accounting for 72% of medical spending.

The income of those who are insured and become ill is augmented by the income transfers from those who remain healthy. To account for this income transfer, it is assumed that all of the ill are insured and that income is increased by an amount equal to medical expenditures, reflecting the assumption that most medical care is paid for by insurance and therefore represents income transfers. Formally, if M is all medical expenditures in the economy, and Y is total income (assumed to approximate all consumption), then from the national income accounts,

$$M/Y = 0.16. \tag{6.10}$$

Assume that the ill represent the 10% of the population and that without insurance, income is distributed so that the ill possess 10% of the income. If 72% of medical care is consumed by the ill who have 10% of the income, then the share of an ill person's income that is devoted to medical care spending is

$$
\begin{aligned}
M^s/Y^s &= 0.72M/0.1Y \\
&= (0.72/0.10)(M/Y) \\
&= (0.72/0.10)(0.16) \\
&= 1.15.
\end{aligned}
\tag{6.11}
$$

That is, spending by those who become ill exceeds their uninsured income by 15%.

The spending share would, however, need to account for the income transfer in the denominator as well. Assume that the income of the ill is increased by an amount that approximates the medical expenditures of the ill or 0.72M. If so, the share of medical expenditures spent by the representative ill consumer after income transfers is

$$M^s/Y^s = 0.72M/(0.1Y + 0.72M). \tag{6.12}$$

Substituting in M = 0.16Y from equation (6.10),

$$
\begin{aligned}
M^s/Y^s &= 0.72M/(0.1Y + 0.72*0.16Y) \\
&= 0.72M/0.22Y \\
&= (0.72/0.22)(M/Y) \\
&= (0.72/0.22)(0.16) \\
&= 0.52.
\end{aligned}
\tag{6.13}
$$

So, medical expenditures of the representative ill consumer are about 52% of total after-transfer spending (income) on average. If the premium payment were subtracted from the denominator in order to isolate the income *transfer* caused by insurance, medical care spending as a percentage of income would be larger. As an estimate of this effect, 2% is added to the 52% to arrive at 54%. This analysis, therefore, uses 54% as a conservative estimate of the representative ill consumer's spending share.

Income Elasticity of Demand

The appropriate income elasticity of demand would again ideally be based on the behavior of consumers who are ill. For example, a $300,000 increase in income might allow a consumer whose liver has failed to purchase a liver transplant procedure, but the same $300,000 would probably not induce a healthy consumer to purchase one. Also, because the income transfer from insurance occurs simultaneously with becoming ill (or almost so), the ideal measure of the income elasticity would not be based on income qua wages and salaries, but rather on wages and salaries plus an income shock equal to income transfers from insurance. Thus, the appropriate income elasticity would capture the behavior of consumers who are ill and who have contingent claims insurance contracts with varying levels of income payoffs and premiums. It is, of course, possible that some of those who are ill and receive a cash payment from insurance may opt to spend the additional income on other consumption rather than medical care, even though they may be seriously ill. The observed relationship between medical care spending and income from all sources would capture this, too. Unfortunately, an estimate of this income elasticity does not exist.

The income elasticities from the RAND HIE measure the effect of increases in income qua wages and salaries on medical care consumption for all HIE participants. Manning and Marquis (1996) estimate this income elasticity at 0.22. This estimate, however, does not capture the effect of income transfers from insurance, nor does it focus on the behavior of the ill. Thus, this income elasticity estimate probably reflects a lower level of responsiveness than would an income elasticity based on the behavior of the ill whose insurance-generated income transfers were counted as income.

Feenberg and Skinner (1994) estimate income elasticities based on tax returns from the late 1960s and early 1970s. According to the tax code at the time, taxpayers could deduct out-of-pocket medical expenditures if they totaled at least 3% of income. Thus, Feenberg and Skinner's estimate would reflect the behavior of ill consumers, but it would not capture the effect of income transfers from insurance. For those who reported such deductions, the income elasticity of demand is estimated at 0.38, again measuring the effect of annual earnings on annual medical expenditures. Although this estimate is also likely to be too low, it is used in the following calculation because, to my knowledge, no better alternative (that uses the household or consumer as the unit of observation) exists. It should be recognized that a larger income elasticity would result in a welfare loss that is smaller still.[3]

Estimates of the Relative Welfare Loss

Marshallian, Hicksian, and new estimates of the relative welfare loss are presented in Table 6.1. If price fell exogenously from $c = 1$ to $c = 0.31$, consumption of medical care by the ill would be 22.1% greater. Measured by Marshallian demand, the magnitude of the welfare loss would reflect this 22.1% increase in consumption. After removing the Hicksian income effect, the pure price effect would result in a 7.9% increase in consumption.[4] This increase is only 36% as large as the increase estimated from the Marshallian demand, and thus the welfare loss is only 36% as large as the welfare loss estimated using Marshallian demand. Finally, if the ill consumer were required to purchase the price decrease (eliminating all the transfers in insurance from those who remain healthy), consumption would be 6.9% greater than original consumption, moral hazard would be only 31% as large as Marshallian moral hazard, and the welfare loss would only be 31% as large as the welfare loss implied by Pauly's (1968) analysis.

Table 6.1.

Estimates of the relative welfare loss from the price effect

	Moral Hazard Increase in Consumption as a Percentage of Original Consumption	Moral Hazard Percentage Increase Evaluated with above Parameters	Moral Hazard Increase as a Percentage of the Marshallian Increase
Marshallian demand	$\eta(c - 1)$	$-0.18(-0.69) =$ $0.221 = 22.1\%$	100%
Hicksian demand	$\Theta\epsilon(c - 1) + \eta(c - 1)$	$0.54(0.38)(-0.69) +$ $0.124 = 0.079 = 7.9\%$	36%
New demand	$[\Theta\epsilon(c - 1) + \eta(c - 1)]/$ $[1 + (1 - c)\Theta\epsilon]$	$0.079/[1 + 0.69(0.54)(0.38)] =$ $0.069 = 6.9\%$	31%

IMPLICATIONS

Pauly's model of the welfare effect of insurance simply requires that the consumer be insured to respond to the lower insurance prices. The present model suggests that it is necessary for the consumer to be both insured and ill to respond to the insurance price. If the latter is a more accurate representation of reality, then income transfers enter the analysis because not all of those who are insured also experience an illness during the period of the insurance contract. If income is transferred from those who remain healthy to those who become ill, and if additional income leads to additional consumption of the insured commodity, then even though a price reduction is used to pay off the contract, a portion of moral hazard is caused by income transfers. This portion can be eliminated by determining the amount of health care that would be consumed if the consumer who became ill simply purchased a contract to obtain the health care at a lower price without any income transfers. This analysis is intended to capture exactly this effect.

The welfare loss from this price effect is smaller than the loss implied by those who interpreted Pauly's original analysis as a movement along the Marshallian demand curve. Under reasonable estimates for the parameters in question, the welfare loss is shown to be only about 31% as large as the loss using Marshallian demand. This estimate depends critically on the accuracy and representativeness of the parameters in question. Future refinements may well concentrate on developing better estimates of all these parameters, especially the income elasticity of demand for those who are insured and ill.

The price effect was determined by eliminating the two income effects of insurance. First, the price reduction that is purchased requires a premium payment in order to exist. This premium payment reduces the amount of income available to purchase medical care, and therefore reduces moral hazard. Second, the price reduction transfers income from the healthy to the ill. This income transfer increases medical care spending and therefore, accounts for a large portion of the moral hazard that was conventionally attributed to price. Both these effects are captured in the above analysis.

This analysis has attempted to determine the price effect of the representative person who consumes medical care. Because the top 10% of medical care spenders account for 72% of all spending, it was assumed that the representative ill consumer would be among this group. These consumers were deemed to be ill based on their spending, although it is clearly possible that some within this group—such as those opting for major plastic surgery—might not be ill. Based on conservative estimates of the medical care spending share and income elasticity of demand, it was estimated that over 2/3 of moral hazard was due to income transfers. This makes sense because a large portion of moral hazard would be represented by those relatively few, but very expensive procedures that would not have been accessible to the ill consumer on an average income were it not for health insurance.

Less than 1/3 of moral hazard spending is due to a price effect. For this portion of moral hazard, the value of the medical care consumed is about 1/2 the cost under the assumption of linear demands. Therefore, a moral hazard welfare loss occurs that amounts to about 1/2 the cost of this medical care. The remaining 2/3 of moral hazard is caused by income transfers and for this portion, the value of the additional care received in excess of the cost is a measure of the welfare gain. The value of the income transfer effect, however, is difficult to estimate based on demand analysis because of the lack of information on willingness to pay for expensive procedures in the absence of insurance. In Chapter 7, I address this issue and attempt to calculate a net value for all of moral hazard, not just the moral hazard from the price effect.

1. The analysis in this section represents Roland Maude-Griffin's contribution to Nyman and Maude-Griffin (2001). The analysis representing the rest of the chapter, however, originally appeared in Nyman (1999b).

2. This 31% average coinsurance rate represented a welfare improvement in the study by Feldman and Dowd (1991) because it resulted in a smaller welfare loss compared with the 0% coinsurance plan.

3. In Chapter 10, I argue that estimates using the country as the unit of observation are probably better estimates of the true income elasticity of demand of the uninsured consumer. These estimate often exceed 1. Therefore, the use of Feenberg and Skinner's (1994) 0.38 is probably conservative.

4. Note that this Hicksian decomposition captures the effect of the income transfers to the ill by using a larger income share figure than would be used to estimate the Hicksian decomposition of an exogenous price decrease.

7 | WELFARE GAIN FROM MORAL HAZARD

OVERVIEW

The main empirical results presented in Chapters 3–6 to support the new theory are the findings that

1. The income elasticity of demand for medical care is greater than zero.
2. Consumers generally prefer uncertain losses to certain losses when confronted with a fair standard gamble choice.
3. The distribution of health care spending is highly skewed.
4. A large portion of a consumer's insurance premium is devoted to covering procedures and episodes that are so expensive that the consumer would not be able to purchase them privately.
5. The welfare loss associated with moral hazard is much smaller than the loss implied using the observed Marshallian demand for medical care.

These empirical results support a theory that postulates that the demand for health insurance is a demand for an income transfer when ill. The new theory is consistent with each of the above empirical results because

1. It allows for income transfers contained in the price reduction to cause moral hazard (consistent with the income elasticity being greater than zero).
2. It reinterprets the demand for insurance as being derived from the demand for income transfer when ill (not the demand for certain losses).

3. It models health care as being consumed primarily by the ill, rather than by all consumers (consistent with the skewed expenditure distribution).

4. It permits the demand for insurance to be related to the demand for access to otherwise unaffordable medical care (because some health care is privately unaffordable).

5. It allows moral hazard to incorporate both inefficient health care (caused by a price effect) and efficient health care (caused by the consumer in the ill state obtaining income transfers that are spent in part on additional medical care).

In this chapter, I focus on the welfare gain from efficient moral hazard. The chapter attempts to answer the question, What empirical evidence is there to suggest that at least a portion of moral hazard spending is the intended result of purchasing insurance, rather than an opportunistic response to a reduced price? That is, what evidence is there to suggest that consumers purchase insurance in order to obtain a transfer of income if they were to become ill, and that this income transfer then allows them to purchase more health care (and other goods and services) than they otherwise would, even though the income transfer occurs as a result of a reduction in the price of medical care? The chapter begins by juxtaposing the theoretical examples of moral hazard against the actual examples of moral hazard that have been documented in the clinical literature.

MORAL HAZARD AS SPECIFIC HEALTH CARE

Theoreticians often use archetypal examples in order to communicate and persuade others of the essential truth of their theory. These examples are powerful because they capture the essence of a theory in a single concept that has unambiguous intuitive appeal. That is, the examples are chosen because their essential truth in support of the theory is obvious and unquestionable. Thereafter, when it is necessary to recall a certain theory, perhaps a complex one, the student may instead recall the example, which contains all of the essential elements supporting the theory but is less demanding cognitively than the theory itself. Of course, the issue with the archetypal example is that, without rigorous scientific investigation, it is not known to what extent the example is representative of all the cases to which the theory claims to apply. It may be intuitively obvious that the example supports the theory and that it is not the only one to do so, but there may be little understanding about the extent to which the example is truly representative.

Conventional health insurance theory has its archetypal examples of moral hazard: designer prescription sunglasses, cosmetic surgeries, and drugs to improve sexual functioning. It is intuitively clear that in most cases, this care would be inefficient if purchased only when insured, and would result in a welfare loss. That is, although the consumer may have sufficient resources to purchase these services, he does not purchase them without insurance. So, if he purchases the care when insured, the change in behavior must be an opportunistic response to the reduced insurance price, rather than an intended response to an income transfer when ill. Thus, moral hazard is inefficient, as conventional health insurance claims that it is.

The new theory has its archetypal examples, too. The main archetypal example that I have used to communicate my theory of the demand for health insurance is the $300,000 liver transplant (first mentioned in Chapter 2). It contains all the essential elements of the new theory. Although a consumer may purchase a liver transplant only when the price is reduced due to insurance, it is clear that the conventional theory does not explain this. Under the conventional theory, it would be assumed that the consumer could have purchased this procedure if uninsured, but preferred not to because the consumer's evaluation of the procedure was too low. The procedure is purchased only when the price is reduced sufficiently to match this low evaluation.

To most of us, however, it seems clear that the purchase of a liver transplant would be considered only by someone who is ill. If ill, however, few consumers could afford to purchase a $300,000 liver transplant procedure privately, despite the fact that a liver transplant is likely to save the ill consumer's life. Thus, the real reason for not purchasing the procedure without insurance is that the consumer does not have sufficient financial resources available, and that the reduced insurance price represents the vehicle by which the ill consumer obtains an income transfer from those who remain healthy. The additional years of life that the consumer gains as a result of the transplant are worth far more than the cost of the procedure, even though the cost of the procedure is very high. Thus, the consumer with health insurance purchases the liver transplant because of the income transfers, and the liver transplant represents an efficient purchase.

Because of the dominance of the conventional theory and the presumption that all additional health care consumed when insured is inefficient, no studies have attempted to estimate the portion of moral hazard that is efficient. Theoretically, a study based on the consumer's income payoff test would do this, but such a study presents a number of practical and ethical difficulties, and had not been done. Although no income payoff test study has ever been conducted, a number of other studies have shown that *ill* consumers purchase more health care when insured. That is, one of the characteristics that distinguishes between the two archetypal examples is whether the health care in question is largely discretionary (as in the case of designer sunglasses) or clearly associated with the presence of an illness (as in the case of a liver transplant). Moreover, if it can also be shown that the insured receive more care but that this care reflects standard practice, then it would be difficult to construct a context in which the moral hazard in question is inefficient.

The study by Overpeck and Kotch (1995) presents a real-world example of moral hazard. Using a sample of 17,110 children under age seventeen from the Child Health Supplement to the National Center for Health Statistics' Health Interview Survey for 1988, the authors compared the rate at which children received medical attention for serious injuries among the insured and uninsured, holding constant (1) having a place for care, (2) maternal education, (3) age, (4) race, and (5) gender. Serious injuries were defined as those that require time in bed, hospitalization, or surgery, or those that limit activities, or those that result in persistent pain or persistent awareness of the injury. The authors found that the rate at which children with injuries received medical attention among the uninsured was only 71% of the rate among the insured. To interpret this finding as evidence of moral hazard, it must be assumed that the rate at which children had injuries at all (regardless of whether they received medical attention following the injury or not) is about the same across insurance status groups. In fact, Overpeck and Kotch (1995) cite studies that found evidence of a correlation between being uninsured and having injuries. Thus, the rate at which children have injuries among the uninsured is likely to be greater than the rate among the insured, so the conclusion that this rate differential represents moral hazard is reasonable and the ratio found by the authors is probably conservative.

These results suggest that when children are injured, insured children receive more medical care than uninsured children do. The additional medical care is related to an illness occurring, and is not discretionary because only those with the illness (injury) would benefit from it and, therefore, consider purchasing it.[1] Moreover, from Overpeck and Kotch's (1995) definition of "serious injury," it appears that the medical attention that those children with insurance receive is warranted, and that, if anything, those without insurance receive less than would be considered standard care. Thus, Overpeck and Kotch's (1995) study suggests that for health care qua medical attention following injuries for children, moral hazard is probably not of the opportunistic, price-related, inefficient variety.

This study is not the only one to find that when ill, the insured receive more care and that the additional care appears to be warranted. Studies have looked at a variety of illnesses and, although far from standardized, found a similar pattern of results. Young and Cohen (1991) found that uninsured patients with acute myocardial infarction were less likely than insured patients to receive coronary artery bypass graft or angioplasty, and that uninsured patients were more likely to die. Yergan et al. (1988) found that uninsured patients who were hospitalized with pneumonia were less likely to have radiographic procedures, consultations, and surgical procedures, and that the uninsured patients had higher mortality rates. Wilson and Sharma (1995) found that patients with diabetes who were hospitalized were more likely to have the proper medications if they were insured. Thomas et al. (1996) looked at emergency room patients who presented with asthma, chest pain, abdominal pain, hand lacerations, head trauma, or first-trimester vaginal bleeding and found that uninsured patients were less likely to fill their prescriptions after discharge.

Stoddard, St. Peter, and Newacheck (1994) found that children with pharyngitis, acute earaches, recurrent ear infections, or asthma were less likely to see a physician for their disease if uninsured. Kuykendall, Johnson, and Geraci (1995) found that uninsured hospitalized patients with coronary atherosclerosis were less likely to undergo revascularization. Greenberg et al. (1988) followed patients with lung cancer and found that the uninsured patients were less likely to receive surgery, radiation therapy, or chemotherapy. Haas and Goldman (1994) found that adults who were hospitalized with acute trauma were less likely to receive surgery, physical therapy, and intensive care if uninsured. They were also more likely to die of their injuries. Fleishman and Mor (1993) found that uninsured AIDS patients were less likely to be admitted to the hospital than insured ones.

These studies suggest that the medical care that economists have conventionally used to exemplify moral hazard is far from typical of the medical care that *is* moral hazard in practice. Theoretically, moral hazard is represented by designer sunglasses, but in practice, it is represented by medical attention for children who have received a serious injury, or coronary artery bypass grafts for persons with a myocardial infarction. This juxtaposition of examples is revealing because intuitively, it is clear that taking one's child to a physician when injured seems prudent and consistent with medical and societal norms, not wasteful and frivolous as conventional theory would predict. While none of these studies is sufficiently comprehensive to evaluate all of moral hazard, the preponderance of evidence from these various clinical studies suggests that a substantial portion of moral hazard is efficient and represents health care that is worth more to the consumer who is insured (and who receives an income transfer from the healthy) than it costs to produce.

EVALUATING MORAL HAZARD

Conventional theory assumes that the observed Marshallian demand for medical care not only determines consumption when insured, but also the willingness to pay for the different quantities of medical care when insured. That is, because conventional theory assumes that becoming insured simply moves the consumer along her uninsured Marshallian demand, the value of all additional medical care is based on the area under the uninsured consumer's Marshallian demand.

The new theory suggests that this is wrong because insurance acts to transfer income to the ill, and as a result, the willingness to pay for medical care increases for every unit of care, shifting outward both the original Marshallian demand and the new demand for medical care described in Chapter 6. But even if this income transfer were not part of the picture, it is important to recognize that willingness to pay is often a misleading measure of value because it depends on the consumer's income. For commodities that have high intrinsic value, but where the lack of sufficient income leads to a misleadingly small willingness to pay, alternative analytical approaches have been used to determine value. The fact that alternative approaches are used to measure high-value commodities raises additional questions about the appropriateness of using willingness to pay to measure the value of medical care, which if lifesaving, is also of high value. As a result, some of moral hazard that has been deemed inefficient due to measuring its value by willingness to pay, may actually be efficient using an alternative evaluative metric.

Using the observed willingness to pay of uninsured consumers to evaluate expensive medical care is inappropriate for exactly the same reason that it would be inappropriate to use the willingness to pay of an indigent person to determine the value he places on food, clothing, or shelter. Although a poor person may be willing to pay only a fraction of the marginal cost of producing these commodities, society recognizes that his willingness to pay is constrained by his resources and that it does not adequately measure the true value of these commodities to the indigent consumer. For example, food actually may be worth far more to the poor person than his willingness to pay—if it keeps him from starving. Society has recognized that the value of food to the poor person often exceeds his observed willingness to pay by a large margin, and as a result, often intervenes with charity or government programs to provide food to those who cannot purchase it privately.

Similarly, the distribution of medical care expenditures is highly skewed. Because such a large proportion of medical care spending is represented by very expensive treatment episodes that may be beyond the resources of those few who become seriously ill, estimating the value of this care by the uninsured consumer's willingness to pay would also be misleading.

Analysts who have sought to determine the value of human life have faced a similar problem, but have solved it by evaluating willingness to pay for an *expected* life, rather than a life. That is, instead of attempting to determine the value of a whole human life by, say, finding how much a person with limited resources says he would be willing to pay to save his life, researchers have essentially focused on how much a person would be willing to pay to save a fraction of his life, and have used fractions that are sufficiently small so that the consumer's true willingness to pay would likely be within his budget. Thus, the value of human life literature consists largely of studies that determine the amount of additional wages that a worker would need to be paid in order to take a slightly riskier job (Viscusi, 1993). Using the same example that appeared in Chapter 5, if workers on average require $500 more in annual wages to take a job that would increase the annual chance of dying by 1/10,000, then the willingness to pay (accept) for 1/10,000 of a life is $500 and by extrapolation, the willingness to accept for one life would be ($500 × 10,000 =) $5,000,000. The value of a life is determined by extrapolating from an expected life, not by attempting to determine the willingness to pay (or accept) for a whole life.[2]

A similar evaluation strategy could be used to obtain willingness to pay estimates for expensive medical care. That is, because insurance is available for medical care, the same extrapolation based on expectations could be done to determine the value of expensive medical procedures if ill. For example, a consumer with $50,000 in resources may only be willing to pay (at most) $50,000 for a liver transplant. But he might be willing to pay as much as, say, $9.33 for insurance that covers a liver transplant in the 1 in 75,000 chance that he would become ill enough to need one. Since the consumer is willing to pay $9.33 for 1/75,000 of a transplant procedure, the entire procedure is worth ($9.33 × 75,000 =) $700,000. This amount is far more than the $50,000 he would be willing to pay for the procedure without insurance, but it better reflects the, say, $100,000 that the consumer would be willing to pay for each of the seven additional years of life generated by the transplant.

The cost-effectiveness literature has also recognized the inadequacy of using observed willingness to pay for expensive lifesaving procedures in evaluating them. As a result, few, if any, cost-effectiveness studies have used the observed willingness to pay to determine the value of a medical procedure. This literature has generally substituted the value of the mortality and morbidity outcomes generated by the procedure in place of the willingness to pay for the procedure itself. As already discussed, the most widely accepted values of a year of life come from labor market studies of the willingness to accept risky jobs. Viscusi (1993) has reviewed the value of life literature and determined that the most reasonable values for a life would be between $3 and $7 million dollars (in 1990 dollars). Hirth et al. (2000) reviewed this literature and converted lives into life years by a standard methodology that included discounting. The authors found that $100,000 is probably a conservative estimate of the value of a quality adjusted year of life because the median value of a life year for these studies was about $265,000 in 1997 dollars. Although $265,000 may be the implied value of one year of life from the market studies, few consumers would be willing (or able) to pay that amount for a procedure that saved one year of life.

So, for medical procedures that have high intrinsic value in terms of their impact on mortality and morbidity, estimates of the value of the procedure from the cost-effectiveness literature would better determine whether the additional procedures represent efficient or inefficient moral hazard. A number of examples of efficient moral hazard have, therefore, already been presented in Table 5.1.

Thus, conventional insurance theory is out of step with standard analytical practices because it bases the value of medical care on the uninsured consumer's demand and willingness to pay. Basing the value of medical care on its outcomes, and evaluating these outcomes at levels determined by the value of life literature, would not only result in more accurate valuation, but it also would raise the values compared with values based on observed demand. Thus, raising the values above the willingness to pay of observed uninsured demand would also imply that a substantial amount of efficient moral hazard exists. Finally, it must be recognized that whatever the true value of health care, the income transfer within all insurance payoffs would allow the ill consumers to exhibit a willingness to pay that is more commensurate with their true evaluation of health care.

AN ESTIMATE OF THE WELFARE GAIN

Becoming insured increases consumption of medical care. According to the new theory, some of the increase is due to the price effect and some to the income transfer effect, but in all cases, the additional medical care itself is assumed to have a positive effect on the welfare of the consumer. An overall welfare loss from moral hazard would be realized only if the cost of the additional care exceeded its value because of the dominance of the price effect.

Literature on Health Insurance and Health

As discussed in the second section of this chapter, evidence from the clinical literature confirms that being insured does increase consumption of medical care (see Brown, Bindman, and Lurie, 1998, for comprehensive review of these studies), but that moral hazard is represented primarily by standard care for common diseases. That is, most of the studies in this literature focused on consumers with specific diseases and showed that ill consumers who were insured were more likely to receive the standard treatment for their disease than those without insurance.

While there is probably little question that this literature establishes a causal relationship between becoming insured and receiving additional health care, the causal relationship between becoming insured and improving one's health is less established. This is because most of the studies of the relationship between health insurance and health are observational, and although many of them hold observed characteristics constant, none of these studies can completely rule out selection or endogeneity biases (Levy and Meltzer, 2001). The observational studies purport to represent the causal relationship:

health insurance → health care → health.

Instead, the empirical evidence of a correlation between health insurance and health could also represent either (1) that an unobserved third variable is correlated with both health insurance and health and is causing them both (selection), or (2) that a consumer's health status is systematically causing him to either purchase insurance or remain uninsured, so that the arrow pointing toward health is actually pointing in the opposite direction, away from health and toward health insurance (endogeneity). The inability to rule out completely these alternative interpretations makes it unclear what the evidence from the observational studies truly means.

Randomized controlled trials eliminate this uncertainty by allocating consumers into health insurance categories—insured or uninsured—at random, and therefore for reasons that are not associated with health. The RAND Health Insurance Experiment (HIE) represents the only study of the relationship between health insurance and health to have a true randomized, experimental design. This study found that for certain categories of participants, the degree of health insurance coverage did have an effect on health. Specifically, Brook et al. (1983) found that increased health insurance coverage improved visual acuity for those participants with poor vision and that it improved diastolic blood pressure for those with high blood pressure and low incomes. The RAND HIE, however, was not powered to determine mortality effects of insurance, so the mortality implications of lower blood pressure were based on results of other studies. This modeling exercise found that for those in the cost-sharing plans, a person in the highest quartile of mortality risk had a higher relative risk ratio (compared with person with average mortality risk) than a similar person in the free fee-for-service plan. Thus, free fee-for-service insurance resulted in a significant 10% reduction in the death rate among low-income participants.

The RAND HIE compared those with greater insurance coverage to those with lesser coverage, but did not compare the insured to the uninsured. This is because all participants, even those in the plans with the least coverage, converted to free fee-for-service as soon as $1,000 in out-of-pocket spending was incurred. As a result, the RAND HIE provides only suggestive evidence of the health consequences of being uninsured. Indeed, the fact that some difference was found at all suggests that a larger health effect would be found if the study were actually to compare the health of those who were completely uninsured to those who were insured.

Natural experiments can eliminate much of the selection and endogeneity problems of observational studies by using data where the consumers are placed in the insured or uninsured categories for reasons not associated with their health or anything that is reasonably correlated with their health. Three large-scale natural experiments appear in the literature and all have found evidence that becoming insured increases health, as measured by decreases in mortality and other morbidity-related variables.[3]

Currie and Gruber (1996a,b) estimated the mortality effects of expansions of Medicaid eligibility for pregnant women and children. Over the period 1979 to 1982, the various states imposed slightly different expansions of their Medicaid programs and at different times. Currie and Gruber took advantage of these variations to measure the effect of becoming insured under Medicaid on health care utilization and mortality rates of children. Currie and Gruber (1996a) found that becoming eligible for insurance under Medicaid increased health care utilization by children and decreased child mortality rates. Specifically, becoming insured represented a significant reduction in child mortality of 1.277 deaths per 10,000 children, compared with a baseline mortality rate of 3.807 deaths per 10,000 children, for a 34% reduction in mortality rates.

Hanratty (1996) estimated the effect of Canada's national health insurance program on infant mortality. When Canada implemented her health insurance program, it was implemented in the various provinces at different times between 1962 and 1972. Using the county as the unit of observation, Hanratty found that the infant mortality rate declined significantly by 4% as a result of national health insurance.

Lichtenberg (2001) used the fact that everyone becomes insured by Medicare at age sixty-five as a natural experiment to determine the effect of insurance on mortality and days spent in bed for those turning sixty-five. Combining a variety of data sets, Lichtenberg found that utilization of ambulatory and inpatient care generally increases abruptly at age sixty-five. Comparing the actual reductions in mortality and morbidity after age sixty-five with trends in these outcomes prior to age sixty-five, Lichtenberg found that the probability of death is about 13% lower after age sixty-five than it would have been in the absence of Medicare. Similarly, days spent in bed are about 13% lower as well. The causal connection is further tested by determining the relationship between utilization and mortality. Lichtenberg found that a sustained 10% increase in the number of physician visits results in a reduction of the death rate by 5%.

Although all of the natural experiments found evidence of an insurance effect on mortality, they did not represent a clean comparison of insured against the uninsured. For example, although the Lichtenberg (2001) study found evidence of a 13% reduction in the probability of death associated with Medicare insurance compared to those without Medicare, many of those without Medicare would have been privately insured. Indeed, because about 85% of the population under age sixty-five are insured, the Lichtenberg study is probably comparing those who are insured under Medicare to those who are predominantly—clearly over 50%—insured anyway. Thus, it would be reasonable to expect that if Lichtenberg were actually able to compare the mortality rates of those with Medicare insurance to those without any insurance at all, the mortality rate differential would exceed 13%. The Currie and Gruber (1996a) study was more likely to be comparing the insured to the uninsured, and as a consequence, being insured under Medicaid was associated with a larger (34%) reduction in mortality.

If the results from these natural experiments are sufficient to allay concerns about selection and endogeneity in the observational studies, then we can use the results from an observational study that compares the health of the insured to that of the uninsured, in order to estimate the welfare gain from becoming insured. One study that makes this comparison for a large representative sample of the U.S. adult population is Franks, Clancy, and Gold (1993).

Estimating the Welfare Gain

Franks, Clancy, and Gold (1993) used data from the National Health and Nutrition Examination Survey Epidemiologic Follow-up Study (NHEFS) to estimate the effect of being uninsured on mortality. The NHEFS collected baseline characteristics on a sample of 6,913 adults aged twenty-five to seventy-four years and followed them for up to sixteen years to determine mortality. In their analysis, the authors excluded those with Medicaid, Veterans Administration, or Medicare insurance at baseline, leaving 5,218 who reported that they were either uninsured or had private insurance. The exclusion of the Medicare participants implies that their results apply best to adults aged twenty-five through sixty-four. The authors found that those who reported being uninsured at baseline had an increased risk of mortality represented by a 1.25 hazard ratio (95% confidence interval of 1.55 to 1.00) compared with those who reported being insured, holding constant the other baseline characteristics. A 25% greater mortality rate for those who are uninsured is consistent with the results from the studies that used data from natural experiments.

Although providing a cleaner comparison than the natural experiments, the mortality rate differential measured by Franks, Clancy, and Gold (1993) represented a certain amount of contamination. This is because insurance status for their sample was only observed at baseline. Migration in and out of being insured would likely have occurred for portions of this population over the sixteen-year follow-up period. This migration, however, would interject a conservative bias into the insurance effect. That is, if the observed persons were all continually uninsured or continually insured over the entire sixteen-year follow-up, the observed mortality effect would probably be greater.[4]

The 1.25 hazard ratio from the Franks, Clancy, and Gold (1993) study was used to estimate the moral hazard welfare gain from becoming insured for a year for an arbitrary group of forty million uninsured consumers. Assuming that these forty million uninsured are uniformly distributed across age categories so that one million uninsured adults are allocated to each of the forty age categories between ages twenty-five and sixty-four, the added years of life expectancy can be estimated using the 1996 Interpolated Abridged Life Table (Public Health Service, 2000). This life table reflects the experience of U.S. residents in the 1990 census, adjusted to 1996. The death rates in the table were assumed to reflect the death rates of those who are continually insured, because about 85% of the population under age sixty-five was insured in 1996.

For ease of computation, the differential effect of one year of insurance coverage on mortality was found by estimating the number of people who would die at each age level due to the 25% greater mortality without insurance, and multiplying this number by the insured life expectancy at that age. The death rates for those under age sixty-five are relatively small, so a 25% increase in the death rate does not represent a large number of lives lost. Still, because each of these lives is lost at a relatively young age, the number of life years lost is relatively high. Therefore, as a result of being uninsured for one year, a total of 1,225,380 life years would be lost for these forty million people, or a loss of about 9/10,000 of the total years of life expectancy of the forty million. If it were assumed that a life year is conservatively valued at $100,000 (Hirth et al., 2000), the value of the one year of moral hazard is about $123 billion.

According to the 1996 Medical Expenditure Panel Survey, the average health care expenditures of those with insurance who were less than sixty-five years of age were $1,918, and for those in the same age group without insurance were $942, for a cost of moral hazard of about $976 per insured person (Cohen et al., 2000). The total cost of moral hazard—that is, the cost of the additional health care due to becoming insured from all sources, including an adverse selection demand effect—is therefore estimated at $39 billion for the same forty million consumers. Thus, the net welfare gain from moral hazard for this arbitrary group of forty million Americans is ($123 billion − $39 billion =) $84 billion, or a welfare gain from moral hazard that is more than three times its cost.

Refinements of the Analysis

A number of refinements might be appropriate. Discounting would reduce the number of life years gained from insurance without increasing the cost of moral hazard. Hirth et al. (2000) found that discounting at a 3% rate reduced the number of life years saved to about 40% of the undiscounted number. The $100,000 figure used in the present calculation essentially represents a measure of the value of a year of life, calculated from the estimated value of a whole life, divided by the *undiscounted* number of years of life remaining. If I were to use, instead, a value of a year of life that was calculated using the number of *discounted* years of life, the value of a life year would increase to the levels—median of $265,000—found by Hirth et al. (2000) using a similar procedure. Thus, while discounting would reduce the number of life years gained from insurance, to be consistent, it would be necessary to also raise the value of each life year from $100,000 to about $265,000. Thus, discounting would reduce the life years saved and simultaneously increase the valuation of a life year, and therefore, would not qualitatively affect the welfare gain calculations.

Another implicit assumption is that a person whose life was saved by insurance would have the same life expectancy of the person represented in the life table. If the life expectancy of the ill person who does not die because of insurance is less than average, the life expectancy gain and the value of the moral hazard would be overstated.

Similarly, the gain from insurance would also be overstated if the estimate of the lives saved does not adjust for a lower quality of life of those who survive because of insurance. For example, if the quality of life weight were reduced from 1 to 0.66—a weight commensurate with the quality of life of persons with metastatic breast cancer who are undergoing chemotherapy, or of those with a migraine headache (Tengs and Wallace, 2000)—the gain would be about 808,751 quality adjusted life years (QALYs), which evaluated at $100,000 would result in a welfare gain that is still over twice the cost.

On the other hand, I have not accounted for the reduced morbidity in the population as a result of insurance. In a natural experiment, Lichtenberg (2001) finds a 13% decrease in days spent in bed for those with Medicare in his study. In an observational study, Baker et al. (2001) used the Health and Retirement Survey from 1992, 1994, and 1996 to relate insurance status to health status for those aged fifty-one to sixty-one at baseline. The authors find that the uninsured have a 63% greater chance of a major decline in self-reported health status than the insured, holding constant age, sex, race, income, smoking status, alcohol consumption, and separate measures of health status at baseline. Similarly, the uninsured were found to have a higher risk of having problems with physical functioning. If the effect of insurance in improving morbidity were included in the moral hazard gain, it would serve to cancel at least some portion of the overestimation due to using longevity estimates that do not account for the shorter lifespan of those who have been ill, and due to using quality of life weights that do not acknowledge the lower quality of life of those who have been seriously ill.

Also not included in the gain is the benefit from those discretionary, opportunistic purchases that are associated with moral hazard by conventional theory but are largely unrelated to health. Under the analysis presented in Chapter 6 and with assumption of linear demands, the value of these inefficient services is still equal to half of their costs. So, if their value were included in the estimation of the value of the moral hazard, it would again cancel some of the overestimation due to inflated estimates of longevity and quality of life. Overall then, this analysis suggests that moral hazard generates a welfare gain that is driven primarily, but not entirely, by the gains from the reduced mortality and that this gain exceeds the cost of all the additional care.

THE WELFARE GAIN FROM MORAL HAZARD
DIAGRAMMATICALLY

This chapter attempts to pull together some of the empirical evidence on the extent to which moral hazard represents efficient purchases. In the second section of this chapter, documented examples of moral hazard from the clinical literature were reviewed. It was suggested that moral hazard typically represents prudent, intentional, and medically necessary procedures, not the frivolous, opportunistic, and discretionary examples of moral hazard that are used to support conventional theory.

In the next section, it was argued that for those procedures that are highly effective in saving lives and at the same time place excessive demands on the consumer's budget, the willingness to pay for these procedures by the uninsured consumer—the metric used by the conventional theory—is an inappropriate measure of value. For these procedures, a more appropriate evaluation methodology would assign a value to a procedure based on the outcomes of the procedure and evaluate those outcomes (that is, life years saved) by prices from the literature on the value of life. The insured willingness to pay would be closer to this value than the uninsured willingness to pay. Thus, some seemingly inefficient moral hazard is in fact efficient.

In the fourth section, it was shown that the results from the natural experiments and from the Franks, Clancy, and Gold (1993) study imply a value of moral hazard that far outweighs its cost. These findings suggest that while moral hazard may represent some inefficiently demanded procedures, efficient procedures that benefit the consumer predominate.

Figure 7.1 illustrates these results. Figure 7.1 modifies Figure 6.2 by adding in the effect of the income transfers. In Figure 7.1, D_M shows the Marshallian demand for medical care for the ill consumer without insurance and indicates that without insurance, M^u would be purchased. D_N shows the demand for medical care for the ill consumer with insurance that pays off by reducing the price to zero. The income transfers increase the demand for medical care. Because of the income transfers, the consumer demands an additional ($M^c - M^u$) of care. Because price reductions are the mechanism used to pay off the contract, the consumer demands an additional ($M^i - M^c$) of care, but the willingness to pay for this additional care reflects the reduced income from paying the premium. The new demand curve is represented by D_N', which is kinked at point b, where the willingness to pay after the income transfers equals the pre-insurance price. The levels of medical care

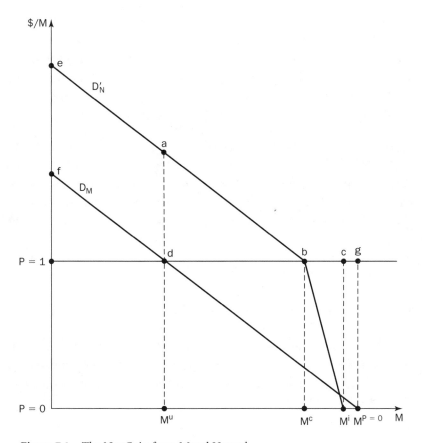

Figure 7.1 The Net Gain from Moral Hazard.

shown as M^u, M^c, and M^i in Figure 7.1 correspond to similarly labeled quantities in Figure 3.1.

In Figure 7.1, the uninsured Marshallian demand, D_M, indicates that if the price had fallen to zero exogenously, the quantity of medical care demanded would be $M^{P=0}$. For the insured consumer who becomes ill and faces a payoff price of 0, quantity M^i is consumed. M^i is less than $M^{P=0}$ because the premium payment required to reduce the price to 0 with insurance reduces income available to be spent on medical care. In contrast to Marshallian demand, a different demand curve would exist for each coinsurance rate, reflecting the different levels of income transfers generated by the various coinsurance rates (see Figure 9.1 and the corresponding discussion).

With regard to the welfare effects, the income transfer effect shifts Marshallian demand outward in the same way that a lump sum transfer of income would shift the ill consumer's Marshallian demand outward with a contingent-claims insurance payoff. As a result, the willingness to pay with insurance would exceed the marginal cost of producing care for all units of M up to M^c, the level of medical care consumption where the insured willingness to pay equals the price (which is assumed to be equal to the marginal cost and constant). An additional $(M^i - M^c)$ units of medical care would also be consumed, generated by the price effect of insurance. For that care, the willingness to pay is less than the marginal cost of producing the care. Thus, moral hazard would be represented by $(M^i - M^u)$, and the welfare change from moral hazard would compare the gain from the additional care, area $M^u abM^i$, to the cost, area $M^u dcM^i$. Figure 7.1 is drawn to show a net welfare gain from moral hazard, consistent with the empirical evidence reported in this chapter. Contrast this gain to the moral hazard welfare loss of area $dgM^{P=0}$ under conventional theory.

In addition to the welfare gain from moral hazard, the income transfers increase the willingness to pay for the original M^u units of care. Therefore, the welfare gain from insurance would need to account for the fact that the value of the original M^u units of care has increased by area eadf. Thus, the income transfers within insurance that pays off by reducing price not only generate additional care that is more valuable than it costs (perhaps, by a factor as large as 3 to 1), but also increase the value of the medical care that would have been purchased without insurance.

CONCLUSIONS

In order to understand the relationship between health insurance and demand for medical care, it is important to recognize that private health insurance is primarily a vehicle for transferring income from those who remain healthy to those who become ill. Although there may be a price effect caused by using price reductions as the payoff mechanism, the welfare consequences of the price effect are small relative to the welfare consequences of the income transfer effect, especially the role of income transfers in making accessible those expensive, lifesaving procedures that would otherwise be unaffordable.

If insurance were expanded in the U.S. to cover the uninsured among the non-Medicare portion of the population, relatively few additional lives would be saved. Nevertheless, because these lives are saved at a relatively young age, they imply a relatively large increase in life years saved. But even more importantly, when these saved life years are evaluated at dollar levels from the value of life literature, moral hazard becomes associated with a net welfare gain.

It must be remembered that income transfers from insurance do not result only in increases in medical care, but also in increases in the amount of other goods and services consumed. Because of diminishing marginal utility of income, the expected utility gain from the other consumption generated by the income transfer when ill also contributes to the demand for insurance, and can alone exceed the expected utility loss from paying the premium when healthy. Thus, insurance has two sources of welfare gains: one related to the additional medical care and the other related to the additional other goods and services purchased that would not have been purchased without insurance.

This analysis alters the nature of the central puzzle associated with the demand for health insurance. Under conventional theory, insurance policies with coverage parameters that are typical of those actually purchased in the U.S. generate such a large moral hazard welfare loss that they make the consumer worse off. For example, Manning and Marquis (1996) estimate that fair health insurance with a 25% coinsurance rate and a $4,000 maximum on out-of-pocket payments—the type that is perhaps closest to current coverage parameters—would result in a net welfare loss of $131 per family in 1995 dollars. Free fee-for-service insurance—the type that most insured families purchased in the 1960s and 1970s—would result in a $1,424 net welfare loss (Manning and Marquis, 1996). Because the tax subsidy largely cancels the loading fee, an appeal to the tax subsidy is not sufficient to explain why such policies were (are) voluntarily purchased. Besides, many similar health insurance policies with large loading fees were purchased by the self-employed, who until recently, were ineligible for the tax subsidy. Thus, under conventional theory, the central puzzle is: why would consumers purchase unsubsidized health insurance?

Under the new theory, the puzzle is just the opposite: why would consumers *not* purchase health insurance if it is so welfare increasing? About 17% of Americans, or about forty million consumers, do not purchase health insurance. If health insurance is so clearly beneficial to the consumer through both the additional medical care and other goods and services available when ill, then why are forty million Americans uninsured? This question is addressed next.

NOTES

1. "Discretionary" medical care is difficult to define because the consumer, even if seriously ill, still decides whether to spend income on health care or other goods and services. Therefore, unless a consumer can be forced to pay for and receive a medical procedure, all health care is discretionary, even for those who are ill. An improved definition would be care that a consumer would benefit from regardless of whether he were ill or not. This definition is not completely satisfactory either, because for much of discretionary care, there is at least some predisposing physical condition—short of acute illness—that makes the health care valuable. For example, designer prescription sunglasses would not be valuable unless the consumer's eyesight was chronically impaired in the first place. Moreover, some health care is discretionary not to the patient but to the patient's physician. More will be said about this type of care in Chapter 8.

Discretionary health care is, perhaps, best defined by what it is not. Nondiscretionary care would be defined as procedures that are only valuable to a consumer with the corresponding disease. For example, a coronary artery bypass graft procedure would be nondiscretionary because no consumer would consider purchasing a bypass procedure unless he were seriously ill with coronary heart disease. In contrast, some plastic surgery would be discretionary because it is not necessary to be disfigured to consider purchasing it. Thus, discretionary care could be defined as any care that is not nondiscretionary in that sense.

2. One issue with this approach is whether the rate at which a worker would trade portions of his life for income is constant. That is, a simple extrapolation from information that the consumer would sell the first 1/10,000 of his life for $500 assumes that each and every 1/10,000th of a life is valued at that same $500 level. Under convexity of preferences, however, it would be assumed that, while the consumer might trade the first 1/10,000 of his life for $500, successive 1/10,000ths would require successively higher income payments. Therefore, a simple extrapolation from information about the first 1/10,000th might dramatically understate the true value of a life.

3. A study by Perry and Rosen (2001) represents a fourth study to use a large natural experiment to investigate the effect of insurance on health status. As Levy and Meltzer (2001) point out, however, this study was not sufficiently powered to find significant results, if they existed.

4. It is interesting to speculate on the direction of the selection and endogeneity effects, were they to exist. One likely selection possibility is that low-income consumers are both uninsured and have lower health statuses. If so, this selection effect would bias the results in favor of finding a larger insurance effect than actually existed. Fortunately, Franks, Clancy, and Gold (1993) include income (and education) in their analysis, presumably eliminating income as a source of bias. On the other hand, endogeneity could still be present. An often-mentioned potential endogeneity effect is that those who are ill (or expect to be) are more likely to purchase insurance. This effect, however, would bias against finding that the insured have better health, making the finding of a 25% reduction in mortality for the insured a conservative estimate of the true effect.

8 | WHY HEALTH INSURANCE IS SOMETIMES NOT PURCHASED

INTRODUCTION

Why do some consumers fail to purchase health insurance? In the theory presented so far, it has been suggested that health insurance is overwhelmingly welfare-increasing, yet about forty million Americans do not have insurance, either privately or through a government program. Why are so many consumers uninsured if health insurance is so valuable? Moreover, because of the access it provides, the new theory suggests that health insurance is especially beneficial for those at the lower end of the income distribution. It is, however, those at the lower end of the income distribution who are most likely to be uninsured (Feldstein, 1999). A convincing explanation must account for this apparent inconsistency.

In this chapter, I discuss the factors that might induce those who would seem to benefit from insurance to do without. The first of these is the availability of charity and government safety net programs such as Medicaid. These programs are especially important because they are focused on low income consumers, those who are most likely to be uninsured.

The second factor, preferences for risk, is speculative in nature. In this section, I develop the outline of a theory that distinguishes between (1) behavior that derives from a Bernoulli utility function that is concave in income, and (2) preferences regarding risk. That is, the theory that I propose postulates that risk preferences are generated separately from the shape of utility as a function of certain income or wealth. Consumers exhibit behavioral tendencies that are based on maximizing expected utility given a concave Bernoulli utility function for certain income, but overlaid on this, consumers have preferences for risk that are independent of the utility function. These risk preferences may either reinforce or oppose, and if strong enough, override the behavioral tendencies that are based on the Bernoulli utility function.

The remaining sections of this chapter consider a number of other factors that are generally thought to enter the decision to insure, and whose influence may be sufficient to induce consumers to remain uninsured. These factors include: high loading fees, inefficient moral hazard, adverse selection, and physician-induced demand. Indeed, any inefficiency in the health care system that leads to higher premiums might contribute to the nonpurchase of insurance. In this chapter, however, the discussion is limited to only those factors that are associated directly with insurance.

CHARITY AND MEDICAID

Consider a model where the consumer again chooses between (1) being insured at coinsurance rate c, with probability π of becoming ill, and (2) being uninsured, but now with charity and government safety net programs, such as Medicaid, available. Assume that the consumer is sufficiently poor so that the medical expenditures required to treat the illness in question exceed her endowed income, or $M > Y^o$. If the consumer chooses to purchase insurance that pays off by reducing the price to 0, her expected utility is the same as specified in Chapter 3:

$$EU_i = \pi U^s(M^i, Y^i) + (1 - \pi)U^h[0, Y^o - \pi(1 - c)M^i] \quad (3.19)$$

$$= \pi U^s[M^i, Y^o + (1 - \pi)(1 - c)M^i - M^i]$$
$$+ (1 - \pi)U^h[0, Y^o - \pi(1 - c)M^i] \quad (3.20)$$

$$= \pi U^s(M^i, Y^o - R) + (1 - \pi)U^h(0, Y^o - R), \quad (8.1)$$

where R is the actuarially fair insurance premium, $R = \pi(1 - c)M^i$. If $c = 0$, then $R = \pi M^i$.

Alternatively, the consumer can choose to remain uninsured and rely on charity or Medicaid (in the U.S.) to pay for the care. Charity and Medicaid stand ready to pay for care as a last resort in the event of illness. While charity is financed many ways, one source is the contributions of those who might use charity in the future. Part of the motivation behind such contributions may be altruism, but part may also be a more selfish insurance motive. That is, charity may represent an implicit social contract: if everyone pays a little when healthy, then an income transfer would be available to each payer if he or she were to become ill. Unlike private insurance, however, there is no quid pro quo obligation to pay a premium in order to receive the income transfer, and many may "ride free." Medicaid is a more formal social insurance where the financing comes from general tax revenues that are generally progressive. Some of those who become ill and qualify for Medicaid have supported the program through tax payments, but many have not. Again, it is not necessary to pay taxes to benefit from the program.

Charity and Medicaid essentially change the coinsurance rate on marginal health care to 0, but they both require some level of front-end private spending in the event of illness in order to qualify for payment of the residual by this third-party source. That is, charity usually pays for the difference between whatever the ill consumer can afford to pay out of her own resources and the cost of the medical services. This is also true of Medicaid, except that the amount that the consumer must pay to qualify is formalized in the "spend down" rules. This qualifying expenditure reduces disposable wealth (and income) substantially, but these programs rarely require the ill consumer to exhaust her resources entirely in order to become eligible. Instead, the ill are allowed to retain some level of income and assets to cover other expenses. In both cases, however, this implies a qualifying "deductible" at the time of illness that varies with the size of the consumer's income or wealth.

If the consumer chooses to remain uninsured and to rely on charity or Medicaid, she would face the following degenerative problem if ill:

$$\max U^s = U^s(M, Y) \qquad (8.2)$$

$$\text{s.t. } Y^o - G(Y^o) = Y \text{ and } M = M^c, \qquad (8.3)$$

where G is the amount of spending that must be incurred at endowed income level Y^o to reduce income sufficiently to qualify for charity or Medicaid, where M^c is the level of medical spending that charity or Medicaid would support, and where $dG/dY^o > 0$. If ill, the consumer would consume at $(M^c, Y^c) = [M^c, Y^o - G(Y^o)]$. If healthy, the consumer would face:

$$\max U^h = U^h(0, Y) \qquad (8.4)$$

$$\text{s.t. } Y^o = Y \qquad (8.5)$$

and consume at $(0, Y^o)$. Thus, the consumer's expected utility if uninsured and relying on charity is

$$EU_c = \pi U^s(M^c, Y^c) + (1 - \pi)U^h(0, Y^o). \qquad (8.6)$$

Consumers purchase insurance if

$$EU_i - EU_c = \pi U^s(M^i, Y^o - R) + (1 - \pi)U^h(0, Y^o - R)$$
$$- \pi U^s[M^c, Y^o - G(Y^o)]$$

$$- (1 - \pi)U^h (0, Y^o) > 0. \tag{8.7}$$

Rewriting this expression to show the potential gains from being insured in each of the health states, the consumer would purchase insurance if

$$EU_i - EU_c = \pi\{U^s(M^i, Y^o - R) - U^s[M^c, Y^o - G(Y^o)]\}$$
$$+ (1 - \pi)[U^h(0, Y^o - R) - U^h(0, Y^o)] > 0. \tag{8.8}$$

If medical expenditures are about the same under private insurance and charity or Medicaid, that is, if there is no difference between the level or quality of care received under charity or Medicaid compared with care financed through private insurance, then the decision to purchase insurance can be simplified to whether the following inequality holds:

$$\pi\{U^s(Y^o - R) - U^s[Y^o - G(Y^o)]\}$$
$$+ (1 - \pi)[U^h(Y^o - R) - U^h (Y^o)] > 0. \tag{8.9}$$

If the qualifying deductible under charity or Medicaid were similar in size to the insurance premium, that is, if $G(Y^o) \approx R$, then the consumer would benefit from remaining uninsured and relying on charity or Medicaid in the event of illness. This is because, even though uninsured, the consumer still has access to medical care if ill, but is able to avoid paying an insurance premium when healthy, a premium that may take a large share of a poor consumer's budget.

The presence of charity or Medicaid reduces the demand for private health insurance primarily because it removes the health consequences of being uninsured. This can readily be seen by comparing inequality (8.8) with inequality (5.2) that shows the gain from insurance when being uninsured implies that the needed medical care is forgone.

Empirical studies show that the presence of charity or Medicaid reduces the demand for private insurance. Cutler and Gruber (1996) and Dubay and Kenny (1997) have investigated the effect of extending Medicaid coverage (to include health care services for pregnant women) on the number of births financed by private insurance. These studies found that, by extending Medicaid coverage to women of child-bearing age, some consumers who would have otherwise been privately insured, dropped their insurance (see Holahan, 1997, for a review).

Johnson and Crystal (2000) use the Health and Retirement Survey to investigate why some Americans aged fifty-one to sixty-one at baseline were uninsured. The authors find that those without private health insurance were able to avoid significant out-of-pocket expenditures by using fewer health care services when not seriously ill, and then relying on Medicaid and charity when seriously ill. Being uninsured at midlife in the U.S., they conclude, does not eliminate access to health care, although it reduces routine care. Johnson and Crystal (2000) suggest that the recent increase in the uninsured among the employed is due to high premiums and the availability of charity and Medicaid care.

Some factors might increase the demand for private insurance. If the quality of care were greater under private insurance than under Medicaid, then this quality differential would represent an incentive to purchase private insurance. Or, if the premium for private insurance were reduced—for example, because of a government subsidy—then the incentive to purchase private insurance would be greater.

Using the 1977 National Medical Care Expenditure Survey (NMCES), Thomas (1994/5) evaluates whether reducing the price of insurance would result in more uninsured families becoming insured. Thomas finds that reducing the price of private insurance—for example, through a subsidy—would probably have only a small effect on increasing the demand for private insurance among the lowest-income groups. A more important impetus to purchasing private insurance, however, appears to be removing the availability of Medicaid. Thomas estimates that removing Medicaid would alone be sufficient to make it likely that even those in the lowest of income groups would purchase private health insurance (that is, improve the probability of purchase to greater than 0.5). Thomas's study suggests that it is indeed the availability of Medicaid that has enticed many of those who would otherwise be insured, to go without.

RISK

With conventional theory, risk and consumers' attitudes toward risk play a central role in explaining the demand for health insurance. With the new theory, risk and risk attitudes play only a minor role. Moreover, whereas risk preferences would generally lead consumers to purchase insurance under the conventional theory, under the new theory, they would most likely lead consumers to do without.

Risk and the Very Poor

If safety nets, such as charity care or Medicaid (or for that matter, programs like food stamps and public housing that provide other goods and services to the poor), were not available, the consumer on the very low end of the income distribution would have a more difficult choice. The choice would be between (1) purchasing health insurance and gaining access to medical care in the event of illness, or (2) not purchasing insurance and taking the chance of becoming ill without access to medical care, but being able to use the dollars saved from not paying the premium to buy other basic commodities—food, shelter, clothing—that are also necessary to sustain life.

In Chapter 5, it was suggested that much of the demand for health insurance is motivated by a demand for access to those expensive procedures that would otherwise be unaffordable, even for those at the median of the income distribution. For those at the very low end of that distribution, more, if not most, of medical care would otherwise be unaffordable. The crucial difference is that, for those around the median of the income distribution, the premium payment represents a loss of income that would be used for largely discretionary purchases. For those at the low end of the distribution (and assuming no safety nets), the premium payment represents a loss of income that would otherwise be used to purchase necessities like food, shelter, and clothing. Thus, at the low end of the income distribution, the utility cost of purchasing health insurance is greater vis-à-vis the value of the other goods and services forgone, compared to those at the middle range of the distribution. Forgoing these necessities (in the nontechnical sense of the word) could have consequences for health similar to those of forgoing medical care when ill.

Inequality (5.2), which is repeated here, represents the formal modeling of this decision when private insurance pays off by reducing the price of medical care to 0:

$$EU_i - EU_u = \pi\{U^s[M^i, Y^o - \pi M^i] - U^s(0, Y^o)\}$$
$$+ (1 - \pi) \{U^h[0, Y^o - \pi M^i] - U^h(0, Y^o)\} > 0. \quad (5.2)$$

If this inequality is positive, then purchasing insurance increases expected utility, compared with being uninsured. If this equation represents the decision of consumers at the very lowest end of the income distribution, the choice is between (1) being insured and incurring a certain loss of πM^i dollars worth of very valuable goods and services, or (2) being uninsured and facing an uncertain loss of M^i worth of medical care, with a probability of π. In the extreme, if forgoing medical care when ill or making a premium payment would both result in mortality, then the consumer at the low end of the income distribution would be better off taking his chances with illness and remaining uninsured, rather than choosing sure death from starvation and exposure.[1] Thus, for survival considerations, the consumer would prefer the risk of death over certain death, and remain uninsured. While this choice is rare for consumers living in developed countries, it may fairly represent the typical choice for consumers living in less developed countries and explain why so little insurance is purchased there.

Even if the health consequences of paying the premium were not as dire as those of forgoing medical care if seriously ill, an indigent consumer might still opt to remain uninsured. That is, even if unrelated to health, the expected utility loss from paying the premium could still be so great that it would be better to be uninsured. If the income and health consequences of becoming insured canceled each other out so that the consumer is indifferent to purchasing insurance or being uninsured—that is, if the left-hand side (LHS) of inequality (5.2) equaled 0—then other factors might enter the decision.

Digression on Gambling and Insurance

One of those factors is risk. However, to understand how risk preferences enter the insurance decision, a digression is necessary. So far in this book, I have followed a traditional model where utility depends on medical care and disposable income, and where different utility functions are specified for each health state, ill or healthy. Underlying this model is the assumption that the demand for medical care is derived from preferences for health, H, and income, Y,

$$U = U(H, Y), \qquad (8.10)$$

and that the production of health depends on medical care,

$$H = H(M), \qquad (8.11)$$

assuming that $dH/dM > 0$, $\partial U/\partial H > 0$, and $\partial U/\partial Y > 0$. Because contingent-claims health insurance is conventionally modeled so that the same medical care is received both with and without insurance, the choice to insure or not is conventionally modeled as a comparison of the income consequences of the two alternatives. If the (expected) income differences are eliminated by assuming actuarially fair insurance, then the decision appears to depend solely on the shape of utility function, and this has been interpreted as the sole source of a consumer's preferences for risk. That is, the effect of risk on the consumer's utility is modeled only indirectly through the relationship between income and utility.

Conventionally, the von Neumann–Morgenstern (vNM) utility function is used to model choice under uncertainty. As was suggested in Chapter 2, this function confounds preferences for risk with preferences for income, and lacks the intuitive appeal of the Bernoulli utility function, which describes the relationship between certain income and utility, rather than lotteries and utility. A Bernoulli utility function that shows diminishing marginal utility of income would result in greater expected utility if fair insurance were purchased, but because of the way that the choice between insurance and no insurance is conventionally specified, it appears as if the consumer is choosing insurance because he prefers certainty to uncertainty. Hence, utility functions that exhibit diminishing marginal utility of income are conventionally referred to as "risk averse" utility functions.

In conventional economic theory, risk preferences derive only from the shape of the utility function. Observed choices involving risk and certainty, therefore, imply the shape of the consumer's utility function. For example, the purchase of fair insurance would imply that the consumer has a concave function, and the purchase of a fair lottery would imply a convex function (see Figure 2.2). Because of this theory, economists have puzzled over why some consumers could purchase insurance and gamble at the same time, a seemingly irrational behavior.[2] Various solutions for this puzzle have been suggested. For example, Friedman and Savage (1948) postulated that while the utility function is concave over most of its range, over some portion, it may be convex, prompting the purchase of a lottery. None of these explanations, however, has gained general acceptance.

The theory presented here would fix the Bernoulli utility function as concave in income because, as argued in Chapter 2, diminishing marginal utility of income is such a fundamental and intuitively unassailable concept. The Bernoulli utility function alone would imply specific behavior for economic problems involving uncertainty. Specifically, the Bernoulli utility function is all that is necessary to explain the purchase of a fair insurance contract in a quid pro quo specification. For example, it would predict that a consumer would pay $100 for a contract that provided a $200 payoff in the event that the consumer became ill with a 0.5 probability and incurred a $1000 loss of income.

On the other hand, a Bernoulli utility function would predict that a consumer would *not* pay $100 for a contract that provided a $200 payoff in the event that the consumer's flip of a fair coin turned up heads and no exogenous loss of income occurred. There is no difference between these two contracts: both the insurance and gambling contracts represent paying $100 for a 0.5 probability of winning $200. The only difference between these two scenarios is a change in the reference point on the Bernoulli utility function from which the payoff is received. Both contracts have exactly the same amount of risk associated with them. However, if the consumer were maximizing expected utility, given a Bernoulli utility function, he would purchase insurance and not make the gamble.

The fair insurance and gambling problems are illustrated generally in Figure 8.1. Panel A of Figure 8.1 shows that the consumer is worse off making a fair wager of $(Y_1 - Y_0)$ for a π probability of winning $(Y_2 - Y_1)$. The gamble is fair because the wager equals the expected winnings: $(Y_1 - Y_0) = -\pi(Y_2 - Y_1)$. The probability of winning, π, is determined, for example, by the probability that a certain number will be chosen in a lottery, or by the probability that a certain number will face upwards after a roll of a die, but these events in themselves do not alter the consumer's reference income level. Thus, the gambler wagers $(Y_1 - Y_0)$ from Y_0 in exchange for a π probability to gain $(Y_2 - Y_1)$ from Y_1, the consumer's income level after the wager is paid. In an attempt to streamline the notation, the operator Δ is introduced, so that, ΔU indicates the change in utility due to a gain or loss of disposable income. So, the expected change in utility, $E\Delta U$, due to the gamble compared with no gamble can be written

$$E\Delta U_g = \Delta U[(Y_1 - Y_0)|_{Y_0}] + \pi \Delta U[(Y_2 - Y_1)|_{Y_1}] < 0. \qquad (8.12)$$

Because the loss of utility from $U(Y_0)$ to $U(Y_1)$ exceeds the expected gain from $U(Y_1)$ to $U(Y_2)$ with a probability of π, this wager results in a net expected utility loss as illustrated in Panel A of Figure 8.1, so the consumer is better off not making the wager.

In contrast, Panel B of Figure 8.1 shows the consumer is better off purchasing an insurance contract costing $(Y_1 - Y_0)$ for a π probability of receiving $(Y_1 - Y_2)$. Again assume the contract is fair, such that $(Y_1 - Y_0) = -\pi(Y_2 - Y_1)$. The probability of winning (π) with this contract, however, is the exogenously determined probability of, say, becoming ill or disabled, which is associated with an exogenous reduction in the consumer's reference income level to Y_3. Thus, the purchaser of this contract pays $(Y_1 - Y_0)$ from income level Y_0 and expects to gain $(Y_2 - Y_1)$ from income level Y_3 with a probability of π. If insurance is fair, the expected change in utility from this insurance contract is

$$E\Delta U_i = \Delta U[(Y_1 - Y_0)|_{Y_0}] + \pi \Delta U[(Y_2 - Y_1)|_{Y_3}] > 0. \qquad (8.13)$$

That is, the loss of utility from paying the premium, from $U(Y_0)$ to $U(Y_1)$, is smaller than the expected gain in utility from obtaining additional income equal to $(Y_2 - Y_1)$ from income level Y_3 with a probability of π. Therefore, the consumer experiences a net gain in utility by purchasing the insurance contract.

Figure 8.1 shows that the gamble and the purchase of insurance are exactly the same quid pro quo contract: the payment of a certain amount in exchange for a claim on a larger amount if certain conditions prevail. Figure 8.1 shows that the only difference between gambling and insurance is the event that triggers the payoff. In gambling, the event does not entail a change in income, but with insurance it does. In both cases, however, the event and any change in income associated with the event are completely separate from the contract itself. This is different from the standard gamble specification of insurance, where the

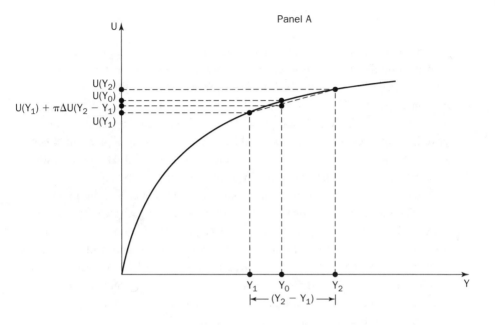

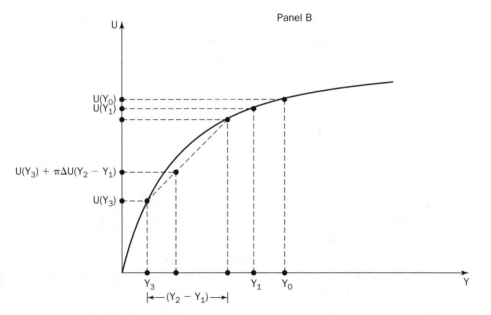

Figure 8.1 Gambling and Insurance Compared.

change in reference income (the loss) appears to be integrated into the insurance contract.

The analysis of insurance presented here uses a slightly different specification than the one first presented in Chapter 3 and used throughout the rest of this book. In previous specifications, it was recognized that when the consumer with insurance becomes ill, he has both paid the premium and received the premium back as part of the payoff. Because these two factors cancel themselves, the analysis of insurance was previously specified in net terms as paying a premium when healthy in exchange for a claim on an income transfer when ill. The above insurance and gambling models can be readily converted into such a specification.

In the above model, the consumer who purchases insurance loses his premium $(Y_1 - Y_0)$ only in the event that he is healthy. If the consumer is ill, his premium, $(Y_1 - Y_0) = -\pi(Y_2 - Y_1)$, is actually paid back as part of the payoff $(Y_2 - Y_1)$. (Or, equivalently, a portion of the payoff represents his premium contribution.) Thus, the consumer is expected to pay a premium, $-\pi(Y_2 - Y_1)$, only when healthy, and has an expected premium of $-(1 - \pi)\pi(Y_2 - Y_1)$. Similarly, the payoff, $(Y_2 - Y_1)$, net of the premium, $-\pi(Y_2 - Y_1)$, leaves $(1 - \pi)(Y_2 - Y_1)$ in income transfers. Because these transfers are made only when ill, the expected income transfer is $\pi(1 - \pi)(Y_2 - Y_1)$. The expected income transfer, $\pi(1 - \pi) \times (Y_2 - Y_1)$, and the expected premium, $-(1 - \pi)\pi(Y_2 - Y_1)$, are exactly the same, so the insurance is still fair. Inequality (8.13) can be rewritten as

$$EΔU_i = ΔU[-\pi(Y_2 - Y_1)|_{Y_0}] + \pi ΔU[(Y_2 - Y_1)|_{Y_3}]$$
$$= (1 - \pi)ΔU[-\pi(Y_2 - Y_1)|_{Y_0}] + \pi ΔU[-\pi(Y_2 - Y_1)|_{Y_0}] \quad (8.14)$$
$$+ \pi ΔU\{[(1 - \pi)(Y_2 - Y_1) + \pi(Y_2 - Y_1)]|_{Y_3}\} > 0.$$

So, removing the canceled premium payment when ill results in

$$EΔU_i = (1 - \pi)ΔU[-\pi(Y_2 - Y_1)|_{Y_0}]$$
$$+ \pi ΔU[(1-\pi)(Y_2 - Y_1)|_{Y_3}] > 0. \quad (8.15)$$

With this interpretation, the expected utility lost from the premium payment if healthy, $(1 - \pi)ΔU[-\pi(Y_2 - Y_1)|_{Y_0}]$, is less than the expected gain from the income transfer if ill, $\pi ΔU[(1-\pi)(Y_2 - Y_1)|_{Y_3}]$, resulting in a net expected utility gain from insurance. This is the same decision rule as inequality (8.13), only specified so as to omit the redundant portion of the premium payment that is both paid and received when ill.

Similarly, a gambler loses his wager, $(Y_1 - Y_0)$, only when a certain number does not appears on a die. When that number appears with a probability of π, he wins and is paid an amount that represents his wager plus the wager(s) of the losing gambler(s), that is, $(Y_2 - Y_1)$. The wager is fair, so $(Y_1 - Y_0) = -\pi(Y_2 - Y_1)$. Therefore, inequality (8.12) can also be rewritten as

$$E\Delta U_g = \Delta U[-\pi(Y_2 - Y_1)|_{Y_0}] + \pi\Delta U[(Y_2 - Y_1)|_{Y_1}] < 0, \qquad (8.16)$$

or eliminating the portion of the wager that is paid and received back when he wins,

$$E\Delta U_g = (1 - \pi)\,\Delta U[-\pi(Y_2 - Y_1)|_{Y_0}]$$
$$+ \pi\Delta U[(1 - \pi)(Y_2 - Y_1)|_{Y_1}] < 0. \qquad (8.17)$$

With this net gain interpretation, the expected loss in utility if the wager is lost, $(1 - \pi)\,\Delta U[-\pi(Y_2 - Y_1)|_{Y_0}]$, is greater than the expected gain in utility from the net winnings if the consumer wins, $\pi\Delta U[(1 - \pi)(Y_2 - Y_1)|_{Y_1}]$, resulting in a net expected utility loss from the gamble.

Before leaving this section, it should be noted that health insurance is fair because the premium equals the expected income payoff, not because the premium equals the expected spending on medical care. With insurance that pays off by reducing price to 0, fair insurance is often defined as the latter equality. By defining fair insurance as equating the premium to expected medical spending, however, conventional theory has misled analysts into linking the spending decision too closely to the insurance contract itself. In part because of this link, it has not been recognized that the income payoff may generate additional medical care spending compared to being uninsured, and that the payoff and spending could be different for that reason.

This simple model demonstrates that the medical spending is really not part of the insurance contract. It only functions to move the consumer to a different point on her Bernoulli utility function for disposable income. Any payoff-triggering event that also moves the consumer to a lower-income level would potentially make an insurance contract valuable. Indeed, comparing a fair insurance contract to the corresponding fair gamble, the defining characteristic of insurance is that the contract is set in a context where the event that triggers the payoff also moves the consumer to a lower point on her Bernoulli utility function. If such a movement does not occur, then the contract is a gamble.

Separating Risk Preferences from the Bernoulli Utility Function

This analysis suggests that it is not risk that consumers are averse to, but rather a loss of income. If a naturally occurring event (that is beyond the consumer's control) could reduce a consumer's income, he may desire to purchase an insurance contract as a hedge against this loss of income, with a payoff that is triggered by the same event. The consumer may have preferences regarding the level of uncertainty associated with the event, but these risk preferences are not primarily what motivates the consumer to purchase insurance. Indeed, it is the uncertainty with which the event occurs that makes possible the purchase of an insurance contract to hedge against the loss. For example, if an event that is associated with a $1,000 loss of income occurs with a probability of 1, the consumer would not be able to gain from paying $1,000 for a fair contract that paid off with $1,000 when the same event occurred. It is only if the event is uncertain that the purchase of an insurance contract will improve the consumer's welfare given the Bernoulli utility function.

Consumers may have preferences regarding risk that are independent of the shape of the Bernoulli utility function. In some cases, consumers may prefer risk. These preferences for risk may even be strong enough to override the expected utility maximizing behavior implied by the concave Bernoulli utility function, and motivate the consumer to either not purchase a fair insurance contract or to purchase a fair lottery ticket. Or, the consumer may find some risks to be desirable whereas others are not, depending on the consumer's preferences. For example, whereas the consumer might be unwilling to face the (exogenous) risk of a $20,000 hospital bill without insurance, he may actually desire to pay $5 to purchase a fair lottery ticket where the probability of winning is small but the payoff is very large. This theory implies that a consumer chooses to gamble not because of the shape of his utility function, but in spite of it.[3]

This theory represents a departure from conventional theory in a number of ways. It differs from both expected utility theory and prospect theory in that it does not rely on switching from concave to convex utility (value) functions to explain behavior. Within the vNM utility function paradigm, it challenges the expected utility theorem that "proves" that for all consumers, the utility of an uncertain lottery is the same as the probability-weighted utilities derived from the certain payoffs of the same lottery. And, by separating risk preferences from the shape of the consumer's utility function, the new theory accommodates a richer array of behavioral responses—regret, framing and "loss aversion," mental accounting and the isolation of separate risks, disappointment, gambling itself, and so on—than is possible under the deterministic and normative conventional expected utility theory.

It is useful to identify a terminology that distinguishes between the behavior that derives from maximizing expected Bernoulli utility of certain income, and the behavior that derives from preferences regarding risk. I will refer to the former as the *maximization of expected Bernoulli utility* (MEBU) motive, and to the latter as the *second-order risk preference* (SORP) motive. For example, assuming that medical care expenditures with and without insurance are the same, the purchase of fair health insurance is consistent with the MEBU motive if a Bernoulli utility function is assumed. The preference for an uncertain loss over certain loss of the same expected magnitude (that is, loss aversion), however, is a manifestation of the SORP motive, as is the observation that not only do consumers make fair wagers, but they often make wagers that favor the house.

The view that risk preferences originate independently of the MEBU motivation and the shape of the consumer's utility function is consistent with the intuition that gambling—especially if it is habitual and involves wagers of large sums of money relative to income or wealth—is an "irrational" act. That is, it is a behavior that someone who is attempting to maximize his expected utility from income would not normally do. This view is consistent with the studies that show that gambling produces physiological changes in the individual that are similar to those associated with euphoria-inducing drugs (Breiter et al., 2001), and that the same pharmaceutical products used to treat drug addictions can also be used to "treat" habitual gambling (Kim et al., 2001). Separating risk preferences from the shape of the utility function also resolves the behavioral anomaly identified by Rabin (2000) and Rabin and Thaler (2001), referred to in Chapter 4. And it explains why society has created voluntary associations such as Gamblers Anonymous for habitual gamblers, but no similar associations for those who habitually purchase insurance.

Accordingly, the consumer's utility function might be modeled as:

$$U = U(H, Y, \Phi) \tag{8.18}$$

where H is health, Y is disposable income, and Φ is a vector of risk-related characteristics, which may include the probability of illness, π, among other things. For the conventional case where medical care expenditures are assumed to be the same with or without contingent-claims insurance, the expected utility leger might be influenced independently by a consumer's second-order risk preferences. Similarly, for the case of those at the low end of the income distribution where the health care is often unaffordable, the decision to purchase insurance would weigh the expected gain from health care (available only with insurance) against the premium cost. Given these gains and costs, less insurance would be sold to those who prefer risk, other things held constant.

In summary, risk preferences may enter the decision to purchase insurance, but they probably have only a secondary influence. The primary motivation to purchase insurance is derived from the utility gained from income transfers when ill.

Some of these income transfers permit the purchase of additional medical care when ill and some permit the purchase of additional consumer commodities when ill and when the reference level of disposable income has shifted on the Bernoulli utility function because of the purchase of some medical care. The important point for this section is, however, that the purchase of insurance probably has little to do with preferences for risk. It is only when the expected utility gain from the income transfers when ill approximates the expected utility loss from paying the premium when healthy that risk preferences may enter the insurance choice in a decisive way. Sometimes these second-order risk preferences may reinforce the motivation to purchase insurance, and sometimes they may detract from it. Thus, another possible explanation for the nonpurchase of insurance is a possible independent preference for risk.

LOADING FEES AND PREMIUMS

Loading fees cover the administrative costs of supplying insurance, specifically, the costs of marketing, underwriting, management, advertising, and claims processing. They may include the normal profits required to raise capital, and economic profits as well. Insurers add loading fees to the expected payoff to arrive at a total premium. In conventional theory, the loading fee portion of the premium is considered the "price" of insurance because it represents the cost of transferring the risk of the medical expenditures from the individual consumer to the insurer. That is, with a conventionally modeled fair contingent-claims policy where the premium equals expected medical care expenditures, the consumer expects to incur the same costs for medical care with or without insurance. Therefore, the price of insurance is the portion of the premium over and above the payment for the expected medical care expenditures (Phelps, 1997).

Under the new theory, the price of insurance is the entire premium. This is because, under this quid pro quo perspective, the premium must be paid in order to have a claim on an uncertain payoff. The payoff may equal the same level of spending on medical care that would have occurred if not insured, but it is likely that the payoff will generate additional expenditures compared with being uninsured. For example, the payoff may represent income sufficient to obtain an expensive transplant procedure that the consumer would not be able to afford without insurance. Therefore, there is no presumption that expected medical expenditures without insurance would be the same as the nonloading-fee portion of the insurance premium.

If it is assumed that the consumer does not derive direct benefit from the loading fees, increases in the loading-fee portion of the insurance premium might reduce the quantity of health insurance demanded. Even though the consumer derives direct benefit from the income payoff, increases in the payoff can also inhibit the consumer from purchasing insurance. For example, long-term care is expensive at about $50,000 per year in a nursing facility. At $50,000 per year, the expected nursing facility expenditures would make the portion of a long-term care insurance premium that covers the expected income payoff so large that many consumers would not be able to afford to purchase price-payoff long-term care insurance. As a result, increases in the expected expenditure portion of the premium could also increase the price of insurance so much that insurance would not be purchased.

The loading fees cover the transactions costs of the insurance contract, and are added to the expected payoff in determining the total premium. In contingent-claims contracts, these fees cover the standard administrative costs—claims processing, marketing, underwriting, and normal profits—but in addition they would include the costs of employing a medical staff to verify that the insured consumer actually has the illness he claims to have and of employing a legal staff to write the complex contingent-claims contracts. Thus, under a contingent-claims contract, these extra administrative costs may inhibit the purchase of insurance.

A price-payoff contract largely eliminates these additional medical and legal administrative costs, and with no necessary increase in expected payoffs. For example, insurance policies could be designed so that the payoffs under a contingent-claims policy were exactly the same as the payoffs under a price-payoff contract with a 0% coinsurance rate (see Figure 3.1 for the case where $c > 0$). If the payoffs are the same, the expected payoffs would also be the same for both contracts, but the loading-fee costs would be lower with the price-payoff contract because it would no longer be necessary to hire the additional clinical and legal staff. Thus, by using price-payoff contracts instead of contingent-claims contracts, the insurer can reduce the premium but keep the same payoff. The additional cost of using price-payoff insurance, however, is represented by the price distortion that generates the inefficient portion of moral hazard.[4] This raises the question of whether consumers actually respond to inefficient moral hazard by purchasing less insurance.

PRICE-RELATED MORAL HAZARD

Under conventional theory, all of moral hazard is deemed to be a price effect, and therefore, a welfare loss to anyone who purchases insurance. If conventional theory were correct, moral hazard would reduce the value of health insurance to such an extent that unsubsidized insurance would not be purchased. The fact that it is purchased may still suggest that conventional theory is correct if consumers simply do not recognize and respond to the deleterious effects of inefficient moral hazard.

Under the new theory, most of moral hazard represents an intentional response by those who purchase insurance to obtain an increase in income if ill. Nevertheless, a portion of moral hazard is inefficient. These opportunistic purchases have costs that exceed their value, and thus represent premium payments that are not matched by expected benefits. If the inefficient portion of moral hazard is sufficiently large, it would discourage consumers from purchasing insurance, unless consumers do not respond to the presence of inefficient moral hazard. Therefore, the same question—whether consumers respond to the presence of inefficient moral hazard—is important in understanding the purchase of insurance under both theories.

One test for determining the answer to this question is to observe the types of services that are covered by insurance. That is, if one can identify a type of service that inefficient moral hazard would likely dominate, but insurance coverage for that service is still purchased, then it could be the case that inefficient moral hazard exists with health insurance but consumers simply do not respond to it.

Dental insurance exists and is purchased, even though we would expect inefficient moral hazard to dominate insurance for this service. This is because dental care is routinely consumed by both the ill and the healthy, and much of it is cosmetic and largely obtained at the discretion of the individual consumer. However, dental insurance is rarely purchased outside of an employee's compensation package, suggesting that the tax subsidy of employee insurance premiums may play a role in its existence.

On the other hand, separate insurance does not now exist for many forms of complementary and alternative medicine, such as aromatherapy, massage therapy, naturopathy, and acupuncture. Many of these alternative treatment modalities could be beneficial to consumers regardless of their health status, and therefore represent services where inefficient moral hazard would likely dominate if insurance existed. That consumers do not now purchase separate insurance for, say, massage therapy suggests that consumers can recognize and do respond to inefficient moral hazard when it exists. The general lack of separate insurance coverage for these alternative treatment modalities suggests that if inefficient moral hazard truly dominated traditional health insurance, as conventional theory suggests it does, it too would not be widely purchased.

Indeed, if the conventional theory were correct that all consumers responded to health insurance as if it were a movement along their observed (uninsured) demand curve, and that all moral hazard was inefficient, health insurance would probably not exist at all. Health insurance would not exist for exactly the same reasons that no one now purchases price-payoff insurance for food or clothing, and that food or clothing insurance does not exist. What makes health insurance viable is the fact that the services that it covers are to a large extent only desired by the ill. Thus, not everyone responds to the price reduction and the price reduction can be used to transfer income from the healthy to the ill. Health insurance, therefore, is viable precisely because so little of health care is consumed by the healthy and because so little of moral hazard is an opportunistic response by the healthy to price.

ADVERSE SELECTION

If an insurance plan experiences adverse selection, it implies that the plan has a disproportionate number of sickly—that is, higher risk—enrollees. If so, the premium would need to reflect the higher-than-average medical expenditures of these consumers, making insurance policies with adverse selection relatively unattractive to the consumer with average health risk. Adverse selection has traditionally been linked to an information asymmetry: the purchaser of insurance knows more about her health status than does the insurer. As a consequence, the insurer is not able to charge risk-adjusted premiums to its various customers.

Under conventional insurance models, the distinction between adverse selection and moral hazard is relatively clean. Moral hazard is any increase in health care consumption that occurs because of becoming insured. Adverse selection is represented by those consumers who purchase more health care because their probability of becoming ill is greater than average. Under the new model, however, overlap occurs. As suggested in Chapter 3, some behavior that has traditionally been viewed as moral hazard is actually a selection demand effect represented by those whose health status makes attractive both the purchase of insurance and the subsequent purchase of additional health care that the uninsured consumer would not purchase. In the example already given, a consumer with myopia might purchase a 0% coinsurance policy because he knows that only, say, 10% of the population has myopia. Therefore, he would receive a 90% discount on the designer prescription sunglasses (assuming that all those with myopia purchased the sunglasses), which he would purchase with insurance, but not without. This behavioral change stems from insuring a consumer with a preexisting condition, which is a selection story. Under the conventional theory, the discount would appear to be 100% and the behavior would appear to be moral hazard, but under the new theory, it is recognized that the discount is actually only 90% and that the behavior is a selection demand effect.

Because the consumer would not have purchased these sunglasses without insurance, this behavior still represents a welfare loss. This loss, however, is attributed to insurers who sell insurance to consumers with above average risk, rather than moral hazard, which represents the consumer of average health risk who consumes more health care once insured. Still, if these losses are sufficiently large, they may inhibit the consumer from purchasing insurance.

PHYSICIAN-INDUCED DEMAND

So far, the role of the physician has been characterized as generally beneficial. In Chapter 3, it was noted that under price-payoff insurance, the insured consumer's physician implicitly verifies that the insured consumer is ill, thereby reducing fraud-monitoring costs that a contingent-claims insurer would need to incur. It was also noted that the physician reduces the degree of substitutability between medical care and other goods and services by restricting medical care to those insured who are ill. As a result, an insured traveler cannot substitute a night's stay in a hospital for a night's stay in a hotel at his discretion.

As is well known, however, physicians are not merely benign agents of their patients, but have their own objectives as well. Because of an asymmetry of information, physicians can prescribe services when they are not needed, thus increasing their incomes and health care costs. Physicians may also prescribe services when they are not needed because of their lack of information or understanding about which type of care is effective. Thus, the demand for insurance could be influenced by premiums that are higher than necessary because they reflect ineffective health care expenditures, thus reducing the quantity of insurance purchased.

CONCLUSIONS

A number of factors may explain why private health insurance is sometimes not purchased. Most important of these is the availability of alternative vehicles—charity and Medicaid—for accessing expensive medical care when ill. Another is preferences for risk, but this factor seems to be of secondary importance. Risk preferences would be important in the extreme case where no safety nets exist and the payment of an actuarially fair premium would reduce consumption to such an extent as to place the consumer's health in jeopardy. While a choice like this between the risk of death without insurance and certain death with insurance may be rare for consumers in the U.S. and other developed countries, it may fairly characterize the general situation facing most consumers in poor countries and explain why so little health insurance is purchased there.

Conventional insurance theory suggests that insurance is purchased because of a preference for certain losses. In Chapter 4, it was shown that the conventional model is fundamentally mis-specified and that risk preferences have almost nothing to do with the demand for insurance because it has repeatedly been documented that consumers tend to prefer a risk of loss to an actuarially equivalent certain loss. In the present chapter, a modification of expected utility theory was proposed suggesting that if risk preferences enter the insurance choice in a decisive way, they would probably serve to override the natural preference for an income transfer when ill, explaining why consumers might not purchase insurance, rather than why they do.

In Chapter 9, the public policies regarding insurance are reexamined in light of the new theory. Because policy has hitherto been based on the wrong theory, a large portion of public policy has been either ineffective or directed at solving problems that largely do not exist. Moreover, some of the problems that do exist have not been properly recognized or appreciated because of conventional theory.

NOTES

1. In his song, "Like a Rolling Stone," Bob Dylan expresses the intuition behind this choice far more clearly than I have:

"When ya ain't got nothin', ya ain't got nothin' to lose."

2. The discussion in this section assumes fair insurance and fair gambles. Of course, it could be rational to simultaneously purchase fair insurance and a gamble with favorable odds. For example, wagering $100 to win $300 in the event of a "heads" appearing on a toss of a fair coin would have the potential to be rational. National lotteries often present favorable odds if the weekly prize has not been claimed for weeks and the expected payoff (taking into account the possibility of multiple winners) from the accumulated prizes exceeds the cost of a lottery ticket.

3. Again, it must be kept in mind that this discussion is about fair wagers and fair insurance.

4. It is interesting to speculate whether insurers adopted price-payoff contracts rather than contingent-claims contracts to reduce the visible transactions costs, replacing them with the less visible welfare cost from inefficient moral hazard.

9 | POLICY IMPLICATIONS

COST CONTAINMENT

Health policy in the U.S. has been greatly influenced by conventional health insurance theory. There is, perhaps, no better example of this than the impact of Pauly's (1968) model of moral hazard on the problem of high and growing health care expenditures.

The growth of U.S. health care expenditures became an issue in the 1970s and 1980s, as the growth of medical expenditures outpaced the growth of the U.S. economy. As a result, U.S. health care expenditures as a percentage of gross domestic product (GDP) grew until by the end of the century (1998) they reached 12.8% (Organisation for Economic Co-operation and Development [OECD, 2001]). At this level, the spending share in the U.S. far exceeded the spending share in any other developed country (OECD, 2001).[1]

Different actors in the economy saw this growth as a problem for different reasons. Because most of the health care expenditures appeared to be borne by firms in the form of fringe benefit payments to employees, U.S. employers saw this phenomenon as affecting their competitiveness on world markets. Because the growth in health care costs sometimes outstripped the growth in worker productivity, employees sometimes saw the premium growth as canceling take-home wage increases and increases in living standards (at least for those who remained healthy). Federal and state governments saw rising health care costs as a problem because they were required—through Medicare and Medicaid—to fund an increasingly larger health care bill.

Economists generally viewed this growth in health care costs as an inefficiency caused by insurance. That is, because the secular growth in health care expenditures coincided with a secular growth in the percentage of households who were insured, it was apparent that some causal link existed between these two phenomena (Newhouse, 1981). Pauly's (1968) analysis provided a readily accessible understanding of the welfare implications of this new spending. Because of the influence of Pauly's analysis, most economists adopted the view that the growth of health expenditures was largely a problem of too much care being consumed at the margin. For example, Enthoven (1980), whose plan for a managed health care system was directed largely at curbing this excessive consumption, characterized the additional health care spending in the U.S. as "flat of the curve" medicine (Enthoven, 1980, pp. 45–51). That is, the additional expenditures represented that portion of the health production function where greater health care resulted in very little, if any, additional health, an argument that was consistent with Pauly's analysis.

As a result of conventional theory, policies directed at reducing health care costs were mainly intended to reduce health care consumption at the margin. The alternative policy of containing costs by reducing the high and rising health care prices was, at best, only of secondary interest. Indeed, because of the conventional theory, some observers saw higher health care prices as beneficial because they canceled at least some portion of the moral hazard that was generated by the insurance-related price reduction (Pauly, 1995).

Demand-side policies were invoked first. Coinsurance rates and deductibles were imposed on health insurance contracts that had traditionally been free fee-for-service plans. Supply-side policies were imposed later. Supply-side policies included: (1) pre-admission screening, mandatory second opinions, concurrent review of services provided to the hospitalized, third-party management of expensive cases, discharge planning, denial of coverage for certain services, and other forms of utilization control, (2) capitated payments, prospective payments, bundled payments, and other payment schemes that rewarded providers for reducing health care consumption, and (3) selection of providers on the basis of practice style. These practices, along with the use of preferred provider arrangements (which were mainly directed at reducing provider fees), constituted what has come to be known as managed care. These policies are analyzed in light of the new theory in the next two sections.

COST SHARING

Compared with traditional insurance policies that pay for all health care expenditures—the type of insurance that was used in the 1950s, 1960s, and 1970s—most insurance policies today require that the beneficiary pay for a portion the health care bill and share in the insurer's costs. Cost sharing was implemented by health insurers with the intent of controlling and reducing their health care expenditures. It found a larger justification in the welfare loss that was associated with moral hazard by conventional health insurance theory.

The major forms of cost sharing that have been implemented by U.S. insurers are coinsurance rates and deductibles. Coinsurance rates usually apply to initial expenditures until a certain level of out-of-pocket spending has been incurred by the enrollee, then any additional spending is free. Deductibles have the same general form, except that the initial rate of cost sharing is 100%. Thus, deductibles differ from coinsurance rates only by degree. Because of this, I focus on the analysis of coinsurance rates. The analysis of deductibles is "left to the reader as an exercise."

Coinsurance and Moral Hazard

As discussed in Chapter 2 and elsewhere, a number of studies have evaluated the welfare implications of raising the coinsurance rate, based on conventional theory. Feldstein (1973) suggested that raising the coinsurance rate to 66% would improve welfare. Feldman and Dowd (1991) suggested that raising the coinsurance rate essentially to the 95% coinsurance plan from the RAND HIE (that is, a 95% coinsurance rate with a $1,000 maximum on out-of-pocket spending before a 0% coinsurance rate was applied to all subsequent expenditures, in mid-1970s dollars) would also improve welfare. Manning and Marquis (1996) suggested that the optimal coinsurance rate approaches 50%, with no maximum on out-of-pocket spending. These prescriptions were all based on the theory that the benefit of insurance derives only from its ability to avoid risk and that all of moral hazard represents an efficiency loss.[2] Thus, according to conventional theory, a change from free fee-for-service coverage to coinsurance coverage would not only reduce U.S. health expenditures, but it would increase welfare at the same time.

As should be clear by now, the new theory suggests instead that the price reduction mainly acts to transfer income from the healthy to the ill, and as a result of this income transfer, consumers purchase more health care and other goods and services. The portion of moral hazard that is caused by the income transfers is efficient because its value exceeds its costs. This efficient moral hazard appears to represent most—perhaps, 70%—of moral hazard. Even more importantly, it is likely to dominate welfare calculations because it appears to have a mortality-reduction benefit that alone is worth a multiple of its costs. Thus, the new theory suggests that imposing or raising coinsurance rates might reduce health care spending, but because there is no mechanism within coinsurance rates themselves that would selectively focus on the inefficient care, there is also no assurance that imposing coinsurance rates would necessarily result in a welfare gain.

Figure 9.1 illustrates the result that imposing coinsurance on free fee-for-service insurance reduces both efficient and inefficient moral hazard. Originally, the uninsured consumer faces a price of 1 and if ill consumes M^u. The consumer who has purchased insurance with a 0% coinsurance rate consumes $M^{i,c=0}$ if ill. Of the additional health care consumed, $(M^{i,c=0} - M^u)$, income transfers from the healthy account for $(M^{n,c=0} - M^u)$ in additional care, and the consumer's purchasing a lower price generates $(M^{i,c=0} - M^{n,c=0})$. If this consumer were required instead to purchase insurance with a 50% coinsurance rate, he would consume $M^{i,c=0.5}$ if ill. Of this $(M^{i,c=0.5} - M^u)$ increase, income transfers from the healthy generate $(M^{n,c=0.5} - M^u)$ in additional care, and the consumer's purchasing a

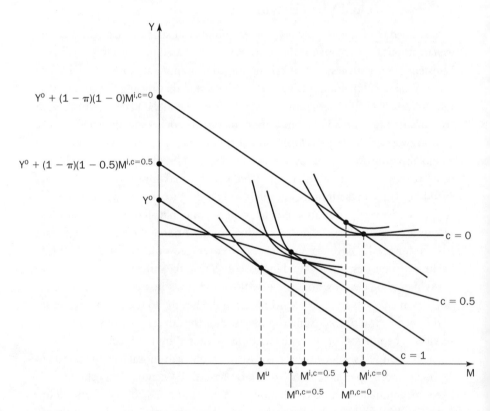

Figure 9.1 Imposing a 0.5 Coinsurance Rate on Insurance That Originally Had a Zero Coinsurance Rate.

lower price generates ($M^{i,c=0.5} - M^{n,c=0}$). As drawn in Figure 9.1, the coinsurance rate would reduce inefficient moral hazard from ($M^{i,c=0} - M^{n,c=0}$) to ($M^{i,c=0.5} - M^{n,c=0.5}$), but it would also reduce efficient moral hazard from ($M^{n,c=0} - M^{u}$) to ($M^{n,c=0.5} - M^{u}$). Thus, in contrast to Pauly's model, coinsurance rates reduce both efficient and inefficient care.

It is important to recognize that the changes illustrated in Figure 9.1 could easily represent the case where imposing a 50% coinsurance rate on erstwhile free fee-for-service reduces the gain in utility from the income transfers more than it reduces the loss in utility from reducing inefficient moral hazard. If so, the imposition of a 50% coinsurance rate could reduce welfare. This could be true for the imposition of any level of coinsurance rate, including very small rates. Therefore, the optimal coinsurance rate under the new theory could very well be 0%.

Insurance contracts with coinsurance rates typically include maximums on out-of-pocket spending. If such stop-losses are present, then increasing the coinsurance rate to any level would imply a smaller reduction of moral hazard because beyond some maximum out-of-pocket spending level, the coinsurance rate reverts to 0%.

Calculating the Effect of Coinsurance on Efficient Moral Hazard

No studies have estimated the effect of coinsurance on efficient and inefficient moral hazard. The ideal study to do this would involve a modification of the consumer's income payoff test referred to previously at various places. Participants would be identified as those who would voluntarily purchase an actuarially fair price-payoff insurance with, say, a 0% coinsurance rate. The participants would then be assigned to different experimental arms: (1) no insurance, (2) purchasing the original fair price-payoff insurance with a 0% coinsurance rate, and (3) purchasing a fair contingent-claims insurance with the same payoffs as the 0% coinsurance. In addition, some participants would also be assigned to (4) purchasing a fair price-payoff insurance with, say, a 50% coinsurance rate, and (5) purchasing a fair contingent-claims insurance with the same payoffs as the 50% coinsurance. Comparisons of actual medical care spending by participants in the various experimental arms would determine the effect of increasing the coinsurance rate from 0% to 50% on efficient and inefficient moral hazard.

The RAND HIE investigated the effect of coinsurance on moral hazard, but the experiment was based on theory that did not recognize the existence of efficient moral hazard. Instead, it held that all moral hazard was an unintended, opportunistic response to an exogenous price change and totally inefficient (Phelps, 1973; Newhouse, 1978a, p. 9). As a result of this theory, the ideal experiment that

RAND researchers sought to achieve was to assign participants at random into arms where consumers faced different prices of medical care, rather than assigning participants to purchase fair insurance policies that differed by coinsurance rate. Although RAND HIE participants were insured, that characteristic was theoretically incidental to much of the intent of the study, and was probably only necessitated because the RAND researchers would not have been able to find a representative sample of the U.S. population that was not insured. In essence, the RAND researchers sought to conduct an experimental demand study where insurance plan assignment was the mechanism and stand-in for assigning participants at random to markets with different medical care prices.

Nevertheless, if the income elasticity of demand of ill consumers is known, the RAND data can be used to illustrate how to calculate the effect of coinsurance rates on efficient moral hazard. In the following exercise, I focus on the inpatient expenditures because they correspond best to the theory that not everyone becomes ill during the insurance contract period, and that those who become ill receive an income transfer from those who remain healthy. The data (from Manning et al., 1987) and derived calculations are summarized in Table 9.1.

Those participants assigned to the free fee-for-service plan in the RAND experiment had average inpatient expenditures of $409 (in 1984 dollars), which is also a measure of the actuarially fair premium if insurance could have been purchased for hospital care alone. Because only 10.3% of the participants were hospitalized,

Table 9.1

Calculation of effect of imposing coinsurance on efficient moral hazard using RAND HIE data (in 1984 dollars)

	RAND 0% Coinsurance	RAND 95% Coinsurance with $1,000 Stop-Loss
Average inpatient spending (= actuarially fair premium)	$409	$315
Probability of hospitalization	10.3%	7.9%
Hospital spending per hospitalized patient	$3,971	$3,987
Out-of-pocket spending	$0	$1,000
Income transfers	$3,971 − $409 = $3,562	$3,987 − $1,000 − $315 = $2,672
Base income	$8,912	$8,912
Total income after transfers	$8,912 + $3,562 = $12,474	$8,912 + $2,672 = $11,584
Percent income increase	40%	30%
Efficient moral hazard increase (income transfer effect)	40% × 0.38 = 15.2%	30% × 0.38 = 11.4%

the expenditures for those who were hospitalized averaged $3,971. Net of a fair premium payment of $409, income transfers were therefore $3,562, representing a 40% increase in income from an average base income of $8,912. Using an income elasticity of 0.38, the 40% increase in income would generate a (40% $\times$ 0.38 =) 15.2% increase in medical care spending compared to spending without insurance. If the RAND experiment had provided data on medical spending without insurance, the efficient moral hazard could have been calculated in dollars.

If the 95% coinsurance plan with a $1,000 maximum on out-of-pocket spending were imposed on those in the 0% coinsurance plan, efficient moral hazard would be reduced. Accordingly, the 95% plan showed an average inpatient spending of $315, a probability of hospitalization of 7.9%, and an average inpatient spending for those who were hospitalized of $3,987. Assuming that anyone who was hospitalized would have incurred out-of-pocket spending of no less than $1,000 at the 95% coinsurance rate, the average income transfer was ($3,987 − $315 − $1,000 =) $2,672. This implied a 30% increase in income from baseline, and only a 11.4% increase in spending from baseline, using the same 0.38 income elasticity. Thus, in this exercise, efficient moral hazard would have been about 1/3 greater in the free fee-for-service plan than with this coinsurance plan.[3] This reduction in efficient moral hazard creates a welfare loss that has not been recognized in previous estimates of the welfare consequences of imposing coinsurance on free fee-for-service insurance.

Rice's Theory

Rice (1992) has added a further misunderstanding to the relationship between moral hazard and coinsurance rates. Rice conceptualizes medical care as including both effective and ineffective care, where effectiveness can be defined generally as the probability that a procedure will achieve its intended health outcome or diagnostic measurement. Rice suggests that as the coinsurance rate increases from 0% of the actual price toward 100%, informed consumers would respond by dropping ineffective care first, then effective care. As evidence that consumers are not informed, he cites the study by Lohr et al. (1986) that shows that in the RAND HIE, consumers were just as likely to forgo efficient care as inefficient care, when the coinsurance rate increased. He concludes that consumers are uninformed about effectiveness of medical care, that the observed demand curve for medical care is an imperfect measure of the value[4] of medical care, and that medical care is overvalued because consumers think that care is effective when in reality much of it is not.

Rice's demand curve, however, is not the standard conceptualization of demand because it allows a characteristic of the commodity—the effectiveness of medical care—to change systematically as quantity increases. Rice's conceptualization is equivalent to describing the demand for transportation services so as the initial units would represent transportation by car and subsequent units transportation by bicycle, and the willingness to pay would vary according to both the convexity of consumer preferences for successive units of transportation services with the same vehicle, and the differing characteristics of transportation in different vehicles. In standard neoclassical demand theory, the characteristics of the commodity are held constant, and demand registers only the consumer's willingness to pay for each successive unit of that well-defined commodity.

Standard demand analysis would therefore postulate separate demand curves for each effectiveness level of medical care. At 0% of the actual price, a certain quantity of high-effectiveness medical care would be demanded and a certain quantity of low-effectiveness medical care would be demanded. If prices were to increase exogenously toward 100% of the actual price, the quantity demanded would be expected to decrease for both types of medical care, consistent with Lohr et al.'s (1986) findings. Therefore, the lack of a differential response to price for high- versus low-effectiveness medical care is not sufficient evidence to conclude that consumers think that medical care is effective when in reality it is not, nor that medical care is overvalued.

The fundamental problem is that Rice appears to equate efficiency with effectiveness, when in fact they are different concepts. Effectiveness is a characteristic of the commodity, while efficiency is a characteristic of the market. Effective medical care can be inefficient if the price that consumers are willing to pay for the care is less than the marginal cost of producing it, and it is produced and sold anyway. For example, consider a diagnostic test that is 100% effective in detecting the existence of some form of slow-growing cancer. A consumer may be willing to pay an amount that exceeds marginal cost for an annual test, but only willing to pay a fraction of the cost for a second test during the same year. Receiving the second test anyway would be inefficient, even though the test is effective. Similarly, relatively ineffective care can be efficient if consumers are willing to pay a price that exceeds the marginal cost of producing the care. For example, a heroic, but relatively ineffective procedure that saves a life only 10% of the time might be efficient if its costs are low relative to its expected value to the consumer.

The difference between these two concepts can also be illustrated with the health production function. During the 1970s and 1980s, there was the presumption that the additional care being consumed in the U.S.—the care that was causing the large increases in health care costs—was relatively ineffective in producing health. Hence, Enthoven (1980, pp. 45–51) characterized the marginal care as "flat of the curve" medicine. For those who were uninsured, however, the additional care to which consumers gained access by virtue of becoming insured was often effective care that was on the steep portion of the health production function. Thus, policies directed at reducing inefficient care had an impact in reducing effective care that was probably also highly efficient. As a result, cost-sharing and denial of coverage through care management may have generated large, but largely unrecognized and unmeasured, welfare losses.

Before leaving this section, it should be noted that Rice (1992) claims that the observed demand for medical care does not accurately measure the value of health care because consumers are uninformed about which type of medical care is effective. Because consumers think that care is effective when in reality it is not, the observed demand overstates the value of the health care.[5] According to the new theory, however, the observed (uninsured) demand curve is inadequate because consumers lack sufficient incomes to show how much they are truly willing to pay for the medical care that does improve their health or extend their lives. Thus, the observed demand understates the value of health care compared to the demand curve after the insurance income transfer. In this sense, the theory described in this book is diametrically opposed to Rice's theory.

In summary then, coinsurance rates are too crude a tool to use to reduce health care costs because they are not focused on inefficient moral hazard alone. While imposing a 50% coinsurance rate on erstwhile free fee-for-service coverage clearly reduces consumption, it would also reduce welfare to the extent that it reduces the utility from consumption of efficient care more than it raises utility from consuming less inefficient care. Moreover, coinsurance rates unambiguously reduce welfare to the extent that they reduce income transfers that would have been used to purchase other goods and services when ill.

MANAGED CARE

The second policy initiative, also motivated by high health care expenditures and the conventional theoretical interpretation of the welfare consequences of these expenditures, is managed care. As suggested above, managed care is an amorphous concept that encompasses a broad range of insurer behaviors, but most managed care plans use some combination of (1) utilization review, (2) payment structures that give incentives to providers to limit care, and (3) selection of providers on the basis of a desirable practice style.

Managed care is directed at reducing moral hazard under conventional theory, but it is also directed at countering the incentive in fee-for-service payment schemes for physicians to induce demand for medical care. That is, if a physician is undecided whether to recommend an additional visit on the basis of clinical factors, the additional fee that the physician gains may be a sufficient incentive to entice the physician to recommend that visit. Thus, managed care is designed to reduce incentives by both consumers and providers to generate inefficient care.

Managed care may hold greater promise for distinguishing between efficient and inefficient moral hazard than coinsurance rates and deductibles. On the other hand, managed care—especially the utilization review function—may be viewed as filtering the decisions of consumers and providers through a screen that generally favors the interests of the insurer. It is unlikely that the consumer's income payoff test for efficient care—that is, whether the ill consumer, if given an equivalent cash settlement instead, would purchase the same care—would be as acceptable to managed care plans as those tests for appropriateness that they currently employ. In addition, because willingness to pay is an individual characteristic, it is difficult to imagine how this criterion could be implemented as rigorously as a plan-wide policy.

Like cost-sharing policies, the central problem with managed care is that in countering the incentives to consume and provide inefficient moral hazard, managed care embodies an incentive for the health plans to decrease the amount of efficient moral hazard as well. While all utilization would theoretically be subject to review in one form or another, expensive procedures tend to receive the closest scrutiny because they add the most to the health plan's costs and therefore, could detract most from the health plan's profits if they were performed. As a result, it is the expensive procedures for which the incentive to deny care is the most pronounced. As suggested in Chapter 5, however, it is precisely the expensive procedures that are also the most likely to be unaffordable, and for which insurance coverage is most valuable to consumers. Therefore, if managed care plans inappropriately scrutinize and deny access to the expensive procedures, they may greatly reduce the value of health insurance to consumers and the welfare gains from insurance.

At this writing, few conclusions can be drawn from the empirical literature regarding the performance of managed care in eliminating inefficient, rather than efficient care. Still, public opinion polls confirm that consumers regard access to care as a desirable characteristic of health plans and have faulted managed care plans for denying access to valuable procedures.[6] If managed care plans deny access to procedures that would have passed the consumer's income payoff test, then managed care would have reduced welfare.[7]

A PRICE-REDUCTION STRATEGY

Under conventional theory, all additional care consumed because of price-payoff insurance represents a welfare loss and should be reduced. Under the new theory, it is more difficult to generate a welfare gain by reducing health care expenditures through a quantity-reduction strategy. Appropriate cost containment policies must be able to distinguish efficient from inefficient moral hazard, and target the latter for elimination. However, because health care expenditures are the product of price and quantity, it is not necessary to rely solely on quantity-reductions to reduce expenditures. Indeed, the new theory suggests that price-reduction strategies would contain costs, and at the same time increase access to care by the uninsured, but without the reduction in efficient moral hazard that is part of all existing quantity-reduction strategies.

One simple approach to cost containment would, therefore, recognize that many health care providers have monopoly control over certain functions or resources. For example, physicians have monopoly control over hospital admissions, prescription drugs, and invasive procedures such as surgeries. Pharmaceutical companies have patents on their drugs. Specialist physicians have monopoly control over specific information and experience, and the skills necessary for successful treatment. Many other provider groups have gained monopoly control over the provision of certain services through state practice acts (Feldstein, 1999). Thus, to contain health care costs, a better policy may be to create a counterveiling monopsony power for purchasers to cancel the monopoly power of providers and health plans.

For example, Pfaff (1990) finds that countries with organized buyers have lower health care costs. If so, policies where the government or a purchasing cooperative negotiates prices with providers and health plans would hold promise. Such policies would encourage counterveiling monopsony power to offset the monopoly power of providers (and health plans) in setting prices, thus reducing price mark-ups and keeping health care costs lower than they otherwise would be. In the U.S., the experience of health care purchasing cooperatives may serve as a useful guide. The California Public Employees' Retirement System, the Federal Employees' Health Benefit Plan, and the Minnesota-based Buyers' Health Care Action Group are all examples of organizations that have acted as buyers' cooperatives at some point.

OPTIMAL HEALTH INSURANCE DESIGN

According to the new theory, the optimal design for a health insurance policy would be to impose some level of cost-sharing or managed care on the inefficient portion of moral hazard and no cost-sharing or care management on the efficient portion. The difficulty in practice, however, is that quantity-reduction policies, such as the imposition of coinsurance rates, apply to all spending (or spending up to some limit) and are not be able to focus on inefficient moral hazard alone.

A more practical approach would be to recognize that each illness has a different moral hazard profile. Some illnesses may have no moral hazard at all, as was illustrated in Figure 4.1 from Chapter 4. Others may have moral hazard where the inefficient portion dominates, as was illustrated in the extreme by Figure 3.4 from Chapter 3. Still others may have moral hazard where the efficient portion dominates, as was illustrated in Figure 3.3. The new theory suggests that optimal insurance would be designed to apply coinsurance rates and managed care differentially to diseases with different moral hazard profiles.

For those illnesses with no moral hazard at all or for those where efficient moral hazard dominates, no cost-sharing or care management would apply. For example, those illnesses that are life threatening or serious and also expensive to treat might be highly correlated with illnesses where efficient moral hazard dominates. These illnesses might include liver failure requiring a liver transplant; a coronary heart disease severe enough to require coronary artery bypass grafts; diabetes, asthma, or other chronic diseases that would require periodic physician visits and regular use of pharmaceuticals; cancers for which expensive surgeries and chemotherapy are often prescribed; and other diseases where the treatments are costly in terms of pain and suffering, as well as expenditures. This means that for both expensive procedures and routine care that is associated with a specific disease, no cost-sharing or care management would be imposed.

An alternative approach would be to impose cost-sharing or case management according to the type of care itself. This approach, however, quickly encounters the problem that some care might be either efficient and inefficient, depending on the disease. For example, a breast implant may be efficient for the breast cancer patient who has undergone a mastectomy, but inefficient for a healthy woman who simply desires a change in her appearance. Relating insurance coverage to the disease solves this problem.

For those illnesses where inefficient moral hazard tends to dominate, cost-sharing or care management could be imposed. In reality, these illnesses would largely be represented by the lack of a diagnosable illness, and might include the routine or preventive care that is associated with being healthy (this case is discussed further in Chapter 10). Thus, the optimal design for insurance under the new theory would be to provide free, first-dollar coverage for beneficiaries that fall ill with a defined set of serious or expensive diseases. For those beneficiaries with less serious or expensive diseases, or for beneficiaries who are generally healthy, provide coverage, but impose cost-sharing or care management.

The fact that most health insurance is provided to employees as in-kind compensation provides an opportunity to create coverage for healthy beneficiaries that still has significant cost-sharing. An employer could determine the expected expenditures under price-payoff insurance coverage for a healthy person and contribute that amount to a medical savings account owned by the employee. This account could only be used to pay for medical care expenditures and would essentially cover any routine or preventive care that the healthy consumer might wish to purchase. At the end of the contract period, however, any residual could be rolled over to the next period. As soon as some reservation level of accumulation is reached, any excess could be either kept in the account or redeemed for cash at the employee's discretion. If the employee were to leave the firm, retire, or select a traditional health insurance plan, the account could be cashed in totally, thus the consumer essentially faces a 100% coinsurance rate for any expenditures out of this account. Each dollar spent from this account would represent the decision of a consumer that essentially is faced with the consumer's income payoff test. The prices that the relatively healthy beneficiary pays for this routine or preventative care would be negotiated by the employer and fee schedules would be made available to the beneficiaries.

In addition, those illnesses that are dominated by efficient moral hazard would be covered by an unlimited insurance policy with first-dollar coverage. This policy would cover the expensive acute care such as hospital and ambulatory procedures, diagnostic tests, chronic care, rehabilitation therapies, hospice, emergency transportation and emergency room care. It would also completely cover office visits and any the other routine care associated with the eligible diseases.[8]

Chernew, Encinosa, and Hirth (2000) suggest an insurance design that is consistent with the spirit of the new theory. They suggest that for severe, observable illnesses, coverage should be almost complete. That is, because of the skewness of the medical expenditure distribution, cost-sharing should not be applied to any inframarginal expenditures. Instead, for those severe, expensive illnesses for which there are multiple medically acceptable treatment paths, the optimal policy would be for the insurer to pay the consumer if a low cost path were chosen, but require a payment from the ill consumer if a high cost path were chosen. Thus, cost-sharing would not affect access, but only purchasing decisions at the margin. This may represent a useful method for eliminating any remaining portion of inefficient moral hazard from care of a disease that has been defined as generally associated with efficient moral hazard by the insurance contract.

INSURING THE UNINSURED

Health economists have not told a consistent story with regard to insuring the uninsured. On the one hand, empirical estimates of the welfare implications of insurance have implied that being uninsured is better than being insured at traditional or even current coverage levels (Feldstein, 1973; Manning and Marquis, 1996). On the other hand, a majority (62% of respondents with an opinion) of health economists in 1995 agreed with the statement, "The U.S. should now enact some [insurance] plan that covers the entire population" (Fuchs, 1996). This, despite near unanimous agreement that moral hazard results in a substantial welfare loss (Fuchs, 1996). Health economists who study developing countries have been known to argue that some new health insurance program is successful because the new enrollees use more health care with the program than they would have used without it. That is, the insurance program is deemed beneficial precisely because it results in moral hazard! Yet, under conventional theory, moral hazard is unambiguously bad for society.

The explanation for this confusion, of course, is that conventional theory is wrong. Moral hazard consists of both an income transfer-generated efficient portion and a price-generated inefficient portion. For low-income consumers in wealthy countries, or for most consumers in poor countries, the efficient portion of moral hazard tends to dominate the inefficient portion. This is because the uninsured are drawn predominantly from the ranks of the poor and as a result, the access implications of insurance suggest that insuring the uninsured would be generally welfare-increasing. Any price-related welfare loss is relatively trivial compared with the income transfer-generated gains of poor consumers. According to the Fuchs's (1996) survey, most health economists must have sensed this intuitively and supported extending insurance to the uninsured, despite the opposite being formally articulated by conventional theory and empirical work. What, then, is the formal basis for government intervention to insure the uninsured?

The Case for Intervention: Medicare

During the original debate surrounding the passage of Medicare, Arrow (1963) argued that the case in favor of insurance was "overwhelming" because, if consumers (1) maximize expected utility, (2) were charged an actuarially fair premium, and (3) exhibit diminishing marginal utility of income, insuring the uninsured would increase welfare. Insurance increases welfare because consumers prefer certain financial losses to uncertain ones that are actuarially equivalent, and are able to realize this preference through insurance. Arrow was right, of course, that the case in favor of insurance was overwhelming, but it was not for the reasons that he suggested. In hindsight, a preference for certainty of financial losses seems like a particularly thin reed to use as the theoretical foundation for a major government program like Medicare.

The new theory suggests that the essence of health insurance is an income redistribution. This redistribution is efficient because the ill derive more utility from the income they gain than the healthy give up from the income they lose, and all have an equal chance (theoretically) of being gainers and losers. In contrast to the single-premium, voluntary, one-period insurance that is discussed in this book, Medicare is a mandatory, two-period insurance with a premium that is based on the consumer's income in the first period. That is, consumers are required to pay into the Medicare fund based on their income when under age sixty-five in return for insurance coverage when age sixty-five and over. There is a prepayment aspect to Medicare because a consumer builds up pool of payments when under age sixty-five to cover his own expenses when age sixty-five or over. There is a social insurance aspect because the wealthy pay larger premiums than the poor and because the young subsidize the premiums of the old.[9] And, there is a standard insurance aspect because the spending in the over-sixty-five period varies from beneficiary to beneficiary, and income is transferred from those who are relatively healthy to those who are relatively ill.

The new theory suggests that best justification for a government intervention such as Medicare is the realization that the premium for one-period insurance (annual insurance, for example, where the premium is paid in the same year that any payoffs are received) would probably be too expensive for many elderly to pay, especially if it were adjusted for the expected expenditures of the elderly. This is not only because those sixty-five and over tend to have larger health care expenditures requiring larger premium payments, but also because they are typically retired and have less income with which to purchase insurance. Without insurance of some kind, consumers with expensive health care episodes may not be able to pay for their health care. Requiring citizens to purchase this two-period insurance is perhaps the only way to finance these potentially large expenditures. Therefore, the best argument in favor of this government intervention is one based on the access value of insurance: without this two-period, mandatory insurance, many of the elderly would not be able to afford a private annual insurance premium and would therefore not have access to the expensive medical care they would require if they were to become ill.

The Case for Tax Subsidies

Compared with the elderly, those under age sixty-five have lower expected expenditures and generally higher incomes (although many have lower net worths). As a result, the central issue for those under sixty-five is generally not the unaffordability of large, risk-rated annual insurance premiums. What, then, is the basis for government intervention?

The current form of government intervention is a tax subsidy: employee insurance premiums are paid for by the employer with the employee's pretax income. According to conventional theory, a tax subsidy is difficult to justify because no market failure can be identified that would argue for the subsidy. Instead, if consumers are uninsured, it appears to reflect a rational appraisal of the net value of insurance, one that is consistent with the empirical evidence that insurance reduces welfare. According to conventional theory, the main problem with a tax subsidy is that it encourages consumers to purchase too much insurance coverage (Feldstein, 1973; Feldman and Dowd, 1991; Manning and Marquis, 1996). That is, it encourages consumers to purchase a lower coinsurance rate than is optimal, which in turn results in a larger moral hazard welfare loss and a larger net loss to society from purchasing insurance. Many economists have called for the repeal of the tax subsidy for precisely these reasons.

In contrast, the new theory suggests that purchasing fair insurance with typical coverage parameters makes the average consumer better off, not worse off. Thus, if some consumers do not purchase insurance voluntarily, it may be because they are not able to afford the premium, especially if the premium includes a large loading fee. A tax subsidy may therefore provide sufficient incentive for the uninsured to purchase insurance.

Under the new theory, a justification for the tax subsidy can be made with standard economic arguments. First, much of the gain from being insured is due to gaining access to otherwise unaffordable procedures. Because we as a society are especially altruistic with regard to health care and generally do not like it when the ill are unable to find appropriate health care, society derives utility when uninsured consumers become insured and, as a result, gain access to care when ill. In contrast, under the conventional theory, altruism would play, at best, a minor role. For example, few members of society would be willing to contribute money to help someone satisfy their preference for certainty of financial losses, but many would be willing to pay at least something to make health care available to those consumers who would not be able to afford care if they became ill. Therefore, an external benefit from health care would justify the tax subsidization of health insurance.

Second, according to Thomas (1994/5) and others, previous government intervention in the form of Medicaid has caused a number of consumers, who would otherwise have been privately insured, to be uninsured. A tax subsidy, especially one directed at these lower income consumers, might entice some of them to purchase private insurance again. If so, they would pay a larger portion of the expected cost of their care, and would reduce the portion presently paid for by the general tax revenues that support Medicaid. Thus, correcting the unintended effects of a previous government intervention is also a legitimate reason for the tax subsidy.

Third, according to the new theory, insurance is often the only mechanism by which poorer consumers can gain access to expensive care. Richer consumers, in contrast, do not need to rely on health insurance to gain access because they have the resources to buy expensive care directly. Therefore, the loading fees that the poor must pay to cover the administrative expenses of health insurers represents a transaction cost that the rich do not need to pay in order to gain access to health care. As a result, a tax subsidy of the premium, especially one targeted at loading-fee expenses that the poor pay, would cancel some of these costs and be justified on equity grounds.

Expanding the number of insured through further subsidizing premiums would not necessarily be expensive. For example, the regressiveness of the existing tax subsidy in the U.S. represents a costless opportunity to rearrange the existing tax spending for greater gain. Instead of structuring the tax subsidy so that it increases with income, the tax subsidy could be redesigned with stricter limits. These limits could be such that they do not reduce the number of insured, but instead reduce the richness of the insurance package received by high-income employees. If so, the tax spending saved could then be targeted to encourage those smaller firms that do not currently offer insurance, to offer it as a fringe benefit. Such a reworking of the tax code could be tax-spending-neutral but welfare-increasing to the extent that more hitherto uninsured workers purchase health insurance.

TECHNOLOGY GROWTH AS MORAL HAZARD

Consider the consumer who would like to purchase contingent-claims insurance, but because of the high costs of monitoring for fraud and of writing complex contracts, such insurance is not available. Instead, the consumer purchases a price-payoff contract that accomplishes the same income transfer.

For the health technology firm, the widespread purchase of price-payoff insurance also implies a dynamic type of moral hazard. The health technology firm knows that demand for its products will not be limited by the income of the typical household, but instead limited by the income of the household enhanced by the aggregate premium contributions in the insurance pool. Moreover, health insurance pays off by reducing price, so the size of the income transfer adjusts as the new, more expensive technology becomes available. Therefore, the firm is not bound by normal budgetary considerations, but can develop technologies that would otherwise require very high incomes to purchase and still be assured of a market (Goddeeris and Weisbrod, 1985; Nyman, 1991).

The prevalence of health insurance has, no doubt, contributed to the secular growth of expensive medical technology. The relationship between health insurance and the growth of medical technology is suggested by the increasing skewness of the medical expenditure distribution. In 1963, the top-spending 1% of the population in the U.S. accounted for 17% of total health care expenditures, in 1970 they accounted for 26%, and in 1987 they accounted for 30% (Berk, Monheit, and Hagan, 1988). Because the growth in skewness is likely to represent expensive new technologies and because these new technologies would not be accessible to many consumers without the income transfers from insurance, an apparent correlation between insurance and technology exists.

Not only does insurance generate technology, but the growth in technology has also increased the demand for insurance. That is, health insurance frees the consumer from being constrained to purchase only those new medical technologies that were within an individual's income. Once the new expensive technologies are developed, however, many consumers are bound to health insurance as the only mechanism for gaining access to them. Thus, as more expensive medical technologies are developed, health insurance becomes increasingly valuable because a larger portion of insurance is devoted to covering otherwise unaffordable procedures.

Under conventional theory, this dynamic moral hazard would be deemed inefficient because it would not have been purchased without insurance. Under the new theory, the new technology could either be efficient or inefficient, depending on the consumer's income payoff test referred to above. Lacking such a test, efficient technologies can be identified through cost-effectiveness analysis. If a cost-utility analysis indicated that a cost of a new procedure was less than $100,000 per QALY saved, it can generally be assumed that the technology is efficient.

The decision of whether to cover the new technology under a certain insurance plan would require a different test. Coverage would depend on whether consumers would purchase price-payoff insurance coverage for that technology alone, given the specifics of the insurance plan in question. That is, coverage decisions cannot be made independently of the consumer's knowing the cost-sharing and care management characteristics of the insurance. Consumers who are like-minded in their evaluation of new technologies would join the similar insurance plans.

CONCLUSIONS

The justification for government intervention differs according to the theory. Under conventional theory, there is little justification for government intervention to encourage the purchase of health insurance. First, the purchase of private health insurance at traditional or current coverage levels results in a welfare loss for society. A tax subsidy would encourage more people to become insured, or it would encourage those who would already have been insured to opt for greater coverage. In both cases, a tax subsidy would result in even larger welfare losses. Second, because the benefit from being insured under conventional theory is the additional utility derived from obtaining a certain, rather than uncertain, financial loss, there is little justification for subsidizing health insurance. Critics of the tax subsidy correctly argue that there is no substantive market failure to justify intervention under this theory.

In contrast, under the new theory, insurance makes the consumer better off. Moreover, the case for government intervention is based primarily on the access value of health insurance and on the altruism that is felt by society toward the consumer who falls ill without access to the needed health care. Because of this external benefit, the private gain from the voluntary purchase of health insurance understates society's gain, and too little health insurance is purchased. The tax subsidy is society's legitimate response to this externality and encourages those who would not otherwise purchase health insurance to purchase it. This externality is the primary justification for the tax subsidy and for any government program that would increase the number of insured.

The different theories imply different cost-containment policies. Under conventional theory, the promotion of cost-sharing and managed care to reduce moral hazard is justified because all of moral hazard is inefficient and welfare-decreasing. Under the new theory, however, cost-sharing and managed care are less desirable because they reduce both efficient and inefficient moral hazard. Optimal insurance design would focus cost-sharing and care management on those illnesses (or more generally, those health states) that generate inefficient moral hazard. Applying cost-sharing or case management to inefficient moral hazard would reduce health care expenditures and increase welfare.

1. Switzerland had the next highest share in 1998, spending 10.4 % of its GDP on health care (OECD, 2001).

2. In a recent exchange, Manning and Marquis (2001) argue that their estimate of the welfare loss from moral hazard in Manning and Marquis (1996) was calculated using a compensated demand rather than a Marshallian demand, and therefore, accounting for an income effect. If so, the welfare loss calculation would be smaller, because the Hicksian income effect would have been removed in the compensated demand estimate. Instead, the authors calculate that using the Marshallian estimate, the welfare loss for the 25% coinsurance plan would be reduced by about $45, or 13%, compared with the compensated estimate. How using a Marshallian demand could result in a smaller welfare loss compared to the welfare loss using a compensated estimate is not explained by the authors, raising questions about what is really being measured.

3. The RAND HIE was more complicated than is represented here. For example, RAND participants received a participation incentive equal to the maximum out-of-pocket spending over the year. This amount was paid monthly on a prorated basis. This payment would have increased income. Against this incentive was the incentive for participants with cost-sharing to drop out of the experiment if an expensive hospitalization loomed, and instead receive care under the participant's previous private coverage. As already noted, those allocated to cost-sharing plans were sixteen times more likely to drop out of the experiment than those in the free plan (Newhouse et al., 1993). As a result, many of the hospitalizations in the cost-sharing plan would have not have appeared in the data, and the rate at which hospitalizations occurred in cost-sharing plans would appear to be smaller than it actually was. Instead of attempting to adjust for these issues, the data were taken at face value for this exercise.

4. Rice (1992) measures the vertical dimension of demand in terms of "utility" rather than the usual willingness to pay or value, both of which are measured in dollars per unit of the commodity.

5. This assumes that the lack of information acts to improve the consumer's appraisal of ineffective care and does not simultaneously diminish the consumer's appraisal of effective care.

6. Bowman (1998) reviews the public opinion polls with regards to managed care. In a Roper poll from December 1997, a series of eleven characteristics of

health care plans were presented to respondents who were then asked which were "absolutely essential." Seventy-five percent of respondents rated "access to immediate care when you feel you need it" as absolutely essential to a health care plan, the highest percentage of any of the characteristics considered. But managed care plans are perceived by the public to have more doubtful access to care than traditional fee-for-service plans. For example, an August–September 1996 Kaiser/Harvard survey asked respondents "if you had a serious medical problem requiring costly treatment, how likely do you think it is that your health plan would pay most of the cost?" Sixty-two percent of respondents with traditional care said that their plan was "very likely" to pay most of the cost, but only 49% of respondents with managed care said their plan was "very likely" to pay. In a February 1998 Gallup survey, 50% of respondents in traditional arrangements trusted their plan to do the right thing "just about always" whereas 32% of respondents in managed care felt the same way. In Harris/Harvard polls conducted in 1994 and 1995, respondents were the non-elderly with significant illness burdens. Twenty-two percent of respondents in managed care plans said that they had problems with not receiving the treatment that their doctor thought necessary, but only 13% of respondents in fee-for-service had these problems. Twenty-one percent of respondents in managed care said they were unable to see a specialist when they had thought that they needed one in the last year, compared with 15% in fee-for-service plans. Seventeen percent of respondents in managed care said they had to wait a long time for a doctor's appointment, whereas 7% in fee-for-service did. Managed care organizations appear to impede access more than traditional plans.

7. Some analysts claim that managed care's ultimate legacy will be to have given providers, especially specialists, the impetus to form cartels in the various market areas. These cartels would possess sufficient market power to raise prices. Again, under conventional theory, this market power appears to be benign to the extent that it counteracts the effect of insurance in lowering prices and creating moral hazard.

8. The product currently sold by Destiny Health Insurance Company, a South African company with U.S. offices in Bethesda, Maryland, and operations in Oak Brook, Illinois, represents an insurance design that is close to the design described here.

9. Medicare premiums increase proportionately with income to a certain level, and then are fixed. Therefore, as a redistributive mechanism, they are generally regressive. Nevertheless, those with higher incomes pay a higher premium for their Medicare coverage.

10 | CONCLUSIONS

THE THEORY SUMMARIZED

The demand for health insurance is the demand for an income transfer in the event of illness. This income transfer allows for the purchase of more health care and other goods and services than would be possible if uninsured. Insurance is purchased because the expected value of the additional health care and other consumer commodities if ill exceeds the expected cost of paying the insurance premium if healthy. Because of the high transactions costs associated with paying off insurance with a lump sum amount, most health insurance contracts pay off by reducing price. Even though price-payoff contracts generate additional transactions costs (the inefficient moral hazard), they are still likely to be more efficient than contingent-claims contracts.

This theory differs from conventional theory. Conventional theory assumes that all moral hazard is inefficient. The new theory holds that some moral hazard—the additional health care purchased because of the income transfers when ill—is worth more to the consumer than it costs to produce. Conventional theory also holds that health insurance is demanded because consumers prefer a certain loss to an uncertain loss of the same expected magnitude. The new theory relies on empirical studies that have shown that just the opposite is true: consumers tend to prefer an uncertain loss to a certain loss of the same expected magnitude. Therefore, preferences for certainty have little to do with demand for insurance.

The new theory suggests that the gain from insurance is related more to the intuitively appealing Bernoulli utility function, than the von Neumann-Morgenstern (vNM) utility function, which confuses preferences for income with preferences for lotteries. For illnesses where medical expenditures are the same with or without insurance, the Bernoulli utility function is sufficient to explain the purchase of fair insurance. Preferences for certainty may still enter the decision to insure, but the primary motivation is the desire to obtain an income transfer when ill.

The new theory emphasizes two constraints. First, without insurance, the ill consumer would generally have no alternative mechanism for gaining access to those expensive procedures that exceed the consumer's resources. This implies that the demand for insurance is related to the expected value of the medical care.

Second, while there is some degree of substitutability between medical care and other commodities for the consumer who becomes ill (for example, an ill consumer might decide between an extra day in the hospital or additional consumer commodities), there is very little substitutability for the consumer who is healthy. This is partially due to the role of the physician in permitting only those who are ill or suspected of being ill to obtain certain types of care (for example, diagnostic procedures, prescription drugs, hospital services, and so on). It is also due to the fact that a healthy consumer derives little utility from most medical care (for example, coronary bypass surgery, chemotherapy, and so on). Only a few types of medical expenditures are so purely discretionary (for example, cosmetic surgery, recreational drugs, and so on) that the healthy could benefit from them, and many of those expenditures can still be traced back to a previous illness. Thus, the new theory emphasizes the role of the probability of illness and the transfer of income from the healthy to the ill.

At a more philosophical level, the new theory emphasizes the quid pro quo nature of the decision to purchase health insurance. That is, the consumer pays a premium for a transfer of income if ill. It does not matter much whether the income is transferred directly in a lump sum payment, or indirectly by reducing price. The purchaser of insurance intends to use this additional income to purchase more health care and other goods and services if he were to become ill. In essence, the decision to purchase additional care and additional consumer goods and services is made at the time the insurance is purchased, but is made in a contingent or expected framework, that is, if the consumer were to become ill.

In contrast, the conventional model emphasizes the financial consequences of illness. It views the financial consequences as a fixed, but uncertain expenditure that the consumer must either pay for himself, or engage insurance to pay. When the consumer pays the premium and purchases insurance, he achieves his goal of certainty. It is only incidentally that insurance has reduced the price of care. Thus, the consumer responds to the lower price opportunistically by purchasing more health care, much as if he happened to be placed by chance in a market with a sale on health care. The decision to purchase the additional care is made after the consumer has purchased insurance and is not part of the original insurance decision. The decision to purchase additional care is also not dependent on becoming ill, because it is assumed that a substantial degree of substitutability between medical care and other goods and services exists regardless of health status.

THE PRICE-PAYOFF MECHANISM, THE VALUE OF HEALTH CARE, AND NATIONAL HEALTH INSURANCE

The price-payoff mechanism in health insurance has misled economists into evaluating the medical care that is consumed with insurance by the same demand curve as would be observed without insurance. In reality, however, the price-payoff mechanism combines the two-step process of contingent-claims insurance into one step. That is, with contingent-claims insurance, the consumer becomes ill and, in the initial step, receives an income transfer that causes the demand for health care to shift out. Then, in the second step, additional health care is consumed because the consumer's willingness to pay for health care has increased.

With price-payoff insurance, the consumer becomes ill and is paid off through a price reduction, but the consumer's response to the price reduction incorporates the same income transfer and increased willingness to pay as with a contingent-claims contract. The consumer's willingness to pay for the last unit of medical care purchased is equal to the low payoff price, but willingness to pay for most of the inframarginal units of medical care has increased because of the income transfer in insurance. Figure 7.1 illustrated this shifting out of the consumer's demand and the increase in willingness to pay in comparison to the observed uninsured demand.

Thus, the new theory suggests that by redistributing income from the healthy to those who are ill, insurance increases the willingness to pay for health care, *including those services that would have been consumed anyway without insurance.* This implies that as health insurance was purchased by an ever-greater portion of the U.S. population in the mid-1900s, medical care became increasingly valuable. This was because, as more people became insured, the U.S. population was able to redistribute its national income more efficiently, allocating more income to those who benefitted from it most, and increasing their willingness to pay.

The policy implications are far-reaching. First, it implies that as health care costs in the U.S. rose because an increasingly larger proportion of the population was insured, there was also a simultaneous, but unrecognized, increase in the value of the health care consumed because of the greater willingness to pay for care by those who became ill with insurance. Thus, the rising health care costs in the U.S. were correlated with an increasing value of health care. This, in turn, implies that policies that were directed at reducing health care expenditures through reducing visits, procedures, and intensity of care—the real use of real resources—were largely directed at solving a problem that did not exist. Instead, focusing cost-containment policies on efforts to reduce health care prices and inefficiencies in the provision of care would have been more beneficial, especially to the uninsured.

Second, it implies that those countries that have adopted national health insurance for all their citizens are more efficient in redistributing and spending their national income than those counties, like the U.S., where some 17% of consumers are left out of the redistribution loop by virtue of being uninsured. Those countries where everyone is insured have more valuable (based on willingness to pay) health care sectors because all citizens are eligible for an income transfer from the healthy in the event of illness. Thus, in contrast to Arrow (1963), who based the case for national health insurance on insurance's ability to convert uncertain financial losses into certain ones, the new theory would base the case for national health insurance on its ability to redistribute national income more efficiently and on the resulting increased valuation of health care (and of other goods and services, net of premium costs) by those newly insured consumers who fall ill and receive an income transfer. This, in addition to society's altruistic desire to see all who are ill gain access to medical care, represents the case for national health insurance.[1]

POTENTIAL WEAKNESSES

This book has concentrated on the strengths of the new theory, but it may have weaknesses, too. In this section, I review four criticisms that could be leveled at the new theory.

Different Income Elasticities for the Healthy and Ill

One apparent weakness stems from the argument that if insurance represents a transfer of income from the healthy to the ill, it implies that the ill gain exactly the same amount of income as the healthy lose, assuming actuarially fair insurance. If the income elasticity for medical care is the same for both the ill and the healthy, the income transfer would increase consumption of medical care by the ill by an amount that is exactly matched by a reduction in medical care consumption by the healthy. Therefore, no net moral hazard effect could occur that is due to income transfers (Pauly, 1983).

This argument depends, of course, on the ill having the same income elasticity as the healthy. In order for the new theory to hold, it would be necessary that the ill exhibit a larger income elasticity for medical care than the healthy, but no such empirical work has compared the responses of these two types of consumers and found the ill to be more responsive to income changes than the healthy.

In existing studies, the income elasticity of demand is typically estimated by the responses of consumers who have insurance. For example, the RAND Health Insurance Experiment (HIE) produced estimates of the participants' responsiveness to income qua wages and salaries, but all participants had insurance with a $1,000 stop loss (in mid-1970s dollars, meaning that once out-of-pocket expenditures exceeded $1,000, a 0% coinsurance rate applied to any additional expenditures, [Newhouse and The Insurance Experiment Group, 1993; Manning et al., 1987]). Thus, the transfer of income that occurs because of insurance is not captured in the income measure used in the RAND estimates. As a result, the RAND HIE found that consumers were relatively unresponsive to wage and salary income, with income elasticities that ranged from 0.2 to 0.4, depending on the plan (Newhouse et al., 1993).

The true effect of income on health care consumption is better captured by the cross-national studies (Parkin, McGuire, and Yule, 1987; Gerdtham et al., 1992; Leu, 1986; Newhouse, 1977; Kleiman, 1974). In these studies, the national medical care expenditures are regressed on some measure of national income. These studies generally find income elasticities that exceed 1, reflecting the reality that if the national income is low, there is less total income available for medical care and less is spent on care on average than in richer countries. In contrast, for studies like Manning and Marquis (1996) and Newhouse and The Insurance Experiment Group (1993) where the unit of analysis is the insured household, if wages and salaries are low, insured consumers can still purchase expensive health care with the income that is transferred to them through insurance. As a result, there would appear to be little responsiveness to income, but in reality, income qua income transfers from insurance has a large effect on the amount of medical care consumed.

For example, consider once again the consumer who becomes ill and needs a $300,000 liver transplant to save his life. With insurance, health care consumption would be about the same, regardless of whether the consumer's wage and salary income was $50,000 or $400,000, because of the (almost) $300,000 in income transfers from insurance. As a result, the observed income elasticity would be low. Without insurance, however, a $300,000 income transfer from insurance would not occur, and the purchase of the expensive procedure would depend critically on the consumer's wage and salary income. Thus, a higher income elasticity of demand would be observed.

Moreover, the true responsiveness to income would be greater for the ill, because it is the ill consumer who has the clinical need for the large health care expenditures. All consumers, healthy and ill alike, might exhibit some common income elasticity for routine or discretionary health care. That is, since purchases of discretionary health care do not depend on health status, the decision to purchase this care would be equally dependent on income for both the healthy and the ill consumers. For example, both a healthy and a chronically ill person might consider purchasing cosmetic surgery and be equally influenced by income. In contrast, only the ill consumer would consider the purchase of expensive medical treatments associated with serious illnesses. For example, no one would consider the purchase of a coronary revascularization procedure unless he had coronary heart disease. For the medical expenditures that are clinically indicated like these, the healthy consumer would exhibit an income elasticity of demand of 0 because he would not purchase the medical care regardless of income, but the ill consumer's demand for medical care would again depend critically on income. As a result of this additional responsiveness to income for clinically indicated care, the income elasticity for all medical care—both discretionary and clinically indicated—would be greater for the ill than for the healthy.

Blank Check Argument

A second potential weakness of the new theory comes from the criticism that, with insurance that pays off with a price reduction, the amount of the income transfer is totally at the discretion of the insured person who becomes ill. It is as if the consumer had purchased a contingent-claims policy where the income payoff was determined by the insured consumer after becoming ill, the consumer simply filling in the amount of a blank check. This blank check argument would imply that the consumer did not have an intended income transfer in mind when he purchased insurance and therefore was not making the decision to purchase insurance on that basis.

One problem with this argument is that the consumer does not have complete discretion over the amount of the income transfer. The income transfer is limited by the amount that can be spent on medical care, and much of medical care spending (hospital admissions, prescription drugs, diagnostic tests, surgical procedures, and so on) must be approved by the consumer's physician. There may be some level of discretionary spending—an extra day in the hospital or an additional office visit—but this discretion is designed to allow additional transfers based on the variable treatment requirements of the patient. Thus, the physician provides a constraint on the amount of additional care that is available to the consumer at the consumer's sole discretion.

More importantly, the consumer generally does not derive satisfaction from consuming health care when there is no clinical reason for doing so. In fact, most health care consumed when healthy would reduce utility. As alluded to above, the consumer would derive negative satisfaction from chemotherapy if the consumer were not sufficiently ill to benefit from it. Even if ill, two courses of chemotherapy are not necessarily better than one, especially if the first was successful. Although not invasive, a CT-scan procedure is only to be endured by the healthy, but claustrophobic, consumer. Hospital stays when healthy would quickly become tedious. Moreover, because almost all medical expenditures represent services, there is little opportunity to resell them on the market to obtain the income. Thus, there is a self-censuring aspect to medical care that would make it difficult to use health insurance simply to fill in the amount of a blank check for an income transfer. These limitations are generally understood by consumers at the time they purchase a price-payoff insurance contract.

Consumer's Income Payoff Test

A third possible weakness in the new theory is the extent to which the consumer's income payoff test actually applies to health care. I have characterized the income transfer effect of insurance that pays off by reducing price as the amount of health care that the consumer would purchase if paid off directly with the equivalent amount of income. Some consumers, however, might take the cash payment and purchase only consumer goods and services, even though society would generally regard the medical care as more valuable. As a result, the income payoff test may be too focused on the consumer's preferences, and not adequately take into account society's values and the external benefit society derives from consumers having access to care. This implies, however, that the consumer's income payoff test is a conservative measure of efficient moral hazard. If society's values were considered, efficient moral hazard would represent a larger portion of total moral hazard.[2]

Health Care for the Healthy

The new theory assumes that health care is consumed only by the ill, but it is clear that some healthy consumers purchase health care. Such an assumption is necessary in order for the ill to receive an income transfer from the healthy. One response is that it is only because of convention or convenience that insurance covers routine and preventative care. Consumption of discretionary health care like this is not really an insurable event, and should be not be covered in the insurance contract.

Still, such care is covered under health insurance. Therefore, a more realistic response is that those who are healthy spend less than they pay into the insurance pool with their insurance premium, and as a result are still net transferers of income to those who are ill. So, for expensive care, there is still a transfer of income from the (relatively) healthy to the (relatively) ill. For those who are healthy, any normal income effect would be in the negative direction because of the income reduction from paying a premium net of smaller health care expenditures.

A useful perspective is that each health state has its own moral hazard profile. For the seriously ill, efficient moral hazard might dominate because both the income transfer and income transfer effect are large, and the pure price effect is small. For those who are healthy and consume routine or preventive care, the income transfer is negative and the income transfer effect small, but the pure price effect could be relatively large, resulting in inefficient moral hazard. Thus, there is a moral hazard profile for every health state, including the state of being healthy, and the differences in net income transfers (both positive and negative) and differences in price effects will affect health care consumption in each health state differentially. Future models may include this refinement.

It should be noted that while this refinement would complicate an empirical analysis, it in no way detracts from the theory of why consumers purchase health insurance. When consumers purchase insurance, they must simply put up with these imperfections in order to obtain an income transfer if ill.[3]

LIMITATIONS

The focus on the consumer in the new theory largely overlooks the role of the physician in sometimes inducing demand for unneeded care. The literature on induced demand and physician agency is, however, well developed. It may therefore be sufficient to acknowledge that such complications exist (see Chapter 8) and that the physician may legitimately or unduly influence the consumer's decisions regarding medical care consumption, with and without insurance.

The analysis found in these pages also does not address the fact that the majority of Americans purchase health insurance through their employer. Therefore, whether most consumers in the U.S. make an intentional decision to purchase insurance is open to debate. Moreover, questions arise regarding whether the employee actually bears the full burden of the health insurance premium, that is, whether the employee's (pretax) wages or salary would be greater by the exact amount of the insurance premium if he were to take an equivalent job at a firm that did not offer health insurance.

The new theory also abstracts from the reality by implicitly assuming that all diseases are discrete events. In reality, some diseases are discrete and some are continuous. That is, sometimes a person may have a disease but it is so mild that no treatment is required, but at other times, it can be severe enough to require treatment. It also abstracts from the reality that for many diseases, there is not just one treatment, but instead, a number of alternative treatments that vary in effectiveness and price. Recognizing this is especially important for the analysis of those diseases with treatments that are otherwise unaffordable without insurance. Refinements of the theory that incorporate these realities would make useful future contributions.

The new theory does address selection by noting that the appropriate price of medical care for those with preexisting conditions is the insurance premium, rather than the coinsurance rate. For example, even though an insurance policy might pay off by reducing the price to 0% of the cost of care, if 50% of purchasers of insurance have the disease in question, the appropriate price for persons who know that they have the disease would be a premium that reflects the 50% probability, rather than the 0% coinsurance price. Other selection issues, such as risk rating and favorable selection, are not addressed.

The scope of this book is limited and does not permit the discussion of inefficiency in the delivery of health care and its connection to insurance. Utilization review, capitated payments, and selected panels of providers are left to others to evaluate. For economists, inefficiencies in delivery of health care have absorbed a great deal of attention and studies have shown and still show that the sector is rife with blatant examples of waste and other forms of inefficiency. These studies, however, paint a distorted picture of the health care sector because they fail to acknowledge the great value that consumers derive from that portion of care that is efficiently delivered. The theory presented in this book, I hope, provides an insight into the true balance between inefficiency and value in the health care sector.

FUTURE EMPIRICAL WORK

This new theory suggests the need for a number of new empirical analyses. First on this list would be a study that decomposes moral hazard into its efficient and inefficient components by essentially performing the consumer's income payoff test. To reiterate, such a study would first identify and recruit as participants those consumers who had voluntarily purchased a specific health insurance policy, for example, a 0% coinsurance rate contract. These participants could then be randomly assigned to three groups: (1) the same 0% coinsurance rate insurance, (2) a contingent claims insurance that paid off in cash amounts equal to the expenditures for the various diseases of the participants who held 0% coinsurance rate insurance, and (3) no insurance. Because the payoffs would be the same for participants in the first two groups, participants in those groups would pay the same actuarially fair premium and the ill participants in those groups would receive the same income transfers. The participants in the third group would not pay a premium. Observed spending differences between groups (1) and (2) would represent inefficient moral hazard, and observed spending differences between groups (2) and (3) would represent efficient moral hazard. This study could be replicated for insurance with other coverage parameters.

The practical difficulty with such a study would be in developing a contingent-claims payoff schedule that was exactly the same as the expenditures under the 0% coinsurance rate insurance. The difficulties in designing a such a payoff schedule provide an insight into why health insurers use a price reduction mechanism for transferring income, rather than a lump sum cash payoff. The ethical difficulty would be in randomizing participants into the arm with no insurance.

Another useful study would attempt to estimate separate income elasticities of demand for those who are ill and those who are healthy. An ideal approach would be to distinguish between those medical procedures that were clinically indicated by the presence of disease and those that were largely discretionary. For each of the clinically indicated procedures, determine those *uninsured* consumers who have the disease and observe the effect that wage and salary income has on their consumption of the standard medical treatment for that disease. Then do the same for a sample of those who do not have the disease. Presumably, the income elasticity of the ill would exceed that of the healthy. Then, conduct the same analysis for each of the purely discretionary procedures, only the ill are defined as anyone who has an acute or chronic disease. Presumably, for the discretionary expenditures, the income elasticities for the ill and healthy would be similar, or at least more so than the income elasticities of demand for, say, a coronary arterial bypass graft procedure for those with and without coronary heart disease. The difficulty with this study is that the true income elasticity could only be determined by those who are uninsured, which would again present recruitment and ethical problems for investigators.

A third study would develop a better estimate of the percentage of the health insurance premium that is devoted to covering medical expenditures that would not otherwise be privately affordable. The estimate developed in this book was based on comparing the net worth of the household at the median of the income distribution with the average expenditures for the top-spending 1% of the population. A better estimate would compare the distribution of health care expenditures to the distribution of net worth to determine which expenditures are unaffordable. Expenditures in excess of net worth for each person could be summed and divided by total health care expenditures to determine the percentage of the fair insurance premium that would go to pay for otherwise unaffordable health care.

A fourth study would attempt to determine the net welfare gain from voluntarily purchased health insurance—unsubsidized and at some well-defined coverage level. This would be a complex study. It would be necessary to distinguish among (1) those diseases for which the insured consumer would purchase no additional health care, (2) those diseases for which the insured consumer would purchase additional health care that would have otherwise been affordable, and (3) those diseases for which the additional health care purchased by the insured consumer would otherwise be unaffordable. Estimates of the mortality and morbidity gains would be necessary to determine the value of the additional health care consumed with insurance. Estimates of the Bernoulli utility function would provide information on the utility cost of the insurance premium and utility benefit derived from the additional other goods and services purchased with the income transfer from insurance. Estimates of the welfare loss from inefficient moral hazard could be obtained using the appropriate parameters and the new demand curve described in Chapter 6. Many important sub-studies would be contained in this one. Once the net gain from a specific insurance policy is determined, the issue of optimal insurance could then be addressed.

A CAUTIONARY WORD

This theory is controversial because, in many ways (for example, by holding that moral hazard is predominantly good, not bad, and that insurance is not demanded to avoid risk), it stands conventional theory on its head. One response to its controversial nature is to minimize the difference between this theory and the conventional one, claiming that the new theory is just part of the conventional theory, but an aspect that has not yet been emphasized. Whatever the motives for such a response might be, it would be a mistake to draw too close a connection between the new theory and the conventional one. There are four areas for which this seems especially true.

First, some observers may note that it is common knowledge that price changes incorporate both income and price effects. Indeed, even students in principles classes are taught the classic Hicksian decomposition of a price change. These critics might argue that the analysis in this book shows that there is only a small difference between the magnitude of the income effect using the conventional Hicksian decomposition and the income transfer effect using the new decomposition. Thus, the difference between the old theory and the new theory is merely a technical one.

This perspective does not fully appreciate the motivation behind the purchase of insurance. According to the new theory, the raison d'être of insurance is an intentional income transfer to those who become ill. This is accomplished in health insurance by means of a price reduction, but the price reduction is just a secondary, transaction-cost-generating feature of health insurance. In the quid pro quo exchange that underlies the health insurance contract, the income transfer is central. The price reduction is simply the mechanism by which the income transfer occurs.

An exogenous price decrease is a completely different phenomenon. By definition, it cannot be caused by the individual consumer, but simply happens to her. The resulting change in her behavior is an opportunistic response to it, and can be traced back to a change in real income and to a relatively higher price for other commodities. If the Hicksian decomposition were to be used to eliminate the effect of income transfers in insurance, the consumer would still be consuming beyond her original budget constraint after the income effect had been removed (compare points H and N in Figure 6.1 from Chapter 6). In the case of insurance, because no exogenous price decrease had occurred, it would be impossible for a consumer to consume beyond her budget constraint if all income transfers had truly been removed. Thus, only the new decomposition eliminates all income transfers. More importantly, only the new decomposition is consistent with the actual quid pro quo contract that is health insurance.

Second, some might agree that risk preferences should be separated from the shape of the consumer's Bernoulli utility function, but argue that the ramifications are merely semantic or philosophical because the measure of the Bernoulli welfare gain under the new theory is exactly the same as with the conventional theory. First of all, the differences in understanding go far beyond semantic differences. If students are told that consumers demand health insurance because they desire to "avoid risk," but empirical studies show that consumers actually prefer the risk of a loss to a certain loss of the same actuarial magnitude, students are far from understanding why consumers demand health insurance.

Moreover, the "demand for certainty" theory has implications that are even more misleading. For example, if consumers choose between an uncertain fixed financial loss or an certain smaller one, the fixed nature of the uncertain financial loss implies that the insurance payoff does not affect its size. Thus, in order to believe the "demand for certainty" explanation, it is also necessary to believe that the income elasticity of demand for medical care is 0. This, too, is contradicted by empirical studies.

Most importantly, the decision to insure can be represented as a choice between certainty and uncertainty, holding the expected income loss constant, in only one of the various possible specifications of that decision: the standard gamble. In the other specifications, it is clear that uncertainty appears both with and without insurance. Thus, the "risk averse" implication is simply an artifact of the specification that economists have traditionally used to model this decision. In fact, consumers are not necessarily averse to uncertainty. They are, however, averse to income losses. Thus, when facing an exogenous income loss that happens to be uncertain, consumers demand an increase in income as a hedge against this exogenous income loss if it were to occur, and purchase a separate quid pro quo insurance contract as a means of obtaining this income. Insurance is demanded because of its income implications, not because of its implications regarding certainty. This difference is not merely semantic.

Third, some might argue that the income effect of insurance has already been identified by de Meza (1983). De Meza compares optimal contingent-claims insurance against optimal saving and optimal borrowing in the face of uncertain illness, and shows that, because income is greater with the insurance payoff (when ill) than with saving or borrowing, and because medical care is a normal good, medical care spending under health insurance exceeds medical care spending when financed by saving or borrowing.

De Meza's (1983) model is an important contribution because it shows that saving, borrowing, and contingent-claims (what he refers to as "indemnity") insurance all act to increase the amount of income available to the consumer if ill, and that consumers purchase more medical care as a result of that additional income. My model differs from de Meza's by showing that a similar increase in income occurs within price-payoff insurance and that the desire for income transfers, rather than a desire for "risk reduction," is at the center of why consumers purchase health insurance. Moreover, my model suggests that because saving and borrowing are usually not feasible financing mechanisms for expensive health care procedures for the seriously ill, a better comparison is between price-payoff insurance and no insurance. Thus, the central comparison is between health care expenditures generated by total income after the income transfer from insurance and expenditures generated by income without insurance, and without saving or borrowing as well.

Last, some might argue that "moral hazard" should refer only to that portion of moral hazard that is caused by purchasing a price reduction, that is, the inefficient portion. They would argue that the efficient portion of moral hazard should be called something else. This would preserve moral hazard as being the welfare-decreasing consequence of becoming insured.

I would argue that a new term would be more confusing than clarifying. The term "moral hazard" is not the province of economists. It is a term that insurers coined to refer to the change in behavior that they have observed when consumers and firms become insured. Insurers focus on the fact that this behavior change often leads to unexpectedly higher payoff costs, and as a result, tend to view any moral hazard as bad. It is left to economists to analyze this phenomenon and determine the true welfare implications of moral hazard for society. Therefore, economists have distinguished between ex ante and ex post moral hazard, and now with this new analysis, between efficient and inefficient moral hazard as well.

INTUITION REVISITED

Economics, at least the micro variety, seeks to understand the behavior of consumers and firms. This book has taken the approach that only those explanations that are rooted in intuition truly contribute to our understanding this behavior. In contrast to economic problems that require complex models—macroeconomic models that simulate and predict the course of the economy, comparative statics models that predict the change in some variable in a complex microeconomic situation, or financial models that predict the peaks and troughs of the stock prices—understanding the consumer's decision to purchase health insurance is relatively straightforward. Indeed, most of the U.S. population has purchased health insurance either directly or through their employer, and as a result, most of us have at least some understanding of why we do it.

Even we economists, therefore, possess some experientially derived intuition regarding the demand for health insurance. We seem, however, to have laid this intuition aside in developing the conventional theory of the demand for health insurance. For example, rather than applying the intuitively appealing Bernoulli utility function, health economists have conventionally favored the vNM utility function, which confounds preferences for income with preferences for lotteries (Arrow, 1951).[4] Conventional models have been specified so that any care that is consumed by an insured consumer can also be consumed by the same consumer without insurance, despite the well-known fact that the distribution of health care expenditures is highly skewed, and despite the intuition that many treatments are so expensive that we personally could not afford them without insurance. Models have been specified so that increases in income do not generate additional health care purchases, despite the clear intuition that we ourselves would purchase more health care with this additional income than without it. Models have been specified so that consumers prefer a sure loss to the risk of an actuarially equivalent larger loss, while the everyday transactional motivation of paying a premium to receive additional income when ill is ignored. Models have been specified claiming that all the additional health care that is consumed when insured is inefficient, despite the intuition that poor people benefit from insurance precisely because of the additional care they would consume, and despite the well-known clinician sentiments that this additional care is, in large part, standard treatments for persons with common illnesses. Why we have overlooked this intuition is a puzzle.

A few explanations suggest themselves. First, some health economists may have been more interested in the mathematical aspects of modeling than in truly understanding behavior of consumers and specifying a model that made intuitive sense. Second, others may have been more interested in the empirical modeling of the issue, and used the conventional theoretical model without scrutiny because it allowed them to perform the desired empirical analysis. Third, economists are trained to focus on the price, so we may have automatically viewed insurance as representing a price change, rather than income transfer. Fourth, others may have understood that insurance represented a transfer of income, so health economists needed a different story—one related to prices—in order to have a say in health policy debates. Fifth, economists may simply be predisposed to finding costs when others find benefits; after all, economics is the "dismal science."[5] A number of these factors may have been at work simultaneously.

Most puzzling of all, however, is how we health economists could have adopted a theory that implies that the voluntary purchase of fair health insurance (at coverage parameters that have traditionally been sold in the U.S.) makes the consumer worse off.[6] Voluntary purchases, almost by definition, make the consumer better off. Therefore, we should have been wary when well-researched empirical studies reported just the opposite. Instead, when faced with the choice between believing that consumers were irrational or that our theories were wrong, we generally opted to believe that we knew more about what was in the self-interest of consumers than they did, and that consumers were acting irrationally by purchasing unsubsidized, low coinsurance rate insurance. The idea that the voluntary purchase of fair health insurance could make consumers better off, therefore, appears to be controversial only to economists. To almost everyone else, it makes perfect sense.

NOTES

1. There is also the general equity goal of redistributing income from the non-poor to the poor—income that can be used to purchase worthy commodities, such as food and medical care. It is assumed that for medical care, this goal is largely achieved with the Medicaid program.

2. The price-payoff mechanism might represent a way to reduce this behavior and internalize the externality.

3. Pauly, in a 1983 response to de Meza (1983), suggests that his 1968 paper was directed at "routine physicians' services, prescriptions, dental care, and the like." It was not directed at the serious, expensive care that represents most health care expenditures, a distinction that was not made in his 1968 article and lost on many who have used his model subsequently. Pauly goes on to point out that, "[i]t is nevertheless true that the relevant theory, empirical evidence, and policy analysis for moral hazard in the case of serious illness has not been developed. This is one of the most serious omissions in the current literature" (Pauly, 1983, p. 83).

4. Arrow writes that, with the von Neumann-Morgenstern utility function, "the utilities assigned are not in any sense to be interpreted as some intrinsic amount of good in the outcome . . . Therefore, all the intuitive feelings which led to the assumption of diminishing marginal utility are irrelevant, and we are free to assume that marginal utility is increasing, so that the existence of gambling can be explained within the theory." (Arrow, p. 425, 1951).

5. Adlai E. Stevenson, III once said, ". . . we Americans are suckers for good news." Perhaps the opposite is true for we economists.

6. It is important to note that I include myself in this group. For many years, I taught my students that Pauly's 1968 "Comment" in the *American Economic Review* was the most important article in the health economics literature.

REFERENCES

Aday, L., E. S. Lee, B. Spears, C. W. Chung, A. Youssef, and B. Bloom. 1993. Health insurance and utilization of medical care for children with special health care needs. *Medical Care*, 31(11):1013–26.

Ahern, M., and H. V. McCoy. 1992. Emergency room admissions: Changes during the financial tightening of the 1980s. *Inquiry*, 29(1):67–79.

Anderson, O. W. 1956. *Family medical costs and voluntary health insurance: A nationwide survey*. New York: McGraw-Hill.

Arnold, P. J., and T. L. Schlenker. 1992. The impact of health care financing on childhood immunization practices. *American Journal of Diseases of Children*, 146(6):728–32.

Arrow, K. J. 1951. Alternative approaches to the theory of choice in risk-taking situations. *Econometrica*, 19(4):404–37.

Arrow, K. J. 1963. Uncertainty and the welfare economics of medical care. *American Economic Review*, 53(5):941–73.

Arrow, K. J. 1965. *Aspects of the theory of risk-bearing*. Helsinki: Yrjo Jahnsson Saatio.

Ayanian, J. Z., B. A. Kohler, T. Abe, and A. M. Epstein. 1993. The relation between health insurance coverage and clinical outcomes among women with breast cancer. *New England Journal of Medicine*, 329(5):326–31.

Baker, D. W., J. J. Sudano, J. M. Albert, E. A. Borawski, and A. Dor. 2001. Lack of health insurance and decline in overall health in late middle age. *New England Journal of Medicine*, 345(15):1106–12.

Berg, J. W., R. Ross, and H. B. Latourette. 1977. Economic status and survival of cancer patients. *Cancer*, 39(2):467–77.

Berk, M. L., and A. C. Monheit. 1992. The concentration of health expenditures: An update. *Health Affairs,* 11(5):145–49.

Berk, M. L., A. C. Monheit, and M. M. Hagan. 1988. How the U.S. spent its health care dollar: 1929–1980. *Health Affairs,* 7:46–60.

Bernoulli, Daniel. 1954. Exposition of a new theory on the measurement of risk. Trans. by Louise Sommer. *Econometrica,* 22:23–36.

Bernstein, P. L. 1996. *Against the gods: The remarkable story of risk.* New York: Wiley.

Billings, J., and N. Teicholz. 1990. Uninsured patients in District of Columbia hospitals. *Health Affairs,* 9(4):158–65.

Blaug, M. 1985. *Economic theory in retrospect.* 4th ed. Cambridge: Cambridge University Press.

Blendon, R. J., K. Donelan, C. V. Lukas, K. E. Thorpe, M. Frankel, R. Bass, and H. Taylor. 1992. The uninsured and the debate over the repeal of the Massachusetts universal health care law. *Journal of the American Medical Association,* 267(8):1113–17.

Bless, H., T. Betsch, and A. Franzen. 1998. Framing the framing effect: The impact of context cues on solutions to the "Asian Disease" problem. *European Journal of Social Psychology,* 28:287–91.

Blomqvist, Åke. Does the economics of moral hazard need to be revisited? A comment on the paper by John Nyman. *Journal of Health Economics,* 20(2):283–88.

Bohm, P., and H. Lind. 1992. A note on the robustness of a classical framing result. *Journal of Economic Psychology,* 13:355–61.

Bowman, K. 1998. *Health care attitudes today: Is the trend toward managed care unpopular? Where do we go from here?* Washington, D.C.: American Enterprise Institute for Public Policy Research.

Braveman, P. A., T. Bennett, C. Lewis, S. Egerter, and J. Showstack. 1993. Access to prenatal care following major medicaid eligibility expansions. *Journal of the American Medical Association,* 269(10):1285–89.

Braveman, P. A., S. Egerter, T. Bennett, and J. Showstack. 1991. Differences in hospital resource allocation among sick newborns according to insurance coverage. *Journal of the American Medical Association,* 266(23):3300–08.

Braveman, P. A., V. M. Schaaf, S. Egerter, T. Bennett, and W. Schecter. 1994. Insurance-related differences in the risk of ruptured appendix. *New England Journal of Medicine,* 331(7):444–49.

Breiter, H. C., I. Aharon, D. Kahneman, A. Dale, and P. Shizgal. 2001. Functional imaging of neural responses to expectancy and experience of monetary gains and losses. *Neuron,* 30:619–39.

Brook, R. H., et al. 1983. Does free care improve adults' health? Results from a randomized controlled trial. *New England Journal of Medicine,* 309(23):1426–34.

Brown, M. E., A. B. Bindman, and N. Lurie. 1998. Monitoring the consequences of uninsurance: A review of methodologies. *Medical Care Research and Review,* 55(2):177–210.

Burstin, H. R., S. R. Lipsitz, and T. A. Brennan. 1992. Socioeconomic status and risk for substandard medical care. *Journal of the American Medical Association,* 266(17):2383–87.

Busuttil, R. W., A. Shaked, J. M. Millis, O. Jurim, S. D. Colquhoun, C. R. Shackleton, B. J. Nuesse, M. Csete, L. I. Goldstein, and S. V. McDiarmid. 1994. One thousand liver transplants: Lessons learned. *Annals of Surgery,* 219:490–99.

Cairns, J. 1992. Discounting and health benefits: Another perspective. *Health Economics,* 1(1):76–9.

Chernew, M. E., W. E. Encinosa, and R. A. Hirth. 2000. Optimal health insurance: The case of observable, severe illness. *Journal of Health Economics* 19(5):585–610.

Cohen, J. W., S. R. Machlin, S. H. Zuvekas, et al. 2000. Health care expenses in the United States, 1996 (AHRQ Pub. No. 01-0009). *MEPS Research Findings,* 12, Agency for Healthcare Research and Quality. Rockville, Md.: Department of Health and Human Services.

Connor, R. A. 1996. More than risk reduction: The investment appeal of insurance. *Journal of Economic Psychology,* 17(1):39–54.

Cook, P. J., and D. A. Graham. 1977. The demand for insurance and protection: The case of irreplaceable commodities. *Quarterly Journal of Economics,* 91:143–56.

Cunningham, W. E., R. D. Hays, K. W. Williams, K. C. Beck, W. J. Dixon, and M. F. Shapiro. 1995. Access to medical care and health-related quality of life for low-income persons with symptomatic human immunodeficiency virus. *Medical Care,* 33(7):739–54.

Currie, J., and J. Gruber. 1996a. Health insurance eligibility, utilization of medical care and child health. *Quarterly Journal of Economics,* CXI:431–66.

Currie, J., and J. Gruber. 1996b. Saving babies: The efficacy and cost of recent changes in the medicaid eligibility of pregnant women. *Journal of Political Economy,* 104(6):1263–96.

Cutler, D., and J. Gruber. 1996. Does public insurance crowd out private insurance? *Quarterly Journal of Economics,* 111:391–430.

de Meza, D. 1983. Health insurance and the demand for medical care. *Journal of Health Economics,* 2(1):47–54.

Donelan, K., R. J. Blendon, C. Hoffman, D. Rowland, M. Frankel, and D. Altman. 1996. Whatever happened to the health insurance crisis in the United States? Voices from a national survey. *Journal of the American Medical Association,* 276(16):1346–50.

Drèze, J. 1961. Les fondements logiques de l'utilite cardinale et de la probabilite subjective. *La decision,* 1961:73–87. Translated as Chapter 3 of Drèze, J. 1987. *Essays on economic decision under uncertainty.* Cambridge: Cambridge University Press.

Druckman, J. N. 2001. Evaluating framing effects. *Journal of Economic Psychology,* 22(1):91–101.

Drummond, M. F., B. O'Brien, G. L. Stoddart, G. W. Torrance. 1997. *Methods for the economic evaluation of health care programmes.* 2d ed. New York: Oxford University Press.

Dubay, L., and G. Kenny. 1997. Did medicaid expansions for pregnant women crowd out private coverage? *Health Affairs,* 16(1):185–93.

Dylan, B. 1967. Like a rolling stone. *Bob Dylan's Greatest Hits.* Columbia Records.

Economic Report of the President: Transmitted to Congress February 1998. 1998. Washington, D. C.: U.S. Government Printing.

Ehrlich, I., and G. S. Becker. 1972. Market insurance, self-insurance, and self-protection. *Journal of Political Economy,* 80:623–48.

Eller, T. J., and W. Fraser. *Asset ownership of households: 1993.* 1995. U.S. Bureau of the census. Current population reports, 70–47. Washington, D.C.: U.S. Government Printing Office.

Enthoven, A. C. 1980. *Health plan: The only practical solution to the soaring cost of medical care.* Reading: Addison-Wesley.

Fagley, N. S. and P. Miller. 1990. The effect of framing on choice: Interactions with risk-taking propensity, cognitive style and sex. *Personality and Social Psychology Bulletin,* 16:496–510.

Falk, I. S. 1936. *Security against illness: A study of health insurance.* Garden city, N.Y.: Doubleday.

Falk, I. S., M. C. Klem, and N. Sinai. 1933. The incidence of illness and the receipt and costs of medical care among representative families: Experiences in twelve consecutive months. *Committee on the Costs of Medical Care, Report 26.* Chicago: University of Chicago Press.

Feenberg, D., and J. Skinner. 1994. The risk and duration of catastrophic health care expenditures. *Review of Economics and Statistics,* 76:333–47.

Feldman, R., and B. Dowd. 1991. A new estimate of the welfare loss of excess health insurance. *American Economic Review,* 81(1):297–301.

Feldman, R., and M. A. Morrisey. 1990. Health economics: A report on the field. *Journal of Health Politics, Policy and Law,* 15(3):627–46.

Feldstein, M. S. 1971. Hospital cost inflation: A study in nonprofit price dynamics. *American Economic Review,* 61:853–72.

Feldstein, M. S. 1973. The welfare loss of excess health insurance. *Journal of political economy,* 81:251–80.

Feldstein, M., and B. Friedman. 1977. Tax subsidies, the rational demand for insurance, and the health care crisis. *Journal of Public Economics,* 7:155–78.

Feldstein, P. J. 1999. *Health care economics.* 5th ed. Albany, N.Y.: Delmar.

Fihn, S. D., and J. B. Wicher. 1988. Withdrawing routine outpatient medical services. *Journal of General Internal Medicine,* 3(4):356–62.

Fleishman, J. A., and V. Mor. 1993. Insurance status among people with AIDS: Relationships with sociodemographic characteristics and service use. *Inquiry,* 30(2):180–88.

Folland, S., A. C. Goodman, and M. Stano. 2001. *The economics of health and health care.* 3rd ed. Upper Saddle River, N.J.: Prentice Hall.

Foster, D. C., D. S. Guzick, and R. P. Pulliam. 1992. The impact of prenatal care on fetal and neonatal death rates for uninsured patients: A "natural experiment" in West Virginia. *Obstetrics & Gynecology,* 79(1):40–5.

Franks, P., C. M. Clancy, and M. R. Gold. 1993. Health insurance and mortality: Evidence from a national cohort. *Journal of the American Medical Association,* 279:737–741.

Franks, P., C. M. Clancy, M. R. Gold, and P. A. Nutting. 1993. Health insurance and subjective health status: Data from the 1987 national medical expenditure survey. *American Journal of Public Health,* 83(9):1295–99.

Freeman, H. E., L. H. Aiken, R. J. Blendon, and C. R. Corey. 1990. Uninsured working-age adults: Characteristics and consequences. *Health Services Research,* 24(6):811–23.

Freeman, H. E., R. J. Blendon, L. H. Aiken, S. Sudman, C. F. Mullinix, and C. R. Corey. 1987. Americans report on their access to health care. *Health Affairs,* 6(1):6–18.

Friedman, Milton 1962. *Price theory: A provisional text.* Chicago: Aldine Publishing Co.

Friedman, Milton, and L. J. Savage. 1948. The utility analysis of choices involving risk. *Journal of Political Economy,* 66(4):279–304.

Fuchs, V. R. 1996. Economics, values, and health care reform. *American Economic Review,* 86(1):1–24.

Gerdtham, U.-G., J. Sogaard, F. Andersson, and B. Jonsson. 1992. An econometric analysis of health care expenditure: A cross-section study of the OECD countries. *Journal of Health Economics,* 11(1):63–84.

Getzen, T. E. 1997. *Health economics: Fundamentals and flow of funds.* New York: Wiley.

Goddeeris, J., and B. Weisbrod. 1985. What we don't know about why health expenditures have soared: Interaction of insurance and technology. *Mt. Sinai Journal of Medicine*, 52:685–91.

Gravelle, H., and D. Smith. 2001. Discounting for health effects in cost-benefit and cost-effectiveness analysis. *Health Economics*, 10(7):587–99.

Greenberg, E. R., C. G. Chute, T. Stukel, J. A. Baron, D. H. Freeman, J. Yates, and R. Korson. 1988. Social and economic factors in the choice of lung cancer treatment: A population-based study in two rural states. *New England Journal of Medicine*, 318(10):612–17.

Haas, J. S., P. D. Cleary, E. Guadagnoli, C. Fanta, and A. M. Epstein. 1994. The impact of socioeconomic status on the intensity of ambulatory treatment and health outcomes after discharge for adults with asthma. *Journal of General Internal Medicine*, 9(3):121–26.

Haas, J. S., and L. Goldman. 1994. Acutely injured patients with trauma in Masachusetts: Differences in care and mortality, by insurance status. *American Journal of Public Health*, 84(10):1605–08.

Hadley, J., E. P. Steinberg, and J. Feder. 1991. Comparison of uninsured and privately insured hospital patients: Condition on administration, resource use, and outcome. *Journal of the American Medical Association*, 265(3):374–79.

Hafner-Eaton, C. 1993. Physician utilization disparities between the uninsured and the insured: Comparisons of the chronically ill, acutely ill, and well nonelderly populations. *Journal of the American Medical Association*, 269(6):787–92.

Hafner-Eaton, C. 1994. Patterns of hospital and physician utilization among the uninsured. *Journal of Health Care for the Poor and Underserved*, 5:297–315.

Hanratty, M. 1996. Canadian national health insurance and infant health. *American Economic Review*, 86(1):276–84.

Hauboldt, R. H. 1996. Cost implications of human organ and tissue transplantations, an update: 1996. Research report, Brookfield, Wisconsin: Milliman and Robertson, Inc.

Hausman, J. A. 1981. Exact consumer's surplus and deadweight loss. *American Economic Review*, 71:662–76.

Health Care Financing Administration. 1995. *Health care financing review: Medicare and medicaid statistical supplement, 1995.* Baltimore: Health Care Financing Administration.

Health Insurance Association of America. 1996. *Who buys long-term care insurance? 1994–95 profiles and innovations in a dynamic market.* Washington, D.C.: Health Insurance Association of America.

Henderson, J. 1999. *Health economics and policy.* Cincinnati: South-Western College Publishing.

Hershey, J. C., and P. J. H. Schoemaker. 1980. Risk taking and problem context in the domain of losses: An expected utility analysis. *Journal of Risk and Insurance,* 47:111–32.

Hicks, J. R. 1946. *Value and capital.* 2d ed. Oxford: Clarendon Press.

Himmelstein, D. U., and S. Woolhandler. 1995. Care denied: U.S. residents who are unable to obtain needed medical services. *American Journal of Public Health,* 85(3):341–44.

Hirshleifer, J. 1976. *Price theory and applications.* Englewood Cliffs, N.J.: Prentice-Hall.

Hirth, R. A., M. E. Chernew, E. Miller, M. Fendrick, and W. G. Weissert. 2000. Willingness to pay for a quality-adjusted life year: In search of a standard. *Medical Decision Making,* 20(3):332–42.

Holahan, J. 1997. Crowding out: How big a problem? *Health Affairs,* 16(1):204–06.

Johannesson, M., and D. Meltzer. 1998. Some reflections on cost-effectiveness analysis. *Health Economics,* 7:1–7.

Johnson, R. W., and S. Crystal. 2000. Uninsured status and out-of-pocket costs at midlife. *Health Services Research,* 35(5) (Part I):911–32.

Kahneman, D., and A. Tversky. 1979. Prospect theory: An analysis of decision under risk. *Econometrica,* 47:263–91.

Kemper, P., B. C. Spillman, and C. M. Murtaugh. 1991. A lifetime perspective on proposals for financing nursing home care. *Inquiry,* 28:333–44.

Kennedy, E. M. 1972. *In critical condition: The crisis in Americas's health care.* New York: Simon and Schuster.

Kennickell, A. B., and J. Shack-Marquez. 1992. Changes in family finances from 1983 to 1989: Evidence from the survey of consumer finances. *Federal Reserve Bulletin,* 78(1):1–18.

Kennickell, A. B., M. Starr-McClure, and A. E. Sunden. 1997. Family finances in the U.S.: Recent evidence from the survey of consumer finances. *Federal Reserve Bulletin,* 83(1):1–24.

Kerr, E. A., and A. L. Siu. 1993. Follow-up after hospital discharge: Does insurance make a difference? *Journal of Health Care for the Poor and Underserved,* 4:133–42.

Kilpe, V. E., H. Krakauer, and R. E. Wren. 1993. An analysis of liver transplant experience from 37 transplant centers as reported to Medicare. *Transplantation* 56:554–61.

Kim, S. W., J. E. Grant, D. E. Adson, and Y. C. Shin. 2001. Double-blind naltrexone and placebo comparison study in the treatment of pathological cambling. *Biological Psychiatry,* 49(11):914–21.

Kirkman-Liff, B., and J. J. Kronenfeld. 1992. Access to cancer screening services for women. *American Journal of Public Health*, 82(5):733–35.

Kleiman, E. 1974. The determinants of national outlay on health, in *The Economics of Health and Medical Care*, ed. M. Perlman. London: Macmillan.

Kogan, M. D., G. R. Alexander, M. A. Teitelbaum, B. W. Jack, M. Kotelchuck, and G. Pappas. 1995. The effect of gaps in health insurance on continuity of a regular source of care among preschool-aged children in the United states. *Journal of the American Medical Association*, 274(18):1429–35.

Kühberger, A. 1998. The influence of framing on risky decisions: A meta-analysis. *Organizational Behavior and Human Decision Process*, 75:23–55.

Kuykendall, D. H., M. L. Johnson, and J. M. Geraci. 1995. Exected source of payment and use of hospital services for coronary atherosclerosis. *Medical Care*, 33(7):715–28.

Lefkowitz, D., and A. Monheit. 1991. Health insurance, use of health services and health care expenditures (AHCPR Pub. No. 92-0017). *National Expenditure Survey Research Findings*, 12, Agency for health care policy and research. Rockville, Md.: Public Health Service.

Leu, R. E. 1986. The public-private mix and international health care costs, in *Public and Private Health Services*, ed. A. J. Culyer and B. Jonsson. Oxford: Basil Blackwell.

Levy, H., and D. Meltzer. 2001. What do we really know about whether health insurance affects health? Paper prepared for the agenda setting meeting of the coverage research initiative, Ann Arbor, Michigan, July 9–10.

Lichtenberg, F. 2001. The effects of medicare on health care utilization and outcomes. Manuscript prepared for presentation at the Frontiers in Health Policy Research Conference, 7 June, Washington, D.C.: National Bureau of Economic Research.

Lohr, K. N., R. H. Brook, C. J. Kamberg, G. A. Goldberg, A. Leibowitz, J. Keesey, D. Reboussin, and J. P. Newhouse. 1986. Effect of cost-sharing on use of medically effective and less effective care. *Medical Care*, 24, Supplement, S32–S38.

Lurie, N., N. B. Ward, M. F. Shapiro, and R. H. Brook. 1984. Termination from Medi-Cal: Does it affect health? *New England Journal of Medicine*, 311(7):480–84.

Lurie, N., N. B. Ward, M. F. Shapiro, C. Gallego, R. Vaghaiwalla, and R. H. Brook. 1986. Termination of Medi-Cal benefits: A follow-up study one year later. *New England Journal of Medicine*, 314(19):1266–68.

Machina, M. J. 1987. Choice under uncertainty: Problems solved and unsolved. *Journal of Economic Perspectives*, 1:121–54.

Machina, M. J. 1989. Dynamic consistency and non-expected utility models of choice under uncertainty. *Journal of Economic Literature,* 27(4):1622–68.

Manning, W. G., and M. S. Marquis. 1996. Health insurance: The tradeoff between risk pooling and moral hazard. *Journal of Health Economics,* 15(5): 609–40.

Manning, W. G., and M. S. Marquis. 2001. Health insurance: Tradeoffs revisited, *Journal of Health Economics,* 20(2):289–94.

Manning, W. G., J. P. Newhouse, N. Duan, E. B. Keeler, A. Leibowitz, and M. S. Marquis. 1987. Health insurance and the demand for medical care: Evidence from a randomized experiment. *American Economic Review,* 77(3):251–77.

Markowitz, H. 1952. The utility of wealth. *Journal of Political Economy,* 60:151–58.

Mas-Colell, A., M. D. Whinston, J. R. Green. 1995. *Microeconomic theory.* New York: Oxford University Press.

Mayers, D., and C. W. Smith. 1983. The interdependence of individual portfolio decisions and the demand for insurance. *Journal of Political Economy,* 91:304–11.

Mayers, D., and C. W. Smith. 1988. Ownership structure across lines of property—casualty insurance. *Journal of Law and Economics,* 31:351–78.

Maynard, A. K. 1991. Developing the health care market. *Economic Journal,* 101:1277–86.

Mishan, E. J. 1971. *Cost-benefit analysis: An introduction.* New York: Praeger.

Mishan, E. J. 1981. *Introduction to normative economics.* New York: Oxford.

Monheit, A. C., M. M. Hagan, M. L. Berk, and P. J. Farley. 1985. The employed uninsured and the role of public policy. *Inquiry,* 22(14):348–64.

Mossin, J. 1968. Aspects of rational insurance purchasing. *Journal of Political Economy,* 76:553–68.

Moy, E., B. Bartman, and M. R. Weir. 1995. Access to hypertensive care: Effects of income, insurance, and source of care. *Archives of Internal Medicine,* 155(14): 1497–502.

Newacheck, P. W. 1992. Characteristics of children with high and low usage of physician services. *Medical Care,* 30(1):30–42.

Newacheck, P. W., D. Hughes, and J. J. Stoddard. 1996. Children's access to primary care: Differences by race, income, and insurance. *Pediatrics,* 97(1):26–32.

Newhouse, J. P. 1974. A design for a health insurance experiment. *Inquiry,* 11:5–27.

Newhouse, J. P. 1977. Medical care expenditure: A cross-national study. *Journal of Human Resources,* 12:115–25.

Newhouse, J. P. 1978a. *The economics of medical care.* Reading, MA: Addison-Wesley.

Newhouse, J. P. 1978b. The structure of health insurance and the erosion of competition in the medical marketplace. In *Competition in the Health Care Sector: Past, Present and Future.* Proc. of a conference of the Bureau of Economics, U.S. Federal Trade Commission.

Newhouse, J. P. 1981. The erosion of the medical marketplace, in *Advances in Health Economics and Health Services Research,* 2d ed. Richard Schffler. Westport, CT: JAI Press.

Newhouse, J. P. 1992. Medical care costs: How much welfare loss? *Journal of Economic Perspectives,* 6(3):3–22.

Newhouse, J. P., and The Insurance Experiment Group. 1993. *Free for all? Lessons from the RAND health insurance experiment.* Cambridge: Harvard University Press.

Nyman, J. A. 1991. Costs, technology, and insurance in the health care sector. *Journal of Policy Analysis and Management,* 10(1):106–11.

Nyman, J. A. 1999a. The value of health insurance: The access motive. *Journal of Health Economics,* 18(2):141–52.

Nyman, J. A. 1999b. The welfare economics of insurance contracts that pay off by reducing price. Discussion paper No. 308. Center for Economic Research, Department of Economics, Minneapolis: University of Minnesota.

Nyman, J. A. 1999c. The economics of moral hazard revisited. *Journal of Health Economics,* 18(6):811–24.

Nyman, J. A. 2001a. The income transfer effect, the access value of insurance and the RAND health insurance experiment. *Journal of Health Economics,* 20(2): 295–98.

Nyman, J. A. 2001b. The theory of the demand for health insurance. Discussion paper No. 311, March, Center for Economic Research, Department of Economics, University of Minnesota.

Nyman, J. A. 2001c. The demand for insurance: Expected utility theory from a gain perspective. Discussion paper No. 313, Center for Economic Research, Department of Economics, Minneapolis: University of Minnesota.

Nyman, J. A., and R. Maude-Griffin. 2001. The welfare economics of moral hazard. *International Journal of Health Care Finance and Economics,* 1(1):23–42.

O'Connell, J. F. 1982. *Welfare economic theory.* Boston: Auburn House.

Organisation for Economic Co-operation and Development. 2001. http://www.oecd.org

Organisation for Economic Co-operation and Development. 2001. *Health data 2001: Table 10, Total expenditures on health, %GDP.* OECD web page, health, statistics. http://www.oecd.org

Overpeck, M. D., and J. B. Kotch. 1995. The effect of U.S. children's access to care on medical attention to injuries. *American Journal of Public Health*, 85(3): 402–04.

Parkin, D., A. McGuire, and B. Yule. 1987. Aggregate health care expenditures and national income: Is health care a luxury good? *Journal of Health Economics*, 6(2):109–28.

Parsonage, M., and H. Neuburger. 1992. Discounting and health benefits. *Health Economics*, 1(1):71–6.

Patrick, D. L., C. W. Madden, P. Diehr, D. P. Martin, A. Cheadle, and S. M. Skillman. 1992. Health status and use of services among families with and without health insurance. *Medical Care*, 30(10):941–49.

Pauly, M. V. 1968. The economics of moral hazard: Comment. *American Economic Review*, 58(3):531–37.

Pauly, M. V. 1983. More on moral hazard. *Journal of Health Economics*, 2(1):81–6.

Pauly, M. V. 1990. The rational non-purchase of long-term care insurance. *Journal of Political Economy*, 98(1):153–68.

Pauly, M. V. 1995. When does curbing health costs really help the economy? *Health Affairs*, 14(2):68–82.

Perry, C. W., and H. S. Rosen. 2001. The self-employed are less likely to have health insurance than wage earners. So what? Working paper No. 8316, National Bureau of Economic Research, Cambridge, Mass.: NBER.

Pfaff, M. 1990. Differences in health care spending across countries: Statistical evidence. *Journal of Health Politics, Policy and Law*, 15(1):1–67.

Phelps, C. E. 1973. *Demand for health insurance: A theoretical and empirical investigation*. Santa Monica, Calif.: RAND Corporation.

Phelps, C. E. 1997. *Health economics*. 2d ed. Reading, Mass.: Addison Wesley.

Pratt, J. W. 1964. Risk aversion in the small and in the large. *Econometrica*, 32:122–36.

Public Health Service. 2000. Interpolated abridged life table, 1996 abridged life table. Total population, Public health service, U.S. Department of Health and Human Services, unpublished data. http://www.cdc.gov/achs/data/lewk2_96.pdf

Rabin, M. 2000. Risk aversion and expected-utility theory: A calibration theorem. *Econometrica*, 68:1281–92.

Rabin, M., and R. H. Thaler. 2001. Anomalies: Risk aversion. *Journal of Economic Perspectives*, 15:219–32.

Ramsey, F. P. 1931. Truth and probability, in *The foundations of mathematics and other logical essays*. London: K. Paul, Trench, Trubner and Co.

RAND Health Insurance Experiment. http://www.rand.org/health/cities

Rice, T. H. 1992. An alternative framework for evaluating welfare losses in the health care market. *Journal of Health Economics*, 11(1):88–92.

Rorem, C. R. 1982. *A quest for certainty: Essays on health care economics 1930–1970*. Ann Arbor, MI: Health Administration Press.

Rothschild, M., and J. E. Stiglitz. 1970. Increasing risk I: A definition. *Journal of Economic Theory*, 2:225–43.

Santerre, R. E., and S. P. Neun. 2000. *Health economics: Theories, insights and industry studies*. Orlando, FL: Dryden Press.

Saver, B. G., and N. Peterfreund. 1993. Insurance, income and access to ambulatory care in King county, Washington. *American Journal of Public Health*, 83(11):1583–88.

Schlesinger, H., and N. Doherty. 1985. Incomplete markets for insurance: An overview. *Journal of Risk and Insurance*, 52:402–23.

Shea, S., D. Misra, M. H. Ehrlich, L. Field, and C. K. Francis. 1992. Predisposing factors for severe, uncontrolled hypertension in an inner-city minority population. *New England Journal of Medicine*, 327(11):776–81.

Short, P. F., and T. J. Lair. 1995. Health insurance and health status: Implications for financing health care reform. *Inquiry*, 31(4):425–37.

Short, P. F., and D. C. Lefkowitz. 1992. Encouraging preventive services for low-income children. The effect of expanding Medicaid. *Medical Care*, 30(9):766–80.

Siu, A. L., F. A. Sonnenberg, W. G. Manning, G. A. Goldberg, E. S. Bloomfield, J. P. Newhouse, and R. H. Brook. 1986. Inappropriate use of hospitals in a randomized trial of health insurance plans. *New England Journal of Medicine*, 315:1259–66.

Slovic, P., B. Fischhoff, and S. Lichtenstein. 1988. Response mode, framing, and information-processing effects in risk assessment, in *Decision Making: Descriptive, Normative, and Prescriptive Interactions*, pp. 152–66, eds. D. E. Bell, H. Raiffa, and A. Tversky. Cambridge: Cambridge University Press.

Slovic, P., B. Fischhoff, S. Lichtenstein, B. Corrigan, and B. Combs. 1977. Preference for insuring against probably small losses: Insurance implications. *Journal of Risk and Insurance*, 44:237–58.

Slutsky, E. E. 1915. On the theory of the budget of the consumer. Translated by Olga Ragusa, 1952. Reprinted in *Readings in Economic Theory*. Homewood, IL: Irwin.

Somers, H. H., and A. R. Somers. 1961. *Doctors, patients and health insurance*. Washington, D.C.: Brookings.

Sorlic, P. D., N. J. Johnson, E. Backlund, and D. D. Bradham. 1994. Mortality in the uninsured compared with that in persons with public and private health insurance. *Archives of Internal Medicine*, 154:2409–16.

Spillman, B. C. 1992. The impact of being uninsured on utilization of basic health care services. *Inquiry,* 29(4):457–66.

Stoddard, J. J., R. F. St. Peter, and P. W. Newacheck. 1994. Health insurance status and ambulatory care for children. *New England Journal of Medicine,* 330(20): 1421–25.

Tengs, T. O., and A. Wallace. 2000. One thousand health-related quality-of-life estimates. *Medical Care,* 38(6):538–637.

Thomas, E. J., H. R. Burstin, A. C. O'Neill, E. J. Orav, and T. A. Brennan. 1996. Patient noncompliance with medical advice after the emergency department visit. *Annals of Emergency Medicine,* 27(1):49–55.

Thomas, K. 1994/5. Are subsidies enough to encourage the uninsured to purchase health insurance: An analysis of underlying behavior. *Inquiry,* 31:415–24.

Tolley, G., D. Kenkel, and R. Fabian. 1994. State-of-the-art health values, in *Valuing Health Policy: An Economic Approach,* pp. 323–44, eds. G. Tolley, D. Kenkel, and R. Fabian. Chicago: University of Chicago Press.

Tversky, A., and D. Kahneman. 1981. The framing of decisions and the psychology of choice. *Science,* 211:453–58.

Tversky, A., and D. Kahneman. 1986. The framing of decisions and the psychology of choice, in *Rational Choice,* pp. 123–41, ed. J. Elster. New York: New York University Press.

Tversky, A., and D. Kahneman. 1988. Rational choice and the framing of decisions, in *Decision Making: Descriptive, Normative, and Prescriptive Interactions,* pp. 167–92, eds. D. E. Bell, H. Raiffa, and A. Tversky. Cambridge: Cambridge University Press.

U.S. Agency for Health Care Policy and Research, Department of Health and Human Services. 1998. *National Statistics by Diagnosis-related Group: HCUP-3 Nationwide Inpatient Sample for 1992 Hospital Inpatient Stays.* Agency for Health Care Policy and Research. http://www.ahcpr.gov

U.S. Bureau of the Census. 1997. *Current Population Reports, Series Household and Family Characteristics: March 1996 (Update). Households, by Age of Householder: 1960 to Present.* Bureau of the Census. http://www.bls.census.gov

U.S. Bureau of the Census. 1997. *HH-3 Households, by Age and Householder: 1960 to Present.* Internet release date: July 3. http://www.census.gov

U.S. Bureau of the Census, Population Division. 1998. Release PPL-91. *United States Population Estimates, by Age, Sex, Race, and Hispanic Origin, 1990 to 1997.* Bureau of the Census. http://www.census.gov

Van Hout, Ben A. 1998. Discounting costs and benefits: A reconsideration. *Health Economics,* 1(7):583–94.

Varian, H. R. 1984. *Microeconomic analysis.* New York: Norton.

Viscusi, W. K. 1993. The value of risks to life and health. *Journal Economic Literature,* 31:1912–46.

Viscusi, W. K., and W. N. Evans. 1990. Utility functions that depend on health status: Estimates and economic implications. *American Economic Review,* 80:353–74.

von Neumann, John, and Oskar Morgenstern. 1944. *Theory of games and economic behavior.* Princeton, N.J.: Princeton University Press.

von Neumann, John, and Oskar Morgenstern. 1947. *Theory of games and economic behavior,* 2d ed. Princeton, N.J.: Princeton University Press.

Weissman, J. S., and A. M. Epstein. 1989. Case mix and resource utilization by uninsured hospital patients in the Boston metropolitan area. *Journal of the American Medical Association,* 61(4):3572–76.

Weissman, J. S., C. Gatsonis, and A. M. Epstein. 1992. Rates of avoidable hospitalization by insurance status in Massachusetts and Maryland. *Journal of the American Medical Association,* 268(17):2388–94.

Weissman J. S., R. Stern, S. L. Fielding, and A. M. Epstein. 1991. Delayed access to health care: Risk factors, reasons, and consequences. *Annals of Internal Medicine,* 114(4):325–31.

Willing, R. D. 1976. Consumer surplus without apology. *American Economic Review,* 66(4):589–97.

Wilson, B. E., and A. Sharma. 1995. Public cost and access to primary care for hyperglycemic emergencies, Clark county, Nevada. *Journal of Community Health,* 20(3):249–56.

Yergan J., A. B. Flood, P. Diehr, and J. P. LoGerfo. 1988. Relationship between patient source of payment and the intensity of hospital services. *Medical Care,* 26(11):1111–14.

Young, G. J., and B. B. Cohen. 1991. Inequities in hospital care. The Massachusetts experience. *Inquiry,* 28(3):255–62.

Zeckhauser, R. 1970. Medical insurance: A case study of the tradeoff between risk spreading and appropriate incentives. *Journal of Economic Theory,* 2:10–26.

Zweifel, P., and F. Breyer. 1997. *Health economics.* New York: Oxford.

INDEX

.